Penguin Books

Mass Psychology and Other Writings

Sigmund Freud was born in 1856 in Moravia; between the ages of four and eighty-two his home was in Vienna: in 1938 Hitler's invasion of Austria forced him to seek asylum in London, where he died in the following year. His career began with several years of brilliant work on the anatomy and physiology of the nervous system. He was almost thirty when, after a period of study under Charcot in Paris, his interests first turned to psychology; and after ten years of clinical work in Vienna (at first in collaboration with Breuer, an older colleague) he invented what was to become psychoanalysis. This began simply as a method of treating neurotic patients through talking, but it quickly grew into an accumulation of knowledge about the workings of the mind in general. Freud was thus able to demonstrate the development of the sexual instinct in childhood and, largely on the basis of an examination of dreams, arrived at his fundamental discovery of the unconscious forces that influence our everyday thoughts and actions. Freud's life was uneventful, but his ideas have shaped not only many specialist disciplines, but also the whole intellectual climate of the twentieth century.

J. A. Underwood was born in London in 1940 and educated at Trinity Hall, Cambridge. He has worked as a freelance translator (from French as well as German) since 1969, translating texts by a wide variety of modern authors including Elias Canetti, Jean-Paul Sartre, Julien Green, and Alain Robbe-Grillet. But it is for his Kafka translations that he is best known; his new translation of *The Castle* (also available in Penguin Books) was joint winner of the 1998 Schlegel-Tieck prize for translation from the German.

Jacqueline Rose is Professor of English at Queen Mary, University of London. She is the author of *The Case of Peter Pan*, *Sexuality in the Field of Vision*, *The Haunting of Sylvia Plath* (winner of the Fawcett Prize for Non-Fiction), *Why War?: Psychoanalysis, Politics and the Return to Melanie Klein*, the Oxford Clarendon Lectures: *States of Fantasy*, the novel *Albertine*, and *On Not Being Able to Sleep: Psychoanalysis in the Modern World*. Her Christian Gauss seminars *The Question of Zion* will be published by Princeton in

2005. She is also editor (with Juliet Mitchell) and translator of *Feminine Sexuality: Jacques Lacan and the École Freudienne*, the editor (with Saul Dubow) of Wulf Sachs's *Black Hamlet* and the translator and editor of Moustapha Safouan's *Jacques Lacan and the Question of Psychoanalytic Training*. She was the writer and presenter of the Channel 4 documentary *Dangerous Liaison – Israel and America*.

Adam Phillips was formerly Principal Child Psychotherapist at Charing Cross Hospital in London. He is the author of several books on psychoanalysis including *On Kissing, Tickling and Being Bored, Darwin's Worms, Promises, Promises* and *Houdini's Box*.

SIGMUND FREUD

Mass Psychology and Other Writings

Translated by J. A. Underwood
with an Introduction by Jacqueline Rose

PENGUIN BOOKS

PENGUIN BOOKS

Published by the Penguin Group
Penguin Books Ltd, 80 Strand, London WC2R 0RL, England
Penguin Putnam Inc., 375 Hudson Street, New York, New York 10014, USA
Penguin Books Australia Ltd, 250 Camberwell Road, Camberwell, Victoria 3124, Australia
Penguin Books Canada Ltd, 10 Alcorn Avenue, Toronto, Ontario, Canada M4V 3B2
Penguin Books India (P) Ltd, 11, Community Centre, Panchsheel Park, New Delhi – 110 017, India
Penguin Books (NZ) Ltd, Cnr Rosedale and Airborne Roads, Albany, Auckland, New Zealand
Penguin Books (South Africa) (Pty) Ltd, 24 Sturdee Avenue, Rosebank 2196, South Africa

Penguin Books Ltd, Registered Offices: 80 Strand, London WC2R 0RL, England

www.penguin.com

Zwangshandlungen und Religionsübungen first published in 1907 in *Zeitschrift für Religions-psychologie*, I (I)
Massenpsychologie und Ich-Analyse first published in 1921 (Lepizig, Vienna and Zurich: Internationaler Psychoanalytischer Verlag)
Ein religiöses Erlebenis first published in 1927 in *Imago*, 14 (1, pp. 7–10)
Die Zukunft einer Illusion first published in 1927 (Leipzig, Vienna and Zurich: Internationaler Psychoanalytischer Verlag)
Der Mann Moses und die monotheistische Religion: Drei Abhandlungen first published in 1938 (Amsterdam: Verlag Allert de Lange)
Ein Wort zum Antisemitismus first published in 1938 in *Die Zukunft: Ein Neues Deutschland Ein Neues Europa*, 7 (2)
This translation first published in Penguin Classics 2004

4

Sigmund Freud's German texts collected in *Gesammelte Werke* (1940–52) copyright ©
Imago Publishing Co., Ltd, London, 1941, 1948, 1950
Translation and editorial matter copyright © J. A. Underwood, 2004
Introduction copyright © Jacqueline Rose, 2004

All rights reserved

The moral rights of the translator and the author of the Introduction have been asserted

Set in 10/12.25 pt Postscript Adobe New Caledonia
Typeset by Palimpsest Book Production Ltd, Polmont, Stirlingshire
Printed in England by Clays Ltd, St Ives plc

Except in the United States of America, this book is sold subject
to the condition that it shall not, by way of trade or otherwise, be lent,
re-sold, hired out, or otherwise circulated without the publisher's
prior consent in any form of binding or cover other than that in
which it is published and without a similar condition including this
condition being imposed on the subsequent purchaser

www.greenpenguin.co.uk

Mixed Sources
Product group from well-managed
forests and other controlled sources
www.fsc.org Cert no. SA-COC-1592
© 1996 Forest Stewardship Council

FSC

Penguin Books is committed to a sustainable future
for our business, our readers and our planet.
The book in your hands is made from paper
certified by the Forest Stewardship Council.

Contents

Introduction

It is a commonplace assumption that psychoanalysis only deals with individuals. More, or worse – loyal to its origins in the social milieu and mind of its founder, Sigmund Freud – the only individuals it deals with are an unrepresentative minority of the respectable, bourgeois and well-to-do. And yet, as Freud points out in the opening paragraph of *Mass Psychology and Analysis of the 'I'*, without the presence of the other, there can be no mental life. 'The antithesis between individual and social or mass psychology,' he writes, 'which at first glance may seem to us very important, loses a great deal of its sharpness on close examination.' We only exist through the others who make up the storehouse of the mind: models in our first tentative steps towards identity, objects of our desires, helpers and foes. The mind is a palimpsest in which the traces of these figures will jostle and rearrange themselves for evermore. From the very earliest moment of our lives – since without the rudiments of contact, the infant will not survive – we are 'peopled' by others. Our 'psyche' is a social space.

With one, short, exception, all the texts in this volume were written after the First World War, while the last one, *Moses the Man and Monotheistic Religion*, was composed while the clouds of the Second World War were gathering across Europe. In fact, you could argue that the whole of Freud's writing life was shadowed by the catastrophe biding its time, waiting in the wings, which was to finally come to its cruel fruition with the outbreak of hostilities in September 1939, barely two weeks before he died. In 1897, two years after the first German publication of *Studies in Hysteria*, the Emperor of Austria, Franz Josef, reluctantly confirmed the anti-Semite Karl

Lueger as mayor of Vienna (he had refused to do so no less than three times).[1] From that point on, no Jew in Austria could ignore the fact that the collective, or mass, identity of Europe was moving against the emancipatory tide. Enlightenment, the belief that a cool-headed reason could rule the world, was a dream; while the despised and dreaded unreason of the night would soon be marching on the streets. In a way this should have been no surprise to Freud. Such inversions were the hallmark of his craft. Nonetheless there are moments in what follows where Freud appears to be struggling to catch up with his own insights. From *Mass Psychology* to *Moses the Man,* his last major work, all the writings in this volume share a question: What drives people to hatred? Even in their dealings with those to whom they are closest, Freud muses, people seem to display a 'readiness to hate', something 'elemental' whose roots are 'unknown'. As if Freud had made two utterly interdependent discoveries that also threaten to cancel or wipe each other out, taking the whole world with them. No man is an island: you are the others who you are. But the mind is also its own worst enemy; and there is no link between individuals, no collective identity, which does not lead to war.

In 1914, Freud had set out the basic terms of what has come to be known as his second 'topography'. A previous distinction between love and hunger, the drives of desire and those of self-preservation, between the other and the 'I', breaks down when he alights upon the problem of narcissism, the subject's erotically charged relationship to her or himself. If you can be your own object, the neat line between impulses directed towards self and those tending towards the other starts to blur. But it is no coincidence that this discovery of subjects hoist on their own self-regard should bring him up so sharply against the question of how we connect to the others around us. How indeed? No longer is it the case that what we most yearn for in others is the satisfaction of our drives; what we are no less in search of, and passionately require, is to be recognized, acknowledged, seen. Freud is often wrongly taken to be interested only in the sexual drives (or, for the truly reductive version, only in 'sex'), but that is half of the story. If we need others, it is not so much to satisfy as *to fashion* ourselves. And in this struggle to conjure, and hold fast, to our identities, there is no limit to what we are capable of. From the outset, identification is ruthless; we devour the others we wish to be: 'Identification [. . .] behaves like a product of the first *oral* stage of libido organization in which the coveted, treasured object was incorporated by eating and was annihilated as such in the process.' Overturning his model of the mind in the face of war, Freud thus arrives at the problem of collective life. But he does so on the back of an analysis that has made such life, in anything other than a deadly form, all but impossible.

What is a mass? At first glance, Freud's answer to this question would seem to be contemptuous. '"The people"', he writes to his fiancé, Martha Bernays, in August 1883, 'judge, think, hope and work in a manner utterly different from ourselves.' (If the scare quotes indicate a caution about his own category, they also suggest his distaste.) In a letter to her sister two years before, he had described them as a 'different species', 'uncanny', knowing the meaning of neither 'fear nor shame'. And yet even here there is a subtext. Anti-Semitism gives a different historic substance and context to what might otherwise appear as no more than a familiar and conservative revulsion against the mob. As a Jew, Freud knows what it is like to be the target of collective hate. In an altercation about an open window during a train journey to Leipzig in the same year, someone in the background shouts out: '"He's a dirty Jew!"' 'With this,' he writes to Martha in December, 'the whole situation took on a different colour [. . .] Even a year ago I would have been speechless with agitation, but now I am different. I was not in the least frightened of that mob.' They were just a group of travellers sharing a train compartment. But under the pressure of race-hatred, the voice of one turns into a 'mob'.[2]

Even when Freud's remarks cannot be softened by such historic allusions, his revulsion seems to be at odds with a far more compassionate, politically nuanced, critique. As he continues his letter of August, it becomes clear that the 'people' are 'utterly different', not due to some inherent failing in their nature, but because they are so beset. The 'poor people', who become just *'the poor'* (my emphasis), are 'too helpless, too exposed, to behave like us'; in their 'lack of moderation' they are compensating for being 'a helpless target for all the taxes, epidemics, sicknesses, and evils of social institutions'. By 1921, when *Mass Psychology* appears, the 'people' have become the 'masses'. Certainly the shift of vocabulary might suggest that any traces of empathy have been lost. The masses are gullible, suggestible, out of touch with reality, blind. Although Freud rejects Gustave Le Bon's idea of a specific herd-instinct, he accepts most of his characterization of a mass as at once all-powerful and a mere straw swaying in the wind. Gathered together individuals become both too heavy (the mass comes into being as *critical mass*) and too light; threatening – 'ready, in its awareness of its own strength, to be dragged into all sorts of atrocities such as might be expected only from an absolute, irresponsible power' – and prone: 'It wants to be dominated and suppressed and to fear its master.' Freud acknowledges that masses are capable of 'great feats of renunciation in the service of an ideal'; they can rise as well as sink. But, whether lofty or base, people en masse are only inspired to an *extreme*. Averse to innovation, conservative; always – since time immemorial – the same.

Above all, the mass, lacking all inhibition, exposes the unconscious of us all: 'the unconscious foundation that is the same for everyone is exposed'. Like the pervert and the hysteric, the mass, from which the bourgeoisie no less fiercely like to distinguish themselves, is showing us something that we all need to see (the mass is also contagious, which means that none of us is immune). Ugly, the mass lifts the veil of the night, releasing humans from cultural constraint – in the mass, man is allowed to do what no individual would dare. At moments, it is as if the mass *becomes* the unconscious – without logic, knowing 'neither doubt nor uncertainty', living a type of collective dream. Freud may be repelled; he may be frightened (despite the bravura of his letter to his fiancé in 1883). But he has also made man in the mass the repository of a universal truth. That human subjects suffer under the weight of repressive cultural imperatives that force them against their nature ('our present-day White Christian culture', to use a later phrase). By the time he writes *The Future of an Illusion* in 1927, that early insight into the poor as the bearers of the worst 'evils' of social institutions has become even more political and precise:

if a culture has not got beyond the point where the satisfaction of some participants requires the oppression of others, maybe the majority (and this is the case with all contemporary cultures), then, understandably, the oppressed will develop a deep hostility towards a culture that their labour makes possible but in whose commodities they have too small a share.

'It goes without saying,' he concludes, 'that a culture that fails to satisfy so many participants, driving them to rebellion, has no chance of lasting for any length of time, nor does it deserve one.'

Although Freud calls his text 'Mass Psychology' (from the German *'die Massen'*), the core of his work centres on two great social institutions, the army and the church, and two intensely intimate conditions – being in love and hypnosis in which, to use his own formula, we are dealing with 'if the expression be permitted' a 'mass of two'. Faced with such moments of awkwardness, most previous translations, notably Strachey's *Standard Edition*, have chosen to translate 'mass' as 'group', giving us a 'group of two members', which no doubt causes less of a conceptual stir. But it is not for nothing that Freud, having first charted his path through the most threatening aspect of behaviour in the mass, lands us in the middle of two of society's most prized and refined collectivities, and at least one of its most cherished states of mind. In our normal run of thinking, there are 'groups' and there are 'masses' – the first of which it is assumed, unlike the second, always keeps its head in bad times. In fact we could say that it is the role of church and army, great policing institutions both, to channel the one into the other, to offer – against any menace in the wider world – the sanctuary of the group. In an ideal world, so this logic might go, there would be no masses, which however fiercely bound together, always seem unruly, as if threatening something loose. Freud's view is more radical, cutting through such precious distinctions. For all their *gravitas* and grace, church and army, in their very ability to generate unquestioning, sacred loyalty, are microcosms of what they most fear. They seed what they are meant to contain.

It is central to Freud's thinking on this topic that what binds people together, for better and worse, is their commitment to an internal ideal. Because we are narcissists, we will only relinquish, or even circumscribe, our self-devotion for something or someone that we can put in the same place. Something that makes us feel good about ourselves. Something that tells us, even if we are a multitude, that somewhere, somehow we are also the only one. And that whatever we do – and this is the killer, so to speak – we are a cut and thrust above the rest. To be part of a group is to push everything hated to the outside (which is why for Freud, along with the more mundane, territorial reasons, nations go to war). Freud's originality, however, is to add to this insight that rivalrous hostility towards the other is integral to the very formation of the group. I will suspend my hatred of the other, and bind my fate with his, if you – mentor, leader, father, God – recognize *me*. Clearly there is something amiss. How can rivalry be redeemed by the clamour for such exclusive attention? In one of his most trenchant, and clinically deceptive formulas, Freud states: '*a primary mass is a number of individuals who have set one and the same object in the place of their "I"-ideal and who have consequently identified with one another in terms of their "I"*' (emphasis original). That is what it means to become as 'one.' I will identify with you but only on condition that the ideal you take for your own has become my internal psychic property. The group is an orchestrated flight into inner superiority, which everyone is then presumed to share. In a paradox Freud never succeeds in unravelling, hostility is suspended by narcissistic acclaim. But what this means is that when men – since it is most often men – band together to go to war, another state of war, barely refined, is most likely to be going with them.[3]

Two things, Freud insists, distinguish his account from the previous literature on which he so copiously draws (only chapter one of *The Interpretation of Dreams* can rival this text for the lengths to which he goes to incorporate other theories on his topic): love relationships: 'Let us remember that the existing literature makes no mention of them'; and the tie to the leader: 'For reasons that are as yet unclear, we should like to attach particular value to a distinction that the existing literature tends to underrate, namely that between leaderless masses and masses with leaders'; again, only a few pages later: 'we would venture now to level a mild reproach against the authors of the existing literature for having done less than justice to the importance of the leader as regards the psychology of the mass'; and even more forcefully towards the end: 'the nature of the mass is incomprehensible if we ignore the leader'. 'The essence of a mass', Freud writes, 'consists in the libidinal attachments present within it.' Love, then, and devotion to the leader are what binds. If the mass is held together by some force: 'to what force could such an achievement be better ascribed than to eros, which holds the whole world together'.

Leaving aside for a moment the fact that the world does not obviously 'hold together', as Freud of course knows well, it is worth pausing here. For psychoanalysis, as Freud explains, 'love' has a very wide range. It includes 'self-love . . . parental and infant love, friendship, general love of humanity, and even dedication to concrete objects as well as to abstract ideas'. To deny the libidinal component of these attachments is only for the 'feeblehearted'. So, Freud concludes, 'we shall try adopting the premise that love relationships (to use an inert expression, emotional ties) also form part of the essence of the mass mind.' It is on this basis that Freud takes us into the analysis of church and army, and from there to the structure of identification for which he offers a fuller analysis in this text than anywhere else in his work (crucially being in love also follows the path of identification when the loved object, requiring like a leader total surrender, usurps the place of the 'I'). So what are these love relationships or emotional ties which bind subjects en masse? They are precisely the experience of *being loved*; or to put it in more clichéd terms, not what I give to you, but what you give, or do for, me. To ignore the role of the leader, Freud writes, is not just a theoretical shortcoming but a practical risk. Under cover of a leader's love or benevolent knowing, even the world at its most perilous feels safe (it was not the realities of the battlefield, he argues, but ill treatment by their superiors, that caused the breakdown of Prussian soldiers during the Great War).

And yet Freud is aware that this love of the leader is a precarious gift. Barely concealed behind any leader is the father who was hated as much as he was revered. In *Mass Psychology*, Freud slowly moves back to the theory first advanced in *Totem and Taboo* of 1913: that society originally came into being on the back of a primordial crime. The brothers banded together to murder the father who controlled all the women of the tribe. Once the deed was done, only guilt, plus the dawning recognition of the danger each brother now represented to the other, caused them to bind together and lay down their arms. Whether you accept the historical account or not – and there are no historical grounds to do so – Freud's myth, as always, is eloquent. Trying to explain how love averts hatred, his intellectual trajectory here, the very movement of his text and of his argument (regressive, as he would say of the mass mind), is to take the reader slowly but surely away from mutuality to murder. How solid can any group identification possibly be if the leader we love and who loves us all as equals is also, deep in the unconscious, the tyrant who must be killed? As if the mass is only held together, like those first brothers, because it is aghast at its own history, its own actual and potential deeds. A mass freezes into place at its own dread. At the heart of Freud's analysis of the mass entity is a self-cancelling proposition. We love the other most, or need most to be loved by the other, when – from that other and from ourselves – we have most to fear. It is a 'miracle', Freud writes, that the individual is willing to 'surrender his "ego"-ideal, exchanging it for the mass ideal embodied in the leader'. Like love, one might say; or the belief that love conquers all.

It is almost too easy to see in Freud's portrait of the leader the outlines of his own personal drama as the founder of psychoanalysis. More simply, to see him as issuing a demand: Love me. After all, ever since the split with Jung in 1914, the year after he wrote *Totem and Taboo*, Freud had reason to fear that the love his followers bore him was laced with a hostility that could threaten his movement. What if his group, instead of being a free association of like-minded individuals, were one of those 'artificial masses', like church and army, in need of 'a certain external compulsion [. . .] to prevent them from falling apart'? The only things preventing a mass from behaving like an 'ill-mannered child', 'impassioned, unsupervised savage', or worse, like a 'pack of wild animals' are the agreed conditions laid down for it to function. When Freud draws on W. McDougall's *The Group Mind* to lay out these requirements – a measure of continuity, a specific conception of the group's 'nature, function, attainments and aspirations', contact with related but differing collective entities, traditions, customs and institutions particularly such as bear on the relationship of its members with one another, a careful grading and differentiation of functions – it reads at least partly as a countdown against bedlam, his own wish to bind the chaos he might himself have unleashed. As if he were describing a model for a psychoanalytic institution that would be a cross between a secret society and a bureaucratic machine. In *Mass Psychology*, we can see Freud already struggling with a dilemma that psychoanalysis as an institution has not solved to this day, even while it is the one institution that recognized that dilemma as foundational to what any subject, any institution, might be. How to aim for perfected organized continuity given the cruel ambivalence lurking within our most cherished forms of allegiance?

In his 1907 paper 'Compulsive Actions and Religious Exercises', which opens this volume, Freud suggests that religious ceremony shares its nature with compulsive or obsessional neurosis, in which subjects ritually perform actions designed to ward off the intolerable burden of a guilt-ridden mind. Condemned to the endless repetition of meaningless gestures, lacking the symbolic weight of the sacred, the compulsive neurotic, with his 'half-funny', 'half-sad' distortion of a private religion, is a clown. Or perhaps a parodist, who mocks the petty rituals that in the modern day and age are thrusting the deeper content and meaning of religious faith to one side (one objection of enlightenment, *Haskalah* Jewry to the orthodox in Freud's time was that they were burying the spirit of Judaism under a tide of observational constraints).[4] If religion apes neurosis, being part of a religious collective also assuages the mind. 'Even one who does not regret the disappearance of religious illusions in today's cultural climate,' Freud concludes in *Mass Psychology*, 'will concede that, while they still held sway, they afforded those in thrall to them their strongest protection against the threat of neurosis.' Mass-formation, and none so powerfully as religious mass-formation, is therefore one of the most effective systems a culture creates to keep its subjects sane. By deluding them with the false consolations of belief; but above all by allowing them to repeat, in the daily actions required of them as testament to that belief, the behaviour of a subject who knows he has a great deal to atone for. 'One might venture to construe' neurosis as 'individual religiousness', Freud writes in the 1907 paper, and religion as a 'universal compulsive neurosis'. The neurotic – this is from the last page of *Mass Psychology* – creates his own 'fantasy world, religion and system of delusion', but in so doing he is merely 'echoing the institutions of humanity in a distorted form'.

In the texts that follow *Mass Psychology* in this volume, the question of faith gradually usurps that of mass-formation only to rejoin, slowly but surely, the man in the crowd. To the end of his life, Freud was convinced that his view of faith as deluded, worse as a reaction-formation akin to a neurotic disorder, was the view that set him most at odds with the surrounding culture. Previous translations have lost the link between religion as *compulsion* (as in *Zwangsneurose*) and Freud's later death drive or repetition compulsion (*Wiederholungszwang*), a link that drives religious sensibility firmly towards the demonic. Less repellent than sexuality, less radically disorienting than the idea of the unconscious, such a vision of religious belief nonetheless threatened to breach the most strongly fortified symbolic ramparts of civilized man. Even when he was writing *Moses the Man* across the *Anschluss* of Austria and his exile to London in 1938, Freud persisted in thinking that his critique of religion placed him at risk. He was a target of persecution first as disbeliever, only then as Jew: 'I should now be persecuted not only for my line of thought but for my "race".' 'The only person this publication may harm,' he writes at a particularly defensive moment in *The Future of an Illusion*, 'is myself.'

In many ways, Freud's critique of religion, laid out most ruthlessly in *The Future of an Illusion*, appears as something of a footnote to his view of the mass. After all, in *Mass Psychology*, the masses discard reality in favour of 'affectivity charged with feelings' (a tautology surely – what is affectivity if not to be charged with feelings?); they never 'thirst after truth'; they 'demand *illusions*'. Although *The Future of an Illusion* is also the text in which Freud most loudly acknowledges their oppression, from its opening section, the masses appear as the concentrate of their worst attributes (lethargic, unreasonable, unpersuadable, incapable of restraint). For anyone wanting to limit the damage, Freud's response to the acrimony unleashed by *The Future of an Illusion* in *Civilization and its Discontents* two years later only makes matters worse. 'The whole thing is so patently infantile, so incongruous with reality, that to one whose attitude to humanity is friendly, it is painful to think that the great majority of mortals will never be able to rise above this view of life.'[5] This does not sound friendly. Galled, humiliated ('it is even more humiliating . . .') – Freud loses patience like an irascible father trying to correct the homework of his child. Unless they happen to be the child whose tale he recounts in *The Future of an Illusion*, precociously distinguished by his love of 'objectivity', who, when told that a fairy story was not true – a story to which other children had been listening 'with rapt attention' – 'assumed a scornful expression and withdrew'. Who, we might ask, is most to be pitied in this story – the boy trapped in his deadening 'matter-of-factness', or the other children, whose reverie he will presumably have torn apart with his contempt? For Freud, engaging with the opponent he conjures for the sake of argument throughout *The Future of an Illusion*, this anecdote is meant to be decisive. Like the child, humanity will stop believing when it grows up: 'a turning away from religion must be expected to occur with the fateful inexorability of a growth process' (note how that 'fateful' places our cool emancipation from faith in the lap of the gods). Nothing in the twenty-first century to date suggests this is the case.

The Future of an Illusion is a diatribe. In many ways it is also, I would suggest, Freud's most un-Freudian text, and one which will return to haunt him in the final years of his life. Religion infantilizes the people, consoles them for the inconsolable, suppresses their wholly legitimate and unanswerable fears. The world is brutish and nature does not care. When we most think to have controlled her, she strikes ('coldly, cruelly, without a qualm'). The elements mock our restraint, the earth heaves and splits open, waters drown, storms blow everything away. This is Freud in imitation of Lear. Add the contingency of human diseases, the random inevitability of our own deaths, and we have every reason to despair: 'there remains an uncomfortable suspicion that the bewilderment and helplessness of the human race is beyond remedy'. To add insult to injury, we heap suffering upon each other: 'passions rage in the elements as they do in the human heart'. Enter religion, which tells us that none of this – in the final, cosmic, order of things – matters. We are protected by a benevolent God who redeems our helplessness even when we are unaware (although believing in Him of course helps). Most simply, we are watched over. Someone is looking. The values of our ideals are, Freud repeats here from *Mass Psychology*, narcissistic in nature. Even more than our Saviour, God is our spectator. The citizens of America, that proclaims itself 'God's own country', share with the Jewish people, although Freud coyly does not name them here, the belief that God has made their nation his own: 'and for one of the forms in which humans worship the deity that is indeed true'. How deep must be the narcissistic wound of humanity, if the only way to redeem it is to feel yourself swelling to the measure of the heavens?

The Future of an Illusion offers Freud's most passionate defence of the order of reason. There is, he insists, no 'higher authority'. *Vernunft* in German, which means reason or even more prosaically 'good, common, sense', has none of the ambiguous flexibility of *Geistigkeit*, central to *Moses the Man*, which, as Jim Underwood stresses in his translation, hovers between 'intellectuality', but with none of the negative connotations of aridity attaching to it in the English, and 'spirituality', as an internal quality with no specifically religious meaning (a term therefore eloquently suspended between heart and brain). 'Reason', on the other hand, brooks no argument (as in 'it stands to reason'). Freud is pitting 'reason' against 'illusion', pitting, at its crudest, the educated elite against the mass – a 'split', as his opponent in the text argues, between the 'philosophical thinker' and the 'uneducated mass'. As Freud describes them, the arguments for religious belief are self-defeating, 'oddly out of harmony with one another': our forefathers believed them; we possess proof from distant times; no justification of belief is permitted or required. This is the logic of the unconscious or what he defines in a famous passage in *The Interpretation of Dreams* as 'kettle logic', the logic of a man defending himself against his neighbour's charge that he has returned his kettle in a damaged state: I never borrowed it; it doesn't have a hole; the hole was there when you lent it to me. But Freud also knows that the illogic of this form of reasoning is a sign that a particularly deep vein of psychic investment (*Besetzung*) has been tapped. Strachey translated *Besetzung* as *cathexis*, the Greek inappropriate, the technicality off-putting for a term meant to indicate our most heartfelt and obdurate attachment both to others and to parts of ourselves. In this translation, we are given instead 'charging', as in an electrical current, which is far closer to the urgency of Freud. Of all people, Freud should know better than to think that you can walk into this part of the mind and try to *reason with it*. No one enters here without being burnt.

Freud allows his fictional opponent to articulate many of these criticisms (this is the only text, apart from his 1926 *The Question of Lay Analysis*, in which Freud personifies one half of the argument he is almost always having with himself). But he does so only the more stubbornly to argue him to the ground. Freud believes not only that religious belief is deluded and infantile, but also that it deprives human subjects of freedom (it is the ultimate form of surrender). Because religion ultimately fails to console humans for death, so it shifts increasingly and inexorably into the domain of human affairs, arrogating to itself the ethical life, whose precepts are meant to keep subjects – in legitimate internal revolt against the constraints and injustices of culture – in their place. At moments, Freud's defence of his position reads like Bertolt Brecht's Galileo whose discoveries, as the Church well knew, were a threat as much to secular as religious authority. 'Truth', states Galileo in Brecht's play, 'is the child of time, not of authority'; 'I believe in the gentle power of reason, of common sense over men.'[6] Compare Freud: 'the voice of the intellect is a low one, yet it does not cease until it has gained a hearing'. (Freud did compare himself directly with Copernicus, as well as with Darwin, for dethroning man from the centre of all things.)

What Freud desires most fervently in this work is that man should generate his ethical precepts out of himself, that he should 'leave God out of it entirely', and 'frankly concede the purely human origin of all cultural institutions and rules'. He does not therefore want the constraint of culture abolished. Unlike some of his later followers, such as Herbert Marcuse and Wilhelm Reich, he was no libertarian; indeed he believed that religion was failing to make man moral, was not taming the 'anti-social drives' *enough*. If man knew himself to be the source of his own authority, he would not seek to overturn the precepts of culture; he would try to *improve* them.

Presumably – if we recall Freud's statement that a culture based on flagrant inequality does not deserve to survive – he would make them more just. Freud's biographer Ernest Jones is convinced that Freud's own interest in religion, which the reader would be forgiven for not picking up here, stemmed not from theological concerns but from 'the ethical teaching', particularly 'on the theme of justice'.[7] 'By withdrawing his expectations from the beyond and concentrating all the forces thus released on earthly existence', Freud concludes near the end of his text, 'he will doubtless manage to make life bearable for all and ensure that culture quite ceases to oppress.' In this he anticipates many of today's critics of fundamentalism. A secular polity would make the world a better place.

And yet there remains something unpersuasive about this text. By the time Freud wrote it, he had become convinced that religion preserved deep inside its unconscious archive a forgotten or repressed historical truth. God is the direct descendant of the primal father; that is why, in our petitions to the deity, our dreadful helplessness is our strongest suit. But if Freud reiterates here his belief in a primary parricide at the origins of all culture, if he allows therefore that religion is a form of reminiscence, and that this historical reality is what endows it with much of its powers, he sweeps past this recognition with remarkable haste. Not to say panic. Of course 'acknowledging the historical value of certain religious teachings increases our respect for them', but that, he insists, in no way invalidates the desire to do away with them. 'Quite the contrary!' It is 'thanks to these historic residues' that the analogy between religion and neurosis can be made; as with the neurotic patient it is time to replace repression with 'ratiocination'. In any case, 'we need make no apology' for departing from 'historical truth' in providing a rational motivation for culture as this truth is so distorted as to be unrecognized by the mass of humanity. This is indeed kettle logic and to see it you do not have to accept Freud's view of primary murder at the origins of mankind: there is a truth in religion; it is so distorted the masses cannot see it anyway; reason is more important than historical truth.

As with *Mass Psychology*, it is as if murder returns to haunt the barely acquired, fragile, rational civility of the tribe. Freud does not know where to put this murder, because he loves his new theory and in *Moses the Man* he will place it at the very core of the Jewish tradition and faith; indeed, murder will become what most intensely ties the Jewish people to their law. The question, as Freud knows only too well, is not whether religion is true but why it has the power to bind its adherents (a fact to which he will ascribe the Jew's ability to survive). What matters, we might say, is not reason and reality, but – to refer again to *Mass Psychology* – the force of human identifications, whether lethal or redemptive (indeed often both). Or, going back to the very beginning of Freud's work, people – and the force of this later writing is to show

how that includes 'peoples' – invent themselves out of their memories; what counts is not the accuracy, but the productivity, not the strictness, but the movement, of the meanings we make. Near the end of *The Future of an Illusion*, Freud agrees that reason can do nothing when religion proclaims a 'superior spiritual essence whose properties are indeterminable and whose purposes are unknowable'. The German here is *'geistigen Wesens'*; a term untranslatable into the English as we have already seen, meaning spirituality or intellectuality or both. In the end, Freud leaves us with the glowing residue of his own conviction – something that cannot be fully determined, grasped or known (like the unconscious we might say). What if religion were determined by tradition, memory, murderousness, by indefinable qualities of being and of the mind? What if – as one of the twentieth century's most famous godless Jews was perhaps best placed to discover[8] – this, or at least some of this, is what it means to belong?

On 6 May 1926, an address by Freud was read to the Vienna lodge of B'Nai Brith (Sons of the Covenant), an order representing Jewish cultural, intellectual and charitable interests originally founded in the United States, to which Freud, outcast as he had felt himself to be in the beginning, had addressed many of his early papers. 'Whenever I felt an inclination to national enthusiasm,' he states, 'I strove to suppress it as being harmful and wrong, alarmed by the warning examples of the peoples among whom we Jews had lived.' 'But,' he continues, 'plenty of other things remained over to make the attraction of Jews and Jewry irresistible – many obscure emotional forces all the more powerful the less they could be expressed in words, as well as a clear consciousness of an inner identity, the intimate familiarity of the same psychic construction.' (*'die Heimlichkeit der gleichen seelischen Konstruktion'*, translated by early psychoanalyst Theodor Reik as 'the secrets of the same inner construction').[9] This identity, which Freud here as elsewhere scrupulously detaches from national passion, was not simple; and, even though he will refer to it on occasion as an essence, in many ways as we will see it was not 'clear'. It was after all the whole burden of his 1919 paper on the uncanny – *'Das Unheimliche'* –

that the *'heimlich'* or 'homely/familiar' is intimately, not to say, eerily related to its opposite. Nonetheless, what Freud is describing is undoubtedly a sense of belonging. Crucially, that sense stems from those same dark, obscure 'emotional forces' ('all the more powerful the less they could be expressed in words') that Freud will turn on so ruthlessly the following year.

In 'A religious experience', written in the same year as *The Future of an Illusion*, Freud tells the story of a young American physician who first discards all religious belief and then is promptly reconverted by an inner command, after witnessing the corpse of an old woman laid out on the dissecting table. Freud, in one of his most reductive moments, traces the conversion to deferred obedience to the father, against whom the young man, appalled by the sight of the 'sweet-faced old woman' (for which read the mother), had momentarily but violently rebelled. And yet he knows that the very simplicity of his own analysis – 'so simple, so transparent' – deceives: 'One cannot avoid asking whether [. . .] anything at all has been gained as regards the psychology of religious conversion.' What, to repeat his own question in *The Future of an Illusion*, are the obscure emotional forces – 'whose properties are indeterminable and whose purposes are unknowable' – on which religious affiliation relies? Or in the words of *Moses the Man*: 'from what springs do some ideas, particularly religious ideas, draw the strength to subjugate individuals and nations alike?' In the final years of his life, under the threat of impending exile, *Moses the Man* erupts as the unfinished business of *The Future of an Illusion*, as the return of its repressed. 'We find to our surprise,' Freud writes in the first Viennese foreword to the last essay of *Moses* (the second was written in England), 'that progress has forged an alliance with barbarism.' Freud knew he had not answered the question of his earlier work; something, in his words, 'remained over'. But it was another ten years, in the last major work of his life, before he offered his final unexpected reply.

If *Moses the Man* returns Freud to the question of religion, it also returns him to that of mass psychology, thus bringing the texts in this volume full circle. The Jewish people become the testing ground of how viable it is to insert the notion of the unconscious into collective life. Much will hang on this, but if anything Freud is now more cautious: 'It was not easy, I admit, bringing the concept of the unconscious into mass psychology' (and, increasingly unsure as he proceeds, 'We do not find it easy to transfer the concepts of individual psychology to mass psychology'). By 1938, this 'mass' has become as much a national, as a religious, entity; at issue now is the strength of religion to subjugate: 'individuals *and nations* alike' (my emphasis). Religion, Freud more or less states, forges nations. Nationhood is, or can be, a religious passion. Freud may have wanted to believe that religious beliefs would go away; but instead he seems to be issuing a rather different warning – against the power of national identities, hardly diminished today, to endow themselves with the aura of the sacred. Faced with the rise of Nazism and the growing prospect of invasion and exile – although until February 1938 he persisted in thinking that the *Anschluss* could be averted – Freud found himself up against nationalism in two of its most radically disconcerting shapes. Both can be felt pressing on his study of Moses. On the one hand, a ruthless and expansive German nationalism, its masses in thrall to their leader (Nazism as hypnotic collectivity in its purest most deadly guise); on the other, the nationalism of a dispossessed people, arising at least partly in response to the excesses of the first, but whose history and inner identity offers – or at least this is Freud's hope and claim here – the possibility of another, more nuanced, form of belonging. Freud does not mention Hitler in this work; he could hardly do so of course as long as he remained in Austria where the bulk of the work was written. But it is, surely, impossible not to see the German leader, traced in a type of grotesque reflection, behind the man held – as Freud puts it in his opening lines – to be the 'greatest son' of the Jewish people. Remember too that Freud up to now has offered no portrait of the leader; in *Mass Psychology* there is no sign of the figure on whom, as he repeatedly insists, his whole analysis depends.

In his address to B'Nai Brith, Freud spoke of 'national enthusiasm' as 'being harmful and wrong, alarmed by the warning examples of the peoples among whom we Jews had lived'. Jewish national belonging must be different. In a famous letter in 1930, after the Arab riots in Palestine, he refused an appeal from Dr Chaim Koffler of the Jewish Agency to add his voice to those of prominent European intellectuals calling for a reversal of British policy on access to the Wailing Wall and on Jewish immigration to Palestine. 'It would have seemed more sensible to me,' he comments drily, 'to establish a Jewish homeland on a less historically burdened land.' Writing to Ferenczi in 1922, Freud had spoken of 'strange secret yearnings in me – perhaps from my ancestral heritage – for the East and the Mediterranean'; but when Arnold Zweig returns from a visit to Palestine in 1932, he describes it as this 'tragically mad land' that has 'never produced anything but religions, sacred frenzies, presumptuous attempts to overcome the outer world of appearance by the inner world of wishful thinking'. 'And', he concludes, 'we hail from there [. . .] our forebears lived there for perhaps half perhaps a whole millennium [. . .] it is impossible to say what heritage from this land we have taken over into our blood and nerves.'[10]

Yet despite this anxious recognition and recoil (in which we can recognize a barely concealed orientalist revulsion towards the East), in his letter to the Jewish Agency, Freud does not rule out the creation of 'a Jewish homeland'. And by 1935, in a letter to Karen Ha-Yesod, the financial wing of the World Zionist Organization, he describes that organization as 'a great and blessed' instrument in its endeavour 'to establish a new home in the ancient land of our fathers'.[11] By then what is at issue for Freud, and not only for Freud, is 'our invincible will to survive'. He would not live to see that will utterly shattered in Europe, nor, after the War, watch its dramatic, invincible rebirth in Palestine. In *Moses the Man*, Freud attempts the almost impossible task of squaring the circle of this tragic historical moment. Can there be a form of survival for a people that does not fatally – fatally, that is, for itself and for the others against whom it stakes its claim to existence – entrench and sanctify itself? Freud does not seem to believe for a minute, as he does for religious faith, that 'national enthusiasm' can be reasoned away. What is the likely fate of a longing that you can only, in his words, 'suppress'?

It may seem odd to suggest that the thesis of *Moses the Man and Monotheistic Religion* is simple; after all the book is, as Yosef Yerushalmi describes it in his magisterial reading – *Freud's Moses: Judaism terminable and interminable* – possibly the 'most opaque of Freud's works'. Published piecemeal and with anxiety, the first two parts in *Imago*, the third with two 'mutually contradictory' prefaces, the first of which stating it will never be published, while the complete text was not published until he died. The work is repetitive and uneven, bearing all the signs of a hesitation only partly explicable by the length of time it took him to write it and the unique historical conditions under which it was composed ('internal misgivings coupled with external constraints'). Freud was never at ease with it: 'I miss the sense of oneness and solidarity that ought to exist between the author and his book'; he could see how it might appear as 'a cast-iron figure resting on feet of clay'; or 'a dancer balanced on the tip of a single toe'. To read Freud's *Moses*, writes Lydia Flem, 'is to read Freud writing *Moses*'.[12] It is in *Moses* that Freud famously describes historical writing, on which he is himself at least partly engaged here, as a corrupt and murderous craft: 'The corruption of a text is not unlike a murder. The problem lies not in doing the deed but in removing the traces.' By the time Freud arrived in England, the work was haunting him 'like an unlaid ghost'. Accompanying him on his last journey, *Moses* is, we could say, Freud's phantom limb (the hysteric of his earliest work returns at the end of his life). In the words of Russian Formalist Viktor Shklovsky, this is writing as '*attenuated tortuous speech*', whose point, as he puts it in words remarkably resonant of psychoanalysis, is to 'examine the object, *to dismember it*, to represent it not only as they [the artists] saw it, *but as they knew it*'.[13]

And yet, despite this oddness ('unorthodoxy' or 'eccentricity' in the words of Strachey), it is one of Freud's most fiercely determined texts. Freud believes that Moses was an Egyptian, a prince, priest, or high official belonging to the ancient monotheistic cult of Aton that was swept away with the death of its founder, the Pharoah Amenhotep or Akhenaton, in 1358 BC. Whereupon, Moses seized a Semitic tribe, slaves of Egypt, as his people and led them to freedom in Canaan on condition that they adopt the religion to which his own people had proved so pitifully inadequate. The people rebel against Moses and murder him (not this time because he owned all the women, but because of the dreadful severity of his law). Monotheism and the crime fade in the life of the nation until, generations later, they meet up with a second Moses, son of the Midianite priest, Jethro, of the cult of the volcanic god Yahweh, to which – in an act of partial historical remembrance and atonement – the religion of the first tribe is slowly but surely assimilated.

Freud takes his thesis of the murder of the first Moses from a then famous work by Sellin published in 1922 (when Freud was told that he had later recanted, he famously replied that Sellin was mistaken and should have stuck to his original idea). He takes the account of the second Midianite priest from the historian Eduard Meyer, and several of his contemporaries, who argued that the Jewish tribes 'from which the people of Israel eventually emerged' took on a new religion at a certain point in time, not at Sinai, as the Bible has it, in the locality of Meribath-Kadesh in a stretch of country south of Palestine. Freud's crucial move – in a theoretical gesture that mimes the story he tells – is to *merge* them. Barely concealed behind the unity of the Jewish people, inside its most intimate, *heimlich*, 'inner identity' is an uncanny, *unheimlich*, doubling (for Freud, doubling is one of the most effective vehicles of the uncanny). Nothing simply belongs. Once again the issue is not the – much contested, dubious – accuracy of his narrative, but its effects. Like a compulsion, Freud's account and his history repeat themselves; 'constant repetitions and recapitulations' to use Strachey's terms. What does it mean to insist, as Freud does here, that a people were founded, their divine election established, not in one unanswerable moment of recognition between the people and their God, not once, but twice? Freud was not alone in pointing to this duality in Jewish history, but he adds and embroiders, making it the driving force of the people. *Moses the Man* – the original title restored in this translation – is therefore something of a misnomer. What type of historical novel was Freud envisaging that cuts its hero into two?

Putting our conclusion in the shortest possible form of words, to the familiar dualisms of that history (*two* peoples coming together to form the nation, *two* kingdoms into which that nation divides, *two* names for god in the source writings of the Bible) we add two new ones: *two* religious inaugurations, the first forced out by the second but later emerging behind it and coming victoriously to the fore, *two* religious inaugurators, both of whom went by the same name, Moses.

It is, as Freud was only too aware, an embarrassment of riches that is also the cruellest act of dispossession.[14] Imagine a child from a broken home with a father and a stepfather, stating in all innocence, as pure matter of fact: 'I do not have one' (meaning 'I do not have *one* father, but *two*').

'All these dualisms,' Freud writes, 'are inevitable consequences of the first, namely that one component of the people had been through what has to be described as a traumatic experience that the other had been spared.' Trauma therefore first splits, and then forms, forges, *fuses* the group. What binds people to their leader is that they killed him, although remembering the deed takes time. When Yerushalmi criticizes Freud for suggesting that the Jews repressed this memory, given that 'the most singular aspect of Jewish tradition [is] its almost maddening refusal to conceal the misdeeds of the Jews', he is, however, missing the psychoanalytic point. It is the characteristic of any compulsion (*Zwang*) that you endlessly berate yourself, that you atone, with unflagging and elaborate ceremonial, for everything apart from the one thing you most fear you might have done. For Freud, the subsequent emergence of Christianity, in which the son lays down his life for humanity, should be read as the next verse of this epic of denial and atonement (it must have been a dead father if only the death of a son can redeem it; and if a voluntary death is the penance, then murder must have been the original crime). But if this narrative has a logic, one which we do not have to accept at every turn, Freud's bold-est move is to place at the heart of the group what it would most like to dispose of. As the new millennium already bears witness, war is almost invariably justified in terms of an outside danger or threat (the other is the aggressor; it is only in order to survive that you kill). Freud offers a counter-history. He takes slaying, at which subjects en masse excel, and hands it back to the people. Even the most innocent of people (and for Freud there are no pure innocents), believe somewhere that they are also culprits. What effect might it have on modern-day rhetoric against terrorism, or on its accompanying refrain of good versus evil, if peoples were seen as driven to their greatest acts of self-empowerment, not to say violence and glory, by guilt?

Moses' Egyptian provenance is central to this narrative, not just because it announces and crowns the losses and dislocations to come (in the opening line Freud acknowledges that he is denying, robbing, depriving the Jewish people of their founder, or, as he puts it, 'their greatest son' – the German *abzusprechen* means more literally to 'take back the saying of'). But because, as Edward Said stresses in his vital re-reading of the work for Israel/Palestine at the present time, it inscribes the Jewish people in a non-European heritage, 'carefully opening out Jewish identity toward its non-Jewish background' (while also attesting, as Egyptologist Jan Assman puts it in his recent study, *Moses the Egyptian*, to the fundamental importance of Egypt in the history of mankind).[15] A model for nationhood that would not just accept the other in its midst, nor just see itself *as other*, but that grants to that selfsame other, against which national and political identities define them-selves, a founding, generic status at the origins of the group. Freud knows that this is a form of sacrilege as well as a huge risk, and not just to himself. After all, it was he who insisted in *Mass Psychology* that panic or breakdown in the mass is the result of loss in belief in the leader, not of legitimate fear, even in the face of real danger. At the very moment when the Jewish people have most reason to fear, when they are faced with the rise of a leader who will set as his aim the destruction of the mass of European

Jews, Freud removes their most ardently possessed figurehead at a stroke. Why? if not, surely, to suggest that it is time for groups to look for less rigid, potentially abject, forms of psychic and spiritual cohesion.

In fact it is possible to read *Moses the Man* as a critique of monotheism *tout court*. The gift that Moses bestows on his people is one that cannot be borne. This monotheism is 'rigid', 'intolerant', expansive and 'imperialist'. Claiming universality, it demands – in a gesture that has nothing to do with a critique of national identity – that 'religion give up its national confines'. As it gained in strength under Amenhotep, it achieved 'ever-greater clarity, consistency, brusqueness'. The father-god it introduces is 'boundlessly dominant', 'jealous, strict and inexorable'. In a word, monotheism is awful (the US policy of 'shock and awe' in the 2003 invasion of Iraq could be said to take its cue from just such monolithic forms of psychic coercion). Monotheism ushers religious intolerance into the world. For Assman, it is a counter-theology because it renders idolatrous ancient polytheisms whose principal characteristic was that of being infinitely *translatable* into each other. Prior to monotheism, peoples worshipped different gods, but no one contested the existence of foreign gods or the legitimacy of foreign forms of worship. When monotheism cries false to strange gods, it shuts itself off and, with it, a whole galaxy of potential connections: 'False gods cannot be translated.'

This was, as Assman calls it, the 'Mosaic distinction', and 'the most outspoken destroyer of the Mosaic distinction was a Jew: Sigmund Freud'. In the long tradition that made Moses Egyptian, either historically (Manetho, Strabo, Toland) or in affinity, as someone initiated into 'hieroglyphic wisdom and mysteries' (Spencer, Warburton, Reinhard and Schiller), it is always the rigid difference between monotheism and a more copious religious profusion that is stressed. Jews were hated. Freud's stated objective in his work was, not as might have been expected, to understand anti-Semitism in the mind of the hater, but 'how the Jew came to attract this undying hatred'. By making Moses an Egyptian, Freud liberates his people from the beginnings of their own theocracy.

The founding moment of an oppressive law and intolerant faith falls outside Jewish jurisdiction. 'Who', Freud asks in a footnote, 'prompted the Jewish writer Heinrich Heine in the nineteenth century AD to complain about his religion as "the plague we dragged along with us from the Nile Valley, the unhealthy ancient Egyptian faith"?' Judaism, to use the expression of Martin Buber in his essay 'The Two Centres of the Jewish Soul', 'itself is not of the Law'.[16] Freud is releasing Judaism from its own obduracy, its rigid ortho-dox strain. It is then perfectly possible to move from here back into the mystical counter-tradition inside Judaism itself. Writing to Jung in 1909, after a numerological discussion of the number 62, Freud states: 'Here is another instance of the specifically Jewish character of my mysticism.'[17] Kabbalah shares with psychoanalysis its belief in hermeneutics and the infinite permutations of words (Freud discusses the plurality of God's name in *Moses*). It also always contained an anarchic streak. Like the sixteenth-century mystical messiah, Shabat Svi, Freud can be seen as an iconoclast, leading his followers and his people, against the Law, into apos-tasy and freedom. (And in the *Zohar*, major document of the Kabbalistic tradition, Moses is an Egyptian).[18]

The Law will not strike. Thus Freud reads Michaelangelo's 'wonderful', 'inscrutable' statue of Moses in the San Pietro in Vincoli in Rome as the prophet frozen in the moment before he breaks the tablets, restraining his anger, reining back his wrath as he descends from Mount Sinai to the spectacle of his backsliding people. He reads him, that is, as curtailing, even if only for a moment, the punishing component of his own God-given Law. There is no higher 'mental achievement', Freud concludes, than such restraint (we can clearly feel the strength of Freud's own efforts, in relation to his increasingly dissident followers, to control himself). Freud visited the statue, which must have played its part in his later study, whenever he was in Rome, as a type of pilgrim-age, creeping out of the 'half-gloom' to 'support the angry scorn of the hero's glance', 'as though I myself belonged to the mob upon whom his eye is turned'. He is therefore Moses *and* the people, split in two like the history of the Jews that he will much later recount. But it is surely noteworthy that the only moment in all his writing when Freud identifies himself with the mob, he does so as *idolator*.[19]

If this were all, then *Moses the Man* might become prime evidence in the case for Freud's rejection of his own Jewish legacy. As critics like Marthe Robert, who take this line, have pointed out, Freud did on occasion refer to his Jewishness as the bearer of hereditary illness, or 'taint'.[20] But Freud is far more equivocal than this. 'It is not even certain,' he suggests, going back over the ground he has just covered, 'that [Moses'] religion was a true monotheism, disputing the divinity of the gods of other peoples.' Freud wants it both ways. Monotheism, together with the violence of its earliest history, is not just 'ruthless', 'intolerant', 'inexorable'; it is also the foundation of ethical life. If anything, Freud makes even stronger in this last work the tie between guilt and justice: 'the act of patricide with which social order, the moral law, and religion had first come into being'. As we have seen, the Jewish people become so forcefully a people because of the murder that first bound them together as a group. Only a buried, unconscious identification of this depth and virulence will work. Because they are always unconsciously atoning, so they are always watching and being watched to ensure that the treatment they mete out to others is fair. Freud famously claims in *The Future of an Illusion* that justice arises out of envy: if I cannot be privileged, no one must.

But if the Jews are a just people, it is also because the Egyptian Moses gave to them a god 'as all-loving as he was all-powerful', who 'held out for men, as their highest goal, a life lived in righteousness and truth'. (Akhenaton described himself in his inscriptions as 'living in *ma'at*' – 'truth, righteousness'.) 'Is it not about time', asks the author of the article on anti-Semitism that Freud cites in the last short essay of this collection, 'we stopped tossing [the Jews] favours when they have a right to *justice*?'

It does not matter therefore that this first Moses was slain; what was finest in his tradition survived and slowly but surely it usurped the law of the volcanic Yahweh who might appear, according to the more obvious historic sequence or turn of events, to have replaced it. Aton had been a pacifist. In his 1912 article on Amenhotep and monotheism, Karl Abraham describes him as the first deity to extol 'love as a power that conquers the world' and Amenhotep (or Ikhnaton, meaning 'he who is agreeable to Aton) as rejecting 'in his ethics all hatred and all acts of violence', subli- mating all aggression to an 'unusually far reaching degree', allow- ing his religion to languish because, out of touch with reality, he lived in the peaceful idyll of his own dreams (Abraham was one of Freud's inner circle but the article is strangely not referred to by Freud).[21] Yahweh was, on the other hand, a conqueror. 'For a people on the point of taking violent possession of fresh places to settle,' Freud writes, 'the god Yahweh was undoubtedly more suit- able.' Now we can perhaps see more clearly the advantages, as well as the fully political import, of having two Moses. Not just to disrupt the crushing monolith of national identity, but also so that Judaism, saved from its most exacting features (and one might add any conquering ambitions), can still be the fount of wisdom in the world. 'No one doubts,' Freud states near the end of the second essay, that 'it was only the idea of this other god that enabled the people of Israel to survive all the blows of fate and has kept it alive into our own day.' Freud, we could say, takes the Jewish people's greatest son away with one hand, and gives him back with the other. The people, or rather the best of the people, survive. Freud could hardly have anticipated that this split between his two figures of Moses, between conquering settlement and a people living in justice, would have such an afterlife, that it would become the most disturbing and intractable legacy to the Jewish people of the founding, ten years later, of the Israeli nation state.

In *Moses the Man*, therefore, the question of faith is slowly but surely displaced by that of tradition: 'in what form is effective tradi- tion present in the life of peoples'? (this is Yerushalmi's basic argu- ment). The point is no longer to dissipate faith with a blast of reason, but to understand, even respect, the unconscious trans- mission of mass or group. To understand why people, from gener- ation to generation – with no solid ground and in the teeth of the most historically unsympathetic conditions – *hold on* (the ties of the mass have shifted into the descent of a people). Individual and collective join at the seam of historical identities transmitted over time – the analogy between the two, Freud insists here, is 'complete'. If not Judaism as Law, then Jewishness as tenuous but tenacious remembrance, in the unconscious memory-traces of the people, passes down through the ages. Freud never stopped believing in the inheritance of acquired characteristics even when science had moved on to genetics (he acknowledges here that biology will no longer have anything to do with this belief). It is, as Yerushalmi says, through Jewishness or *for Jewishness* that Freud's Lamarckianism also survives (Ernest Jones, in his discussion of *Moses*, describes it as the 'weakest link'). Something is passed down even if we do not know how: 'our forebears lived there [. . .] it is impossible to say what heritage from this land we have taken over into our blood and nerves.' However much you try to destroy the law of the father, you are obedient to him at least in this. Forever. Pushing it, you could argue that the very concept of 'deferred obedience', not to mention the primal murder of the father and indeed the whole Oedipal structure – all reiterated here – are intended to secure this legacy, as violently repudiated as it was clung to by Freud (Oedipus stating most simply that man kills his father and then must identify with the father he kills – the dead father enters the soul).

Turning to the future, we could say that the question of his Jewish identity propels Freud towards the idea of 'transgenerational haunting', a concept forged by Hungarian emigré analysts Maria Torok and Nicolas Abraham, significantly in the aftermath of this historical moment, as they tried to understand the silent persistence of the Holocaust in the minds of second-generation Jews. A child can be the bearer of the unspoken and often unspeakable legacy of her or his parents (the legacy passes in the unconscious not in the bloodstream).[22] You do not need Lamarck to believe that the sins and suffering of the fathers are visited on the sons. 'The deeper motives for hatred of Jews,' Freud writes, 'are rooted in the remote past, they operate out of the unconscious of nations.'

What cannot be known or spoken is therefore the key. In 1930, in the Preface to the Hebrew edtion of *Totem and Taboo*, Freud made this, his perhaps most famous statement about his Jewish identity:

No reader of [the Hebrew version of this book] will find it easy to put himself in the emotional position of an author who is ignorant of the language of holy writ, who is completely estranged from the religion of his fathers – as well as from every other religion – and who cannot take a share in nationalist ideals, but who has never repudiated his people, who feels that he is in his essential nature a Jew and who has no desire to alter that nature. If the question were put to him: 'Since you have abandoned all these common characteristics of your countrymen, what is there left to you that is Jewish?' he would reply: 'A great deal and probably its very essence.'[23]

No faith, no language, no nationhood – as Said stresses, Freud defines himself here as Isaac Deutscher's non-Jewish Jew; but for all that, or even *because of that*, he is Jewish in essence.

In the third and final essay, 'Moses, His People, and Monotheistic Religion', written across the passage into exile, things take a new turn. It is in this essay that Freud argues that the Jewish people are the bearers, and originators, of *Geistigkeit*, an intangible quality that, as we have already seen, represents the best of intellectuality (without the aridity), the best of spirituality (without religious constraint). Unquestionably an advance or progress (*Fortschritt*, the *fort* is the mark of the irrevocable, as in 'from this time on' or 'no turning back'), *Geistigkeit* stands for that moment when man's beliefs achieved a level of abstraction without which there would never have been ethics, justice, truth. It rides the distinction between paternity and maternity, the one a logical inference, the other an unavoidable empirical fact (motherhood is something affirmed by the evidence of the senses). The supreme achievement is to worship a god 'one cannot see'. And it leads humans to acknowledge 'spiritual powers' which, although they cannot be grasped by the senses, manifest 'undoubted even super-powerful effects'. This without so much as a backward glance to *The Future of an Illusion* in which, as we saw, any such powers were deeply suspect (although the question of emotional forces of 'indeterminable properties' and 'unknowable purposes' was already there).

Now to define a force as intangible or unknowable is to accord it the highest praise: ask Freud what is left to him that is Jewish and he would reply: 'A great deal and probably its very essence,' although he continues, 'he could not now express that essence clearly in words.' 'We are as a group a mystery,' Wulf Sachs, Lithuanian Jew and first practising psychoanalyst in South Africa writes to Freud from Johannesburg on 1 August 1939 in response to reading *Moses the Man*, 'to ourselves and others.'[24] In the middle of writing the work, Freud writes to his sister-in-law Barbara Low after the death of psychoanalyst David Eder: 'We were both Jews and knew of each other that we carried this miraculous thing in common, which – inaccessible to any analysis so far – makes the Jew.'[25] *Geistigkeit*, we could say, is Freud's attempt to give substance, though that is not quite the right word, to this essence. Or to solve the mystery, while preserving it, keeping its miraculous nature intact.

Above all, this achievement of *Geistigkeit* makes the Jewish people of value *to themselves*. The Jews were not just chosen by their leader, the qualities his faith bestowed on them gave them infinite worth in their own minds: 'The "I" feels elated, it takes pride in renouncing the drives.' Moses, and through him his god, chooses the people. As Yerushalmi points out, by retaining this from the Bible Freud turns his back on modern secular-Jewish liberalism for which such an idea had become an embarrassment. In fact Moses does not just choose his people; he *creates* them – Freud is pushing to its furthest conclusion the argument of *Mass Psychology* that without a leader the mass cannot exist. Not for nothing does Freud entitle one section of his work 'The great man' (whose 'implacability' in dismissing everything told about other gods as 'lies and deceptions' now becomes 'superb'). Like all good leaders, but going one better, Moses raises the masses in their own eyes: 'all such advances increase self-esteem, making people proud'.

Through Moses, 'the self-esteem of the Jews' became, uniquely among faiths, 'anchored' inside their religious belief (we could say, tautologically, that their proudest possession becomes their pride). This is what gives the Jewish people their 'toughness'. *In extremis*, the Jews take as their mantle the narcissism of the group. They become, so to speak, the supreme embodiment of culture's good opinion of itself: 'the satisfaction that the ideal gives to those involved in a culture is narcissistic in nature'. In the process they become a people in whom Freud himself can likewise once again take pride. That Yahweh was finally usurped by the god of Moses is 'evidence of a special psychic aptitude in the mass that had become the Jewish nation'. By the end of *Moses the Man*, the Jews, who make their first appearance as 'a bunch of culturally back-ward foreign immigrants', have completed the transformation from mass into people; they have become an *elite*.

Freud therefore turns Moses into an Egyptian, lets the stranger into the tribe. He castigates the ruthlessness of monotheism, breaks apart the unity both of the people and their faith. He places murder at the origins of the group. But this is, finally, no simple icono-clasm. The integrity, the narcissistic unity and at-oneness of the group, *returns*. Identity, as Jewish identity, reaffirms itself. How could it not in 1938? In this final essay, Freud leads the Jewish people into their true inheritance (*Moses the Man* can be read equally as betrayal or as boast). But he has done so at a time and in the framework of an analysis which suggests that identity, while it may indeed be necessary for the survival of subjects and peoples, also places the whole world in peril. The problem, not least for the Jewish people, will not go away. Writing to Gershom Scholem in reply to his criticisms of her study of Eichmann in 1963, Hannah Arendt argues: 'the greatness of the people was once that it believed in God, and believed in him in such a way that its trust and love towards him was greater than its fear. And now this people believes only in itself? What good can come out of that?' She was respond-ing to Scholem's assertion: 'Of course I do not believe in God; I believe in the Jewish people.'[26]

It seems therefore futile to try and decide whether Freud's essay on Moses puts him on the inside or outside of Jewish tradition. The only viable answer must surely be both. Freud defined himself as Jewish in 'essence' even as he feared – and not just for the obvious historical reasons – that psychoanalysis was being seen as a 'Jewish national affair' (ironically given their falling out, it was only Jung's appearance on the scene that he believed would allow psychoanalysis to escape this danger). What Freud does teach us, however, in a struggle present on almost every page of his own text, is how hard it is for any collectivity to avoid the potentially militant self-possession of the clan. Perhaps Freud was trying to do the impossible. How do you save a people at one and the same time from the hatred of others *and* from themselves?

Freud's ideal was Jabneh, the first Torah academy, where the life of learning became the highest aim. 'The fact that Rabbi Jochanan ben Zakkai immediately after the destruction of the Temple obtained from the conqueror permission to establish the first academy for Jewish knowledge,' he wrote in a 1938 letter to Dr Jacob Meitlis of the Yiddish Scientific Institute in Vilno, 'was for me always one of the most significant manifestations of our history';[27] Jabneh also appears in *Moses*: 'henceforth it was holy scripture and the spiritual effort that held the scattered nation together'. But Freud also identified with Moses the hero, seeing his life as the founder of psychoanalysis in terms of conquest in a hostile world (the 'Man Moses' in the title restored in this translation redeems the faith). Psychoanalysis offers us the spectacle of a Janus-faced discipline or way of thinking, at once combative, and – turned to what Freud terms here 'the darkness of the inner life' – in retreat.

'A Comment on anti-Semitism', which appeared in a German journal in Paris in November 1938, was, as a gloss appended to the title stated, the first of Freud's works to be published after his exile from Vienna. It consists almost entirely of a long quotation from an article – 'so extraordinary that I selected excerpts from it to use myself' – about whose source, as the last lines of the piece establish, Freud is completely unclear. Commentators have therefore speculated that Freud himself is the author of a critique of anti-Semitism that he has chosen to place in the mouth of a non-Jew, as if to say: in his analysis of Moses he could only do so much; in the end the persecutor must look to himself. But whether these are Freud's own words or not, the effect is the same. Either way, by copiously citing or by inventing, the distinction breaks down, the two fuse. As they must if race hatred is ever to end, Jew and non-Jew speak with one voice, cross over to the other's place. Wonderfully encapsulating the hardest part of his endeavour, this last piece thus performs in the very form of its writing the task whose difficulty Freud proclaims more or less on every page of all these texts. Issuing its challenge to the crisis of the times and beyond, the journal in which the article appeared was called *The Future: a new Germany, a new Europe*.

In each of the works collected here, psychoanalysis steps outside its own doors, claims its status as fully social analysis, whether between people (empathy, identification, hypnosis and loving) or across the generations (memory, tradition, faith). Even when we dream, we are not alone. Our most intimate psychic secrets are always embedded in the others – groups, masses, institutions and peoples – from which they take their cue, playing their part in the rise and fall of nations. Not to recognize this is, finally, the greatest, most dangerous, illusion of them all.

Jacqueline Rose, 2004

Notes

1. See Dennis B. Klein, *Jewish Origins of the Psychoanalytic Movement*, Chicago, IL, 1981; Carl E. Schorske, *Fin-de-siècle Vienna – Politics and Culture*, Cambridge 1981; Steven Beller, *Vienna and the Jews 1867–1938*, Cambridge 1989.
2. *Letters of Sigmund Freud*, selected and edited by Ernst L. Freud, London 1960, cited Marthe Robert, *From Oedipus to Moses – Freud's Jewish Identity*, translated by Ralph Mannheim, Littman Library of Jewish Civilisation, London 1974, pp. 46–7.

3. For a discussion of some of these internal paradoxes, see Mikkel Borch-Jacobsen, *The Freudian Subject*, translated by Catherine Porter, London 1988, chapter 3 'The Primal Band'; also 'The Freudian Subject: from politics to ethics', translated by Richard Miller and X. P. Callahan, in *The Emotional Tie: psychoanalysis, mimesis and affect*, Stanford, CT, 1992.

4. For a discussion of Freud in relation to *Haskalah*, see Marianne Krull, *Freud and his father*, translated by Arnold Pomerans, New York 1986, and also Yosef Hayim Yerushalmi, *Freud's Moses: Judaism terminable and interminable*, New Haven, CT, 1991, pp. 62–3.

5. *Civilization and Its Discontents*, 1930, translated by David McLintock, New Penguin Freud, London 2002, p. 12.

6. Bertolt Brecht, *The Life of Galileo*, 1955, translated by Desmond I. Vesey, London 1963, pp. 54, 42.

7. Ernest Jones, *Sigmund Freud: Life and Work*, vol. 3, *The Last Phase 1919–1939*, London 1957, p. 375.

8. Letter of 9 October 1918 from Sigmund Freud to Oskar Pfister, *Psychoanalysis and Faith, The Letters of Sigmund Freud and Oskar Pfister*, London 1963, p. 63.

9. Sigmund Freud, 'Address to the Society of B'Nai Brith', *The Standard Edition of the Complete Psychological Works of Sigmund Freud*, vol. XX, pp. 273–4 (translation modified); Reik's translation is cited by David Bakan who discusses the implications of Freud's use of *'heimlich'* in *Sigmund Freud and the Jewish Mystical Tradition*, London 1990, pp. 305–19.

10. Letter to Chaim Koffler, cited from *Freudiana: From the Collections of the Jewish National and University Library Jerusalem*, cited by Yerushalmi, *Freud's Moses*, p. 13; Letter to Arnold Zweig, from *The Letters of Sigmund Freud and Arnold Zweig*, New York 1970, cited by Yerushalmi, p. 15; Letter to Ferenczi, cited Jones, *Sigmund Freud*, vol. 3, p. 88.

11. *Freudiana*, cited Yerushalmi, p. 13.

12. Lydia Flem, *Freud the Man – an intellectual biography*, New York 2003, p. 159.

13. Viktor Shklovsky, 'Art as Technique', 1917, *Russian Formalist Criticism*, edited by Lee T. Lemon and Marion J. Rees, Lincoln, NE, 1965, p. 23, italics original; Shklovsky, *Mayakovsky and His Circle*, London 1972, p. 17, emphases mine.

14. For a very strong discussion of *Moses* in relation to the idea of dispossession and dissociation, see Phillipe Lacoue-Labarthe and Jean-Luc Nancy, 'The unconscious is de-structured like a language', and 'From where is psychoanalysis possible?', *Stanford Literary Review*, 6, 1991, 8, 1992.

15. Edward Said, *Freud and the non-European*, response by Jacqueline Rose, introduced by Christopher Bollas, Verso and the London Freud Museum 2003; Jan Assman, *Moses the Egyptian: the memory of Egypt in Western Monotheism*, Cambridge, MA, 1997.

16. Martin Buber, *Mamre: essays in religion*, Melbourne, Australia 1974, cited Bakan, *Sigmund Freud and the Jewish Mystical Tradition*, p. 117.

17. Freud to Jung, 16 April, 1909, *The Freud/Jung Letters*, edited by William MacGuire, London 1974, p. 220.

18. See Bakan, *Sigmund Freud and the Jewish Mystical Tradition*.

19. Freud, 'The Moses of Michaelangelo', 1914, *Standard Edition*, vol. XIII, p. 213.

20. Marthe Robert, *From Oedipus to Moses*, p. 95; the thesis is central to Robert's study.

21. Karl Abraham, 'Amenhotep IV: a psychoanalytic contribution towards the understanding of his personality and of the monotheistic cult of Aton', 1912, *Clinical Essays and Papers on Psychoanalysis*, London 1955.

22. Nicolas Abraham, 'Notes on the Phantom: a complement to Freud's metapsychology', in *The Shell and the Kernel*, vol. 1, edited, translated, with an introduction by Nicholas T. Rand, Chicago, IL, 1994.

23. Freud, *Totem and Taboo: some points of agreement between the mental lives of savages and neurotics*, 1913, *Standard Edition*, vol. XIII, p. xv.

24. Wulf Sachs to Sigmund Freud, 1 August 1938, *Archive of the Freud Museum*.

25. Freud, *Letters*, cited Robert, p. 35.

26. Hannah Arendt to Gershom Scholem, 24 July 1963, *The Jew as Pariah: Jewish Identity and Politics in the Modern Age*, New York 1978, p. 247.

27. Letter to Jacob Meitlis, 'The Last Days of Sigmund Freud', *Frontier*, 18, September 1981, cited Bakan, p. 49.

Translator's Preface

Most translators try to make themselves invisible, so being asked to contribute a 'Translator's Preface' is a bit like being told, 'Come on out – we can see you!' That is disingenuous, of course (there is no point, when translating an author who so often discusses linguistic issues, in striving officiously to remain invisible), but perhaps not entirely. However, the reader does need to have at least one question addressed: Why a new English translation of Freud?

Much has been written about this, some of which I have read. In this context, let me stress three points:

1) I am a full-time freelance translator of average education. I do nothing else; I am not a critic, for example. I simply take a German (or French) text and render it as faithfully as I can into English. All right, this is also disingenuous: I carry my own 'baggage' (as indeed the reader does), and it will inevitably skew any rendition I make (as the reader's 'baggage' will tend to skew his or her understanding). But I see my job (and try very hard to practise my job) as being to manufacture a transparent illusion of equivalence.

A fuller account of my approach to translation will be found in my 'Translator's Preface' in *Franz Kafka: Stories 1904–1924* (Macdonald, 1981; Abacus, 1995).

2) James Strachey, who translated many of Freud's writings himself and edited the English Standard Edition the *Collected Psychological Works of Sigmund Freud*, was a practising psychoanalyst, not a professional translator. He 'put a lot in', which to a translator is like breathing on a window (reducing its transparency).

Worse, faced with Freud's rather special use of an unexceptional German word (*Besetzung*), he threw professional integrity to the winds and invented a 'translation' (the famous 'cathexis', together with its associated adjective 'cathectic', and even a dreadful verb, 'to cathect', now to be found in the *Concise Oxford Dictionary*).

James Strachey performed a great service in almost single-handedly introducing Freud to the English-speaking world (and readers who want more guidance through the labyrinth of Freud's enormous output are recommended to consult the very thoroughly annotated *Standard Edition*). However, he did not simply translate Freud; he also, to some extent, traduced him.

3) Freud was an amazing man. From a tiny base he generated a vast body of work that changed the way we who come after him think. He did this not systematically, not to any particular purpose, but in sheer profusion. He sought to educate, to 'lead people out'. In retrospectively 'ism-ing' him, we shackle a great liberator.

My source texts were as follows:

Zwangshandlungen und Religionsübungen (1907) ['Compulsive actions and religious practices'], *Gesammelte Werke, chronologisch geordnet*, vol. VII, *Werke aus den Jahren 1906–1909*

Massenpsychologie und Ich-Analyse (1921) ['Mass psychology and Analysis of the "I"'] Fischer Taschenbuch Verlag, Frankfurt am Main, 1993

Ein religiöses Erlebnis (1927) ['A religious experience'], *Gesammelte Werke, chronologisch geordnet*, vol. XIV, *Werke aus den Jahren 1925–1931*

Die Zukunft einer Illusion (1927) ['The future of an illusion'], Fischer Taschenbuch Verlag, Frankfurt am Main, 1993

Der Mann Moses und die monotheistische Religion (1938) ['Moses the man and monotheistic religion'], Fischer Taschenbuch Verlag, Frankfurt am Main, 1975

Ein Wort zum Antisemitismus (1938) ['A comment on anti-Semitism'], photocopy of original article in *Die Zukunft. Ein neues Deutschland, ein neues Europa*, 7, Paris, 25 November

1938 (kindly supplied by the Freud Museum, 20 Maresfield Gardens, London NW3 5SX).

Original notes are translated from the above texts; my additional contributions (a translator, once lured out of hiding, finds it hard to return) appear between square brackets, as do English translations of German titles in Freud's notes.

Compulsive Actions and Religious Exercises

I am certainly not the first to have been struck by the similarity between the so-called 'compulsive actions' of nervous people and the routines by means of which the believer testifies to his piety.[1] What makes me so sure of this is the label 'ceremonial', which has been attached to some of those compulsive actions. However, that similarity seems to me to be more than merely superficial, as a result of which one might, on the basis of some understanding of how neurotic ceremonial comes about, venture arguments by analogy regarding the mental processes of religious life.

People who perform compulsive actions or ceremonial, together with those who suffer from compulsive thinking, compulsive imaginings, compulsive impulses, and the like, belong to a special clinical entity for whose affliction the term in common use is 'compulsive neurosis'.[2] But let no one try to derive the peculiar nature of this ailment from its name, because strictly speaking other kinds of pathological mental phenomenon have the same claim to this so-called 'compulsive character'. In place of a definition we must currently make do with detailed knowledge of such conditions, for it has so far proved impossible to reveal what is probably the deep-seated criterion of compulsive neurosis, the presence of which one nevertheless feels one detects, in its various manifestations, all over the place.

Neurotic ceremonial consists in little routines, add-ons, restrictions, arrangements, performed in connection with certain everyday actions in ways that are always the same or are subject to regular change. Such activities give us the impression of mere 'formalities'; they appear totally meaningless to us. They appear

3

no different to the sick person himself, and yet he is unable to leave them out, for each deviation from the ceremonial is punished by unbearable fear, instantly compelling him to make good the omission. Quite as petty as the ceremonial actions themselves are the occasions and activities that the ceremonial embroiders, makes more difficult, and invariably also draws out, e.g. dressing and undressing, going to bed, satisfying bodily needs. The execution of a ceremonial may be described by, as it were, substituting for it a series of unwritten rules. For instance, in the bed ceremonial the chair must stand in such and such a (specific) position beside the bed and the clothes lie folded on it in a particular order; the blanket must be tucked in at the foot end, the sheet smoothed flat; the pillows must be distributed just so, the body itself must lie in a precisely determined position; only then may the person go to sleep. In mild cases, the ceremonial resembles that kind of exaggeration of a customary, quite legitimate arrangement. However, the special conscientiousness of its execution and the fear experienced when something is omitted mark the ceremonial out as a 'holy action'. Disturbances of it are in the main poorly tolerated; the public eye, the presence of others during performance, is almost always debarred.

Compulsive actions in the broader sense are something that all activities are capable of becoming if embroidered with little add-ons, lent rhythm by means of pauses and repetitions. One will not expect to find a sharp line of demarcation between 'ceremonial' and 'compulsive actions'. Most compulsive actions have their origin in ceremonial. In addition to these two, the substance of the ailment is formed by prohibitions and preclusions (aboulias), which in fact simply continue the work of the compulsive actions, in that, so far as the sick person is concerned, some things are not allowed at all, others only if a prescribed ceremonial is observed.

Interestingly, both compulsion and prohibitions (having to do one thing, not being allowed to do another) initially concern only solitary human activities and for a long time leave a person's social behaviour unaffected; people with such an ailment are thus able for many years to deal with it and conceal it as a private matter.

4

Also, many more people suffer from such forms of compulsive neurosis than doctors know about. Moreover, concealment is made easier for many sufferers by the fact that during part of the day they are quite capable of fulfilling their social obligations, having devoted a number of hours, in Melusina-like solitude,[3] to their secretive doings.

It is easy to see where the similarity between neurotic ceremonial and the sacred actions of religious ritual is located, namely in qualms of conscience when something is omitted, in total isolation from all other activity (no interruptions allowed), and in meticulous conscientiousness of performance. Just as striking, however, are the differences, some of which are so glaring as to make the comparison a sacrilegious one: the greater individual variety of ceremonial actions in contrast to the stereotypical nature of ritual (prayer, proskinesis, etc.); their private character as opposed to the public, communal nature of religious observance; but one difference above all, namely that the small add-ons of religious ceremonial are by intention meaningful and symbolic whereas those of neurotic ceremonial appear silly and meaningless. In this the compulsive neurotic offers a half-funny, half-sad distortion of a private religion. However, precisely this most crucial difference between neurotic and religious ceremonial is removed if, aided by the technique of psychoanalytical investigation, we work through to an understanding of compulsive actions.[4] In the context of such investigation, the appearance of silliness and meaninglessness attaching to compulsive actions is utterly destroyed and the reasons for that impression revealed. We learn that compulsive actions are altogether meaningful in every little detail, serving key interests of the personality and expressing experiences that continue to influence and thoughts that carry an emotional charge for that personality. They do this in two ways: either as direct or as symbolic representations. It follows that they need to be read either historically or symbolically.

I ought at this stage to furnish one or two examples designed to elucidate this assertion. Anyone familiar with the findings of psychoanalytical research in connection with psychoneuroses will not be surprised to hear that what is represented through the medium of compulsive actions or ceremonial stems from the most private, usually sexual experience of the person concerned:

a) A young woman I was observing had a compulsion to swivel the washbasin around several times after washing. The significance of this ceremonial action lay in the proverbial saying: 'Pour no dirty water away before you have clean.' The action was intended to warn her beloved sister and to prevent her from divorcing her unsatisfactory husband until she had formed a relationship with someone better.

b) A woman living apart from her husband obeyed a compulsion at mealtimes to leave the best part, e.g. eating only the edges of a piece of roast meat. This sacrifice was explained by the date of its origin. It had first appeared the day after she refused her husband marital intercourse, i.e. renounced the best part.

c) The same patient could in fact sit only on one chair and had difficulty getting up from it. For her, the chair symbolized (with reference to certain details of their married life) the husband to whom she remained faithful. To explain her compulsion, she hit on the sentence: 'It is so hard to part from a (man, chair) one has once sat upon.'

d) She was in the habit, for a time, of repeating a particularly striking and meaningless compulsive action. She would run out of her room into another, in the middle of which stood a table, pull the tablecloth that lay on it straight in a certain way, ring for the maid, who then had to approach the table, and dismiss her again with a trivial order. As she tried to explain this compulsion, it occurred to her that the tablecloth concerned had a stain on it and that she always placed the cloth in such a way that the maid could not help seeing the stain. The whole thing, it turned out, reproduced an experience from her marriage, which had subsequently presented her mind with a problem to solve. Her husband had been overtaken, on their wedding night, by a not unusual misfortune. He found himself impotent and 'came running many times during the course of the night out of his room into hers' in order to repeat the attempt, perhaps this time successfully. In the morning he said he would inevitably feel ashamed in front of the hotel chambermaid when she came to make the beds. Consequently, seizing a bottle of red ink, he poured its contents over the sheet. However, he did this so clumsily that the red stain appeared in what, for his purpose, was a most unsuitable place. In other words, with her compulsive action she was playing wedding night. 'Bed and board [table]' together constitute marriage.

e) When she adopted a compulsion to write down the number of each banknote before she spent it, this too was explicable historically. Back in the days when she had been contemplating leaving her husband if she found another man more worthy of her trust, while staying at a spa she accepted the courteous attentions of a gentleman about the seriousness of whose intentions she was nevertheless in doubt. Short of coins on one occasion, she asked him to change a five-crown piece for her. He did so, pocketing the large metal disc and saying chivalrously that he meant never to part with it because it had passed through her hands. At subsequent meetings she was often tempted to ask him to produce the five-crown piece for her – as a way, so to speak, of satisfying herself as to whether she could believe his tributes. She refrained from doing so, however, on the excellent grounds that coins of the same value are impossible to tell apart. Consequently her doubts remained unresolved, leaving her with this compulsion to write down the numbers of banknotes, numbers that distinguish each individual note from every other of the same denomination.

These few examples, plucked from the wealth of my experience, are simply intended to illustrate the proposition that everything about compulsive actions is meaningful and can be explained. The same applies as regards ceremonial proper, except that here the proof would need to be cited at greater length. I am very conscious of how far these explanatory remarks about compulsive actions seem to be taking us from the range of ideas covered by religion.

A key element of this ailment is that the person obeying the compulsion practises it without realizing its significance (its principal significance, at least). Only through the effort of psycho-analytical therapy is the patient made aware of the meaning of the compulsive action and hence of the motives behind it. We put this important state of affairs into words by saying that compulsive actions serve to express *unconscious* motives and imaginings. That would seem to imply a fresh difference from the practice of religion, but remember: the individual worshipper also, in the main, performs religious ceremonial without enquiring into its significance, whereas of course the priest and the scholar will no doubt be aware of the usually symbolic meaning of the ritual. However, the motives compelling a person to practise religion are outside the awareness of all believers or are represented in their conscious minds by professed motives.

Analysing compulsive actions has already enabled us to gain some understanding of their causation and of the chain of motives defining them. The person suffering from compulsion and prohibitions can be said to behave as if under the control of a *guilty conscience* of which, however, that person knows nothing – in other words, an unconscious guilty conscience, as we have to call it, disregarding any conflict between the components of that phrase. That guilty conscience has its source in certain early mental processes. However, it finds constant refreshment in the *temptation* that is renewed in connection with each real-life occasion; on the other hand, it produces a perpetually lurking *anticipatory anxiety*, an expectation of calamity that is associated, through the concept of *punishment*, with the internal perception of temptation. In the early stages of ceremonial formation, the sick person is still aware of having to do this or that, otherwise some calamity will occur, and as a rule the sort of calamity that can be expected is still spelled out to his consciousness. The always demonstrable connection between the occasion for the appearance of the anticipatory anxiety and the substance with which it threatens is already masked so far as the sick person is concerned. Ceremonial thus begins as a *defensive* or *affirmative* action, a *protective measure*.

The guilty conscience of the compulsive neurotic corresponds to the protestations of the pious that they know that in their hearts they are grievous sinners; the value of defensive and protective measures appears to attach to the pious exercises (prayers, invocations, etc.) with which they preface each daily activity and particularly every exceptional undertaking.

A deeper insight into the mechanism of compulsive neurosis comes from taking into proper consideration the original fact underlying it: this is invariably the *repression of a drive-impulse* (a component of the sex drive) that was contained in the person's constitution, was allowed to find expression for a while during childhood, and subsequently fell victim to suppression. A special *conscientiousness* directed at the targets of that drive is brought into being as the drive is repressed. However, this psychical reaction-formation does not feel sure of itself; it feels constantly under threat from the drive lurking in the unconscious. The influence of the repressed drive is experienced as temptation, while the fear that usurps the future as anticipatory anxiety emerges in connection with the very process of repression. The repression process that leads to the compulsive neurosis should be termed an imperfectly successful one that increasingly threatens to fail. It therefore invites comparison with an unresolvable conflict; fresh psychical exertions are constantly required in order to counterbalance the continuous pressure exerted by the drive. Ceremonial and compulsive actions thus arise partly as defence against temptation, partly as a shield against expected calamity. Against temptation, protective actions soon seem inadequate; that is when prohibitions appear, designed to keep the temptation situation well at bay. Prohibitions replace compulsive actions, clearly, just as a phobia is designed to obviate the hysterical seizure. On the other hand, ceremonial represents the sum total of the conditions under which other things, not yet the subject of absolute bans, are allowed – very like the way in which the ceremonial of a church wedding signifies to the pious that sexual enjoyment, normally sinful, is now permitted. It is further in the nature of compulsive neurosis, as of all similar affections, that its expressions (symptoms, including compulsive actions) fulfil the condition of a compromise between warring mental

9

powers. In other words, they also invariably bring back something of the desire they are designed to prevent; they serve the repressed drive no less than the agencies repressing that drive. Indeed, as the illness progresses, the original actions, concerned more with defence, come increasingly to resemble the forbidden actions through which, in childhood, the drive was allowed to find expression.

Of these circumstances, something like the following would also occur in the field of religious life. The formation of religion, too, seems to be based on suppression, on the *renunciation* of certain drive-impulses; however, these are not (as in the case of neurosis) exclusively sexual components but selfish, anti-social drives, albeit usually not without a sexual element. After all, the guilty conscience resulting from unexpunged temptation and anticipatory anxiety as fear of divine punishment became familiar to us in the field of religion earlier than in that of neurosis. Possibly because of the admixture of sexual components, possibly as a result of general properties of drives, in the religious life too, suppression of drives turns out to be an inadequate, impermanent affair. Total relapses into sin are in fact more frequent with the pious person than with the neurotic, accounting for a new class of religious activities, namely penances, for which the counterparts can be found in compulsive neurosis.

We saw it as a peculiar, degrading quality of compulsive neurosis that ceremonial attaches to minor actions of everyday life and finds expression in silly rules and restrictions applying thereto. This striking feature of the organization of the clinical picture becomes comprehensible only when we learn that the mechanism of psychical *displacement*, which I first discovered in connection with dream-formation,[5] governs the mental processes of compulsive neurosis. A limited number of examples of compulsive actions have already made it clear how, as a result of the displacement of real, significant matter onto a minor substitute (e.g. from husband to chair), the symbolism and the detail of performance come about. It is this displacement tendency that goes on and on altering the symptomatic picture and eventually makes what seem to be the most trivial matters into the most important and the most urgent. Unmistakably, there is a similar tendency towards the displacement of psychical value in the religious field – and it works in the same direction, with the result that little by little the petty ceremonial of religious observation becomes the essential element, having thrust religion's thought content aside. That is why religions are also subject to reforms that begin in fits and starts, seeking to install the original value relationship.

The compromise character of compulsive actions as neurotic symptoms will be least clearly recognizable in the corresponding religious activity. And yet in this respect too one is put in mind of neurosis when one recalls how often all actions tabooed by religion (expressions of the drives suppressed by religion) are performed precisely in the name of and for the supposed benefit of religion.

Faced with these correspondences and analogies, one might venture to construe compulsive neurosis as the pathological counterpart of the development of religion, calling neurosis individual religiousness and religion a universal compulsive neurosis. The key correspondence might be said to consist in the underlying decision not to exercise constitutionally given drives; the crucial difference in the nature of those drives, which in the case of neurosis are of exclusively sexual origin, in the case of religion of egoistic origin.

A progressive renunciation of constitutional drives, exercise of which might provide the 'I'[6] with primary pleasure, seems to be one of the foundations of human cultural development. Part of that drive repression is performed by religions in that they prompt the individual to sacrifice his libidinal side to the deity. 'Vengeance is mine', says the lord. One gains the impression from the development of the ancient religions that much of what men had renounced as 'wantonness' had been surrendered to god[7] and was still permitted in god's name; in other words, ceding them to the deity was how men and women freed themselves from the tyranny of wickedly anti-social drives. So it is no accident that the ancient gods had every human quality (together with the misdeeds that flowed therefrom) ascribed to them in infinite measure, and there is no inconsistency in the fact that people were still not permitted to justify their own wantonness by the divine example.

(1907)

Notes

1. [Let no one look for political correctness in a text bearing the date 1907; in any case, German linguistic gender (the word for 'person' is feminine, for instance) is irrelevant in English. For 'he', 'his', etc. used in this sort of context, the reader is asked to read 'he/she', 'his/her', etc. throughout.]

2. See Leopold Löwenfeld, *Die psychischen Zwangserscheinungen* ['Psychical Compulsive Phenomena'] 1904.

3. [Freud made many allusions (he was very widely read, particularly in literature, mythology and archaeology) that the modern reader may not appreciate without some expansion. The lovely mermaid Melusina, subject of a French legend, accepts marriage to a human on condition that he does not seek her out on a Saturday. He does so, of course, and, having found her in her bath and discovered that her body ends in a fish's tail, loses her when she returns to the sea from which she came.]

4. See [Sigmund] Freud, *Sammlung kleiner Schriften zur Neurosenlehre* ['Collected shorter pieces on the theory of neurosis'], Vienna 1906 (3rd edition, 1920).

5. See [Sigmund] Freud, *Die Traumdeutung* (1900) [translated into English by James Strachey as *The Interpretation of Dreams, Standard Edition*, vols 4–5.]

6. [All things considered, it seemed best to render these central concepts (the 'I', the 'It', and the 'Above-I') in English but to capitalize them and place them within inverted commas. I realize that repeatedly coming across, for example, 'I' in place of the more usual *ego* will tend to break the reader's stride in a way that is not strictly relevant to Freud's purpose. However, may I ask the reader to bear in mind three rather obvious things:

i. Freud could himself have used Latin words for these concepts; the choice was open to him.

ii. The German words he did use are quite ordinary (though of course he does not use them in ordinary ways). Giving the concepts Latin labels makes them seem unnecessarily 'strange'.

iii. The 'above' in 'Above-I' (like the traditional 'super' in *super-ego*) does not of course make it 'better' than the 'I'; it merely means that it stands in a certain relationship to the 'I'.]

7. [There is a problem here. In German, of course, all nouns (and that includes the various *Götter*) are capitalized. If for no other reason than to reflect this lack of differentiation, I should be inclined to make *all* the deities in this translation, however unique, start with a small 'g'. However, the shock effect of this would distract the reader in a way that is not relevant to Freud's purpose (so, except in *Moses the Man* . . ., I'll only do it this once!). Could I simply ask that, in these texts, 'God' should be registered without the 'baggage' that modern English usage, by capitalizing the word, unthinkingly takes as read?

Moses the Man . . . is clearly an exception in this respect, being in part about the very emergence of monotheism (the context normally posited for writing 'God') and therefore requiring, on the part of the English translator, very frequent decisions as to whether or not to capitalize the deity referred to in the German text – decisions that are in a very specific way irrelevant to Freud's purpose and that are in any case not for the translator to make. In *Moses the Man* . . ., therefore, I have stuck to my original inclination and written 'god' throughout.]

Mass Psychology and Analysis of the 'I'[1]

I

Introduction

The antithesis between individual and social or mass psychology, which at first glance may seem to us very important, loses a great deal of its sharpness on close examination. Individual psychology is of course directed at the person in isolation, tracing the ways in which he seeks to satisfy his drive-impulses, but only rarely, in specific exceptions, is it able to disregard the relationships between that individual and others. In the mental life of the individual, the other comes very regularly into consideration as model, object, aid and antagonist; at the same time, therefore, and from the outset, the psychology of the individual is also social psychology in this extended but wholly justified sense.

The individual's relationships with his parents and siblings, love-object, teacher, and doctor (in other words, all the ties that have hitherto formed the preferential targets of psychoanalytical investigations) can claim to be ranked as social phenomena, which sets them in opposition to certain other processes (called by us *narcissistic*) in which drive-satisfaction eludes or forgoes the influence of others. The antithesis between social and narcissistic (Bleuler[2] might say *autistic*) mental acts thus falls very much within the sphere of individual psychology and does not lend itself to distinguishing the latter from social or mass psychology.

In the said relationships with parents and siblings, lover, friend, teacher, and doctor, the individual invariably experiences only the influence of one or a very small number of persons, each of whom has acquired enormous importance for him. The fact is, people have got into the habit, when discussing social or mass psychology, of disregarding these ties and treating the simultaneous influencing of the individual by a large number of persons with whom he has some sort of connection (whereas in many other respects they may be strangers to him) as a separate object of investigation. In other words, mass psychology deals with the individual as member of a tribe, people, caste, class institution, or as one element in an assemblage of human beings who at a particular time, and for a specific purpose, have organized themselves into a mass. Following this rupture of a natural context, the obvious next step was to regard the phenomena that emerge in such special conditions as manifestations of a special drive not susceptible of being traced back further, the social drive (or *herd instinct*, or *group mind*[3]), which does not come out in other situations. However, we may well object that we find it difficult to attribute such great importance to the numerical factor as to make it possible for number alone to rouse a new and otherwise unactivated drive in the life of the human mind. Our expectations will thus be directed towards two other possibilities: that the social drive is perhaps not an original, irreducible one and that the origins of its formation may be found in a smaller circle – that of the family, for instance.

Mass psychology, although it is only in its earliest stages, embraces a still incalculable wealth of individual problems and sets the investigator innumerable tasks that have not even been properly separated as yet. Merely classifying the various forms of mass formation and defining the psychical phenomena to which they give expression require a major effort of observation and description and have already given rise to a copious literature. Anyone measuring this slim booklet[4] against the great bulk of mass psychology will have every right to suppose that the intention here is to deal with only a few points from all this material. There will indeed be only a small number of questions in which the depth research of psychoanalysis takes a particular interest.

Notes

1. [See 'Compulsive Actions and Religious Exercises', note 6.]
2. [Swiss psychiatrist Eugen Bleuler (1857–1939).]
3. [These two phrases appear in English in the original text.]
4. [Freud's essay first appeared as a separate publication.]

II

Le Bon's portrayal of the mass mind

Rather than preface these remarks with a definition, it would seem more useful to begin by referring to the published literature and extracting from it a few particularly striking and typical facts that the investigation can take as its starting-point. We shall achieve both by quoting an excerpt from Le Bon's (rightly) famous book, *La psychologie des foules*.[1]

Let us remind ourselves of the facts of the case. If psychology, which traces the predispositions, drive-impulses, motives and intentions of the individual through to his actions and into the individual's relationships to those closest to him, had done its job completely and rendered all these connections transparent, it would suddenly find itself facing a fresh and as yet unperformed task. It would be required to explain the astonishing fact that, given a certain condition, the individual whom it has come to understand will feel, think and act quite otherwise than expected, that condition being incorporation into a body of people that has taken on the quality of a 'psychological mass'. But what is a 'mass', how does it acquire the ability so decisively to influence the mental life of the individual, and in what does the mental change it imposes on the individual consist?

Answering these three questions is the task facing theoretical mass psychology. Clearly, the best way to tackle them is by starting with the third. It is observation of the altered reaction of the individual that is the stuff of mass psychology; the fact is, every attempt to explain something needs to be preceded by a description of what is to be explained.

Now, over to Le Bon. He writes:

The most striking peculiarity presented by a psychological crowd is the following: Whoever be the individuals that compose it, however like or unlike be their mode of life, their occupations, their character, or their intelligence, the fact that they have been transformed into a crowd puts them in possession of a sort of collective mind which makes them feel, think and act in a manner quite different from that in which each individual of them would feel, think and act were he in a state of isolation. There are certain ideas and feelings which do not come into being, or do not transform themselves into acts except in the case of individuals forming a crowd. The psychological crowd is a provisional being formed of heterogeneous elements, which for a moment are combined, exactly as the cells which constitute a living body form by their reunion a new being which displays characteristics very different from those possessed by each of the cells singly.[2]

Taking the liberty of interrupting Le Bon's account with comments of our own, we beg to remark at this point: if the individuals in the mass are bound together to form an entity, there must presumably be something binding them together, and that binding medium might be precisely what characterizes the mass. Le Bon, however, leaves this question unanswered, dealing instead with the way in which the individual changes in the mass and describing the change in terms that chime well with the basic premises of our depth psychology.

It is easy to prove how much the individual forming part of a crowd differs from the isolated individual, but it is less easy to discover the causes of this difference.

To obtain at any rate a glimpse of them it is necessary in the first place to call to mind the truth established by modern psychology, that unconscious phenomena play an altogether preponderating part not only in organic life, but also in the operations of the intelligence. The conscious life of the mind is of small importance in comparison with its unconscious life. The most subtle analyst, the most acute observer, is scarcely successful in discovering more than a very small number of the unconscious motives that determine his conduct. Our conscious acts are the outcome of an unconscious substratum created in the mind in the main by hereditary influences. This substratum consists of the innumerable common characteristics handed down from generation to generation, which constitute the genius of a race. Behind the avowed causes of our acts there undoubtedly lie secret causes that we do not avow, but behind these secret causes there are many others more secret still which we ourselves ignore. The greater part of our daily actions are the result of hidden motives which escape our observation.[3]

In the mass, Le Bon believes, individual acquisitions are effaced, which means that the uniqueness of the individual disappears. The racial unconscious comes to the fore, the heterogeneous is swamped by the homogeneous. We would say that the psychical superstructure that had developed so variously in individuals is eroded away, enfeebled, and the unconscious foundation that is the same for everyone is exposed (activated).

In this way, it is alleged, an average nature of the individuals forming the mass comes about. However, Le Bon finds that those individuals also evince fresh qualities, ones they did not possess before, and he looks for the reason in three different factors:

The first is that the individual forming part of a crowd acquires, solely from numerical considerations, a sentiment of invincible power which allows him to yield to instincts which, had he been alone, he would perforce have kept under restraint. He will be the less disposed to check himself from the consideration that, a crowd being anonymous, and in consequence irresponsible, the sentiment of responsibility which always controls individuals disappears entirely.[4]

From our standpoint, we should not need to place so much emphasis on the emergence of fresh qualities. All we should want to say is that, in the mass, the individual finds himself in conditions that allow him to shed the repressions of his unconscious drive-impulses. The apparently fresh qualities that the individual then exhibits are in fact expressions of that unconscious, along with which, as we know, everything wicked in the human mind comes enclosed; the disappearance of conscience or sense of responsibility in such circumstances does not present our understanding with any difficulty. We had long contended that the core of what is called conscience is 'social anxiety'.[5]

The second cause, which is contagion, also intervenes to determine the manifestation in crowds of their special characteristics, and at the same time the trend they are to take. Contagion is a phenomenon of which it is easy to establish the presence, but that it is not easy to explain. It must be classed among those phenomena of a hypnotic order, which we shall shortly study. In a crowd every sentiment and act is contagious, and contagious to such a degree that an individual readily sacrifices his personal interest to the collective interest. This is an aptitude very contrary to his nature, and of which a man is scarcely capable, except when he makes part of a crowd.[6]

We shall return to that last sentence later, basing an important supposition on it.

A third cause, and by far the most important, determines in the individuals of a crowd special characteristics which are quite contrary at times to those presented by the isolated individual. I allude to that suggestibility of which, moreover, the contagion mentioned above is neither more nor less than an effect.

To understand this phenomenon it is necessary to bear in mind certain recent physiological discoveries. We know today that by various processes an individual may be brought into such a condition that, having entirely lost his conscious personality, he obeys all the suggestions of the operator who has deprived him of it, and commits acts in utter contradiction with his character and habits. The most careful observations seem to prove that an individual immerged for some length of time in a crowd in action soon finds himself – either in consequence of the magnetic influence given out by the crowd, or from some other cause of which we are ignorant – in a special state, which much resembles the state of fascination in which the hypnotized individual finds himself in the hands of the hypnotizer. [. . .] The conscious personality has entirely vanished; will and discernment are lost. All feelings and thoughts are bent in the direction determined by the hypnotizer.

Such also is approximately the state of the individual forming part of a psychological crowd. He is no longer conscious of his acts. In his case as in the case of the hypnotized subject, at the same time that certain faculties are destroyed others may be brought to a high degree of exaltation. Under the influence of a suggestion, he will undertake the accomplishment of certain acts with irresistible impetuosity. This impetuosity is the more irresistible in the case of crowds than in that of the hypnotized subject, from the fact that, the suggestion being the same for all the individuals of the crowd, it gains in strength by reciprocity. [. . .]

We see, then, that the disappearance of the conscious personality, the predominance of the unconscious personality, the turning by means of suggestion and contagion of feelings and ideas in an identical direction, the tendency to immediately transform the suggested ideas into acts; these, we see, are the principal characteristics of the individual forming part of a crowd. He is no longer himself, but has become an automaton who has ceased to be guided by his will.[7]

I reproduce this quotation at such length in order to confirm that Le Bon really does explain the state of the individual in the mass as a hypnotic one – rather than merely comparing it with such a state. It is not our intention here to contradict Le Bon, we simply wish to stress that the last two reasons for the change affecting the individual in the mass, namely contagion and heightened suggestibility, are clearly not of the same kind: indeed, contagion is also said to be an expression of suggestibility. Moreover, Le Bon's text does not seem to us to draw any sharp distinction between the effects of the two factors. Possibly the best way to interpret what he says is by relating contagion to the effect that the individual members of the mass have on one another, whereas the manifestations of suggestion in the mass, which are equated with the phenomena of hypnotic influence, point to a different source. But to what? We cannot help seeing it as a substantial shortcoming that one of the chief players in this assimilation, namely the person who, for the mass, occupies the place of the hypnotist, is not mentioned in Le Bon's account. He does, though, distinguish this unexplained fascinating influence from the contagious effect that individuals have on one another, as a result of which the original suggestion is reinforced.

One other important viewpoint as regards assessing the mass individual:

Moreover, by the mere fact that he forms part of an organized crowd, a man descends several rungs in the ladder of civilization. Isolated, he may be a cultivated individual; in a crowd, he is a barbarian – that is, a creature acting by instinct. He possesses the spontaneity, the violence, the ferocity, and also the enthusiasm and heroism of primitive beings [. . .].[8]

Le Bon then dwells particularly on the reduced intellectual performance that the individual experiences in consequence of being swallowed up in the mass.[9]

Let us now leave the individual and turn to the description of the mass mind, as outlined by Le Bon. There is not a single feature of it, the derivation and placing of which would cause the psychoanalyist problems. Le Bon even shows us the way by pointing to the congruence with the mental life of 'savages and children'.[10]

The mass is impulsive, inconstant and excitable. It is 'guided almost exclusively by unconscious motives'.[11] The impulses that the mass obeys may, depending on circumstances, be noble or cruel, heroic or cowardly, but at all events they are so imperious that no personal interest, not even that of self-preservation, is able to assert itself.[12] Nothing about it is premeditated. It may desire things passionately, but never for long; it is incapable of any long-term intention. It cannot abide any delay between its desire and realization of the thing desired. It has a sense of omnipotence; for the individual in the mass the concept of impossibility vanishes.[13]

The mass is extraordinarily suggestible and credulous; it is uncritical; the improbable does not exist so far as it is concerned. It thinks in images that evoke one another by association, as they appear to the individual in states of free fantasizing, images that no reasonable agency gauges in terms of their congruence with reality. The feelings of the mass are always extremely simple and extremely effusive. The mass, in other words, 'knows neither doubt nor uncertainty'.[14]

It instantly goes to extremes: in it a suspicion, once voiced, turns immediately into 'incontrovertible evidence', a seed of antipathy becomes 'furious hatred'.[15]

Itself tending to every extreme, the mass is also only excited by immoderate stimuli. Anyone seeking to move it needs no logical calibration in his arguments but must paint with the most powerful images, exaggerate, and say the same thing over and over again.

Since the mass has no doubt about what is true or false and is at the same time aware of its immense strength, it is as intolerant as it is accepting of authority. It respects strength and is only moderately influenced by the good, which it sees simply as a kind of weakness. What it expects in its heroes is brawn, even a tendency to violence. It wants to be dominated and suppressed and to fear its master. Basically conservative in all things, it has a deep aversion to all innovation and progress and an immeasurable reverence for tradition.[16]

In order to reach a correct assessment of the morality of masses, it is important to consider that when people are together in a mass all individual inhibitions fall away and all the cruel, brutal, destructive instincts that lie dormant in the individual as a leftover from primitive times are roused to free drive-satisfaction. However, masses are also capable, under the influence of suggestion, of great feats of renunciation, disinterestedness, and devotion to an ideal. Whereas personal advantage is more or less the only driving force present in the case of the isolated individual, in masses it very seldom predominates. The individual may even be said to be rendered moral by the mass.[17] Whereas the intellectual output of the mass is invariably way below that of the individual, its ethical behaviour can rise as far above that level as it can descend below it.

Certain other features of Le Bon's account further highlight the justification for identifying the mass mind with the mind of the primitive. In masses, the most antagonistic ideas may exist alongside one another and accommodate one another without their logical contradiction giving rise to conflict. This is also the case, however, in the unconscious mental lives of individuals, of children, and of neurotics, as psychoanalysis proved long ago.[18]

The mass is also subject to the truly magical power of words, which are capable of conjuring up the most fearful storms in the mass mind and also of calming them.[19] 'Reason and arguments are incapable of combating certain words and formulas. [These] are uttered with solemnity in the presence of crowds, and as soon as they have been pronounced an expression of respect is visible on every countenance, and all heads are bowed. By many they are considered as natural forces, as supernatural powers.'[20] One need think no further, in this context, than the taboo on names amongst primitives, of the magical forces that, for primitives, attach to names and words.[21]

And finally, masses have never known the thirst for truth. They demand illusions, they cannot do without them. 'The unreal has almost as much influence on them as the real. They have an evident tendency not to distinguish between the two.'[22]

This predominance of the life of the imagination and of illusion, as borne by unsatisfied desire, are things that we have pointed out as characterizing the psychology of neuroses. We found that what matters for neurotics is not ordinary objective reality but psychical reality, that a hysterical symptom is grounded in fantasy rather than in the rehearsal of actual experience, the guilty conscience of a compulsive neurotic in the fact of an evil design that was never carried out. Indeed, as in dream and hypnosis so in the mental activity of the mass: examination of reality retreats before the strength of affectively charged wishful feelings.

What Le Bon says about leaders of masses is less well thought out and does not let laws shine through so clearly. He says that, as soon as living beings come together in certain numbers, be they a herd of animals or a multitude of people, they instinctively place themselves under the authority of a head.[23] The mass is a docile herd, never capable of living without a master. So powerful is its thirst to obey that, should anyone appoint himself its master, it will instinctively bow down to him.

If the needs of the mass favour the leader in this way, the leader must nevertheless possess personal qualities that suit the mass. He must himself be in thrall to a powerful belief (in an idea) if he is to inspire belief in the mass; he must possess a powerful, commanding will that the will-less mass breathes in from him. Le Bon goes on to talk about the various types of leader and the means by which they influence the mass. In general, he derives the importance of leaders from the ideas of which they are themselves fanatical supporters.

Furthermore, he ascribes to such ideas as well as to leaders a mysterious, irresistible power that he calls 'prestige'. Prestige is a type of dominance that an individual, a piece of work, or an idea exercises over us. It paralyses our entire critical faculty and fills us with astonishment and respect. It should arouse a sentiment similar to that of the fascination of hypnosis.[24]

He draws a distinction between acquired or artificial prestige and personal prestige. The former is conveyed, in the case of persons, by name, wealth, reputation; in the case of notions, works of art and the like it is conveyed by tradition. Since in all cases it draws upon the past, it can do little to explain this puzzling influence. Personal prestige attaches to a small number of persons, who become leaders as a result; it causes everyone to obey them as if under the effect of a magnetic spell. However, prestige of any kind also relies on success and will be eroded by failures.[25]

One does not gain the impression that, in Le Bon's work, the role of leaders and the emphasis on prestige are brought into proper harmony with his quite brilliant portrayal of the mass mind.

Notes

1. [Published in 1895, *La psychologie des foules* was Gustave Le Bon's most popular work, and an (uncredited) English translation appeared in the following year (Gustave Le Bon, *The Crowd*, London 1896). The English version of Le Bon's book ought perhaps to have used the word 'mass' (rather than 'crowd'), since the text also deals with large bodies of

people who are not physically assembled in one place. The German translation, by Dr Rudolf Eisler, bore the title *Psychologie der Massen*.]

2. [Le Bon, *The Crowd*, op. cit. p. 6. Quotations from Le Bon's book are given in the original English translation (so that they refer, for instance, to 'instincts' where Freud will have read *'Trieben'* – now commonly rendered into English as 'drives').]

3. [Ibid., pp. 7–8.]

4. [Ibid., p. 10.]

5. A certain difference between Le Bon's view and our own [this is Freud writing] stems from the fact that his concept of the unconscious does not entirely coincide with that adopted by psychoanalysis. For Le Bon, the unconscious contains mainly the deepest characteristics of the race mind, something that individual psychoanalysis leaves out of account in any case. While not forgetting that the nucleus of the 'I' (the 'It', as I later called it), to which the 'archaic inheritance' of the human mind belongs, is unconscious, we also separate off the 'unconsciously repressed', which springs from part of that inheritance. This concept of the repressed is absent in Le Bon.

6. [Le Bon, *The Crowd*, op. cit., p. 10.]

7. [Ibid., pp. 10–13.]

8. [Ibid., p. 13.]

9. Compare Schiller's distich:

> Jeder, sieht man ihn einzeln, ist leidlich klug and verständig;
> Sind sie in corpore, gleich wird euch ein Dummkopf daraus.

[Every man, seen as an individual, is tolerably shrewd and sensible; see them *in corpore*, and you will instantly find a fool.]

10. [Le Bon, *The Crowd*, op. cit., p. 17. This is one of a small number of instances where Freud's text so closely paraphrases the original (which he appears to have read in the German translation) that I have found it natural actually to quote from the English translation.]

11. [Ibid., p. 18. Freud notes at this point:] Unconscious is used correctly by Le Bon in the descriptive sense, where it does not simply mean 'repressed'.

12. [Ibid., p. 18.]

13. See also *Totem und Tabu* [*Totem and Taboo, Standard Edition*, vol. XIII, p. 1] III, 'Animism, Magic and the Omnipotence of Thought'.

14. [Le Bon, *The Crowd*, op. cit., p. 35.] In interpreting dreams, to which of course we owe our best knowledge of the unconscious life of the mind, we follow the technical rule that doubt and uncertainty are left out of account in dream narration and each element of the manifest dream is treated as equally assured. We derive doubt and uncertainty from the effect of the censorship to which dreamwork is subject, and we assume that primary dream thoughts are ignorant of doubt and uncertainty as critical functions. As content they may of course, like anything else, occur in the remains of the day [or the 'day's residues', as *Tagesreste* is often translated] leading to the dream. [*The Interpretation of Dreams, Standard Edition*, vols IV–V.] (See *Traumdeutung*, 7th edition, 1922, p. 386.)

15. [Le Bon, *The Crowd*, op. cit., p. 35.] The same intensification of all emotional impulses to extremes, to excess, also belongs to the affectivity of the child and is found in dream life, where, thanks to the isolation of individual emotional impulses that prevails in the unconscious, a mild irritation experienced during the day comes out as a death wish directed at the person responsible, or a hint of some temptation becomes the driving force behind a criminal action represented in the dream. This fact prompted Dr Hanns Sachs to remark splendidly: 'What the dream has shown us in terms of relations to the present (reality), we then wish to seek out in consciousness, too, and we should not be surprised if the monster we saw under the magnifying-glass of analysis reappears as an infusorian.' (See *Traumdeutung*, op. cit., p. 457.)

16. [Le Bon, *The Crowd*, op. cit., p. 42.]

17. [Ibid., p. 45.]

18. In the small child, for example, ambivalent emotional attitudes towards the people closest to him exist in parallel for a long time without one interfering with the expression of its opposite number. If the two do eventually come into conflict, often that conflict is resolved by the child changing the object and shifting one of the ambivalent impulses on to a replacement object. It is also possible to discover from the history of the development of a neurosis in adults that a suppressed impulse frequently survives for a long time in unconscious or even conscious fantasies, the content of which naturally runs directly counter to a dominant striving without an intervention of the 'I' against the thing rejected by it arising from that antithesis. The fantasy is tolerated for quite some time until suddenly, usually following an intensification of its affective charge [*Besetzung*], conflict between it and the 'I' comes about, with all that that implies.

As the development of the child into a mature adult progresses, there is in any case an increasingly far-reaching *integration* of the personality, a bringing-together of the individual drives and tendencies that have grown up within it independently of one another. The analogous process in the realm of the sexual life has long been known to us as a bringing-together of all sexual drives in definitive genital organization (*Drei Abhandlungen zur Sexualtheorie*, 1905 [*Three Essays on Sexual Theory*]). Incidentally, many very familiar examples (among them, those natural scientists who, so far as the Bible is concerned, have remained fundamentalists) show that the unification of the 'I' may be subject to the same disturbances as that of the libido. – [*Addition 1923*:] The various possibilities of a subsequent disintegration of the 'I' form a separate chapter of psychopathology.

19. [Le Bon, *The Crowd*, op. cit., p. 100.]
20. [Ibid., pp. 100–01.]
21. See *Totem und Tabu*, op. cit.
22. [Le Bon, *The Crowd*, op. cit., p. 58.]
23. [Ibid., p. 118.]
24. [Ibid., p. 133.]
25. [Ibid., p. 145.]

III

Other appreciations of collective mental life

We have used Le Bon's account as an introduction because, in its emphasis on the unconscious life of the mind, it chimes so neatly with our own psychology. However, we do need to add that in fact none of the assertions made by this author contributes anything new. Everything adverse and disparaging that he says about expression of the mass mind had already been said by others before him with the same finality and the same hostility; it has been reiterated in identical terms since the earliest days of literature by thinkers, statesmen, and poets.[1] The two propositions containing Le Bon's most important views (that of the collective inhibition of intellectual performance and that of the heightening of affectivity within the mass) had been formulated by Sighele slightly earlier.[2] Basically, the only things left as peculiar to Le Bon are the two standpoints of the unconscious and the comparison with the mental life of primitives, though these too had of course been touched on many times before him.

Also, however, the description and appreciation of the mass mind given by Le Bon and the others have by no means gone unchallenged. There is no doubt that all the phenomena of the mass mind described above had been correctly observed, but other expressions of mass formation having precisely the opposite effect can also be identified, and from these a very much higher assessment of the mass mind must be deduced.

Le Bon himself was prepared to concede that the morality of the mass may in certain circumstances be higher than that of the individuals making it up, and that only collective entities are capable of a high degree of selflessness and dedication. 'Personal interest is very rarely a powerful motive force with crowds, while it is almost the exclusive motive of the conduct of the isolated individual.'[3]

Others assert that it is in fact only society that lays down the standards of morality for the individual, whereas the individual, as a rule, somehow falls behind these high demands. Or that in exceptional circumstances the phenomenon of enthusiasm will occur in a collectivity, which in the past has made the most splendid mass achievements possible.

As regards intellectual achievement, it is true that the great decisions of mental endeavour, the discoveries and solutions that truly matter are possible only for the individual working in isolation. But the mass mind, too, is capable of inspired intellectual creations, witness above all language itself but also folksong, folklore, and other things besides. Moreover, it is an open question how much the individual thinker or writer owes to the stimuli of the mass within which he lives, whether he is any more than the perfecter of a mental effort to which at the same time others have contributed.

Given these total contradictions, in fact, it would seem that the work of mass psychology must proceed in vain. Yet it is a simple matter to find a more hopeful way out of the problem. Probably what has happened is that very different formations have been lumped together as 'masses', and that these need to be distinguished from one another. The remarks of Sighele, Le Bon and others relate to masses of a short-lived kind that form rapidly from individuals of different types as a result of a transient interest. Quite clearly, their accounts were influenced by the nature of revolutionary masses, particularly those of the great French Revolution. The contrary assertions stem from evaluations of the stable masses or social entities in which people spend their lives and that are embodied in the institutions of society. Masses of the first kind sit on the back of the latter, so to speak, as short but high waves ride the longer swell of the sea.

McDougall, who in his book *The Group Mind* takes the above contradiction as his starting-point,[4] finds the solution of the same in the organization factor. In the simplest case, what he calls the

33

'group' has no organization at all or none to speak of. Such a mass he describes as a 'crowd'. He admits, however, that a crowd does not readily assemble without at least the beginnings of organization taking shape within it, and that it is in just such simple masses that many of the fundamental facts of collective psychology are particularly easily discernible.[5] If members of a crowd who have drifted together by chance are to form anything like a mass in the psychological sense, it is necessary for those members to have something in common, a shared interest in some object, a similar emotional orientation in a specific situation, and (I would add: therefore) 'some degree of reciprocal influence between the members of the group'.[6] The stronger this 'mental homogeneity', the more readily a psychological mass will be formed from those individuals and the more striking will be the external manifestations of what we may term a 'mass mind'.

Now, the oddest and at the same time the most important phenomenon of mass formation is the way in which it stimulates in each individual an 'exaltation or intensification of emotion'.[7] It is possible, according to McDougall, to say that people's affects[8] rarely (in different circumstances) rise to the heights they may attain in a mass; in fact, it is an enjoyable experience for those concerned to abandon themselves so unreservedly to their passions and in the process be swallowed up in the mass, losing their feeling of individual separateness. McDougall explains this feeling on the part of individuals of being carried away in terms of what he calls the 'principle of direct induction of emotion by way of the primitive sympathetic response'[9] – in other words, the emotional 'contagion' we have already encountered. The fact is, the perceived signs of an affective state are such as automatically to evoke the same affect in the person doing the perceiving. This automatic compulsion will be the stronger, the more people are seen to exhibit the same affect simultaneously. The individual's critical faculties will then fall silent, and he will allow himself to slip into the same affective state. In the process, however, he will heighten the excitement of the others who had aroused him, and thus the individual's own affective charge will increase as a result of reciprocal induction. Unmistakably in evidence here is a kind of compulsion to match others, to stay in tune with the many. The coarser, simpler emotions have more chance of spreading through a mass in this way.[10]

This mechanism of affect enhancement is further assisted by a number of other influences proceeding from the mass. The mass impresses the individual as an untamed force and an invincible threat. Momentarily, it has taken the place of the whole of human society, which is the seat of authority, whose punishments are feared, and for whose sake individuals have inflicted so many inhibitions upon themselves. There is clearly danger in opposing the mass, and safety for the individual lies in following the example of those around him – if need be, even 'running with the pack'. In obedience to the new authority, a person may disable his earlier 'conscience', yielding to the lure of the pleasurable sensations he can be sure of gaining through a removal of his inhibitions. On the whole, then, it is not so strange that we should see the individual in the mass doing or sanctioning things on which, in his customary living conditions, that same individual would have turned his back, and we may even entertain the hope of being able, in this way, to lift something of the shadow so often cast by that enigmatic word 'suggestion'.

The proposition of the low order of intelligence within the mass is one that McDougall, too, does not contradict.[11] He says that lesser intelligences pull greater ones down to their level. The latter are inhibited in their operation because the enhancement of affectivity in any case creates unfavourable conditions for correct intellectual work, also because individuals are intimidated by the mass and their thinking lacks freedom and because, for each individual, awareness of responsibility for his performance is diminished.

McDougall's overall verdict regarding the psychical performance of a simple, 'unorganized' mass is no kinder than that handed down by Le Bon. Such a mass is extremely excitable, impulsive, passionate, fickle, inconsistent, irresolute but at the same time prepared to take extreme action, susceptible only to the coarser passions and more basic feelings, exceptionally suggestible, foolish in its thinking, vehement in its opinions, capable of taking in only the simplest and hastiest conclusions and arguments, easily influenced, easily unsettled, lacking in self-awareness, self-respect and any sense of responsibility, but ready, in its awareness of its own strength, to be dragged into all sorts of atrocities such as might be expected only from an absolute, irresponsible power. In other words, it tends to behave like an ill-mannered child or like an impassioned, unsupervised savage in an unfamiliar situation; in the worst instances, its behaviour bears more resemblance to that of a pack of wild animals than to that of human beings.

Since McDougall contrasts the conduct of highly organized masses with that described here, we shall be particularly interested to learn in what such organization consists and by what factors it is engendered. The author lists five such 'principal conditions' for the mental life of the mass to be raised to a higher level.

The first fundamental condition is a measure of continuity in the existence of the mass. This may be substantive or formal – substantive if the same people remain in the mass for some time, formal if within the mass certain positions have evolved that are allocated to individuals who succeed one another.

The second is that a specific conception of the nature, function, attainments and aspirations of the mass should have taken shape within the individual member in such a way that, for that individual, an emotional relationship with the mass as a whole can result.

The third is that the mass should come into contact (for example, through competition) with other, similar collective entities that nevertheless differ from it in many respects.

The fourth is that the mass should possess traditions, customs and institutions, particularly such as bear on the relationship of its members one with another.

The fifth is that, within the mass, there should exist a structure that finds expression in the specialization and differentiation of what each individual is expected to do.

When these conditions are met, says McDougall, the psychical disadvantages of mass formation are removed. People protect themselves against the collective diminution of intellectual performance by taking the solving of intellectual tasks away from the mass and reserving it to individuals within the mass.

It seems to us that the condition McDougall described as the 'organization' of the mass can with greater justification be described in different terms. The task consists in conferring upon the mass the very qualities that once characterized the individual and that, so far as the individual is concerned, formation of the mass effaced. Because the individual (outside the primitive mass) possessed continuity, self-awareness, traditions and habits, a special job to do and a special place to occupy, he kept himself apart from others with whom he was in contention. For a while, as a result of joining the non-'organized' mass, the individual had lost these qualities. Accepting, then, that the aim is to furnish masses with the attributes of the individual, we are reminded of a profound remark made by Wilfred Trotter,[12] who saw the tendency towards mass formation as a biological extension of the multicellular make-up of all higher organisms.[13]

Notes

1. See also text and bibliography in B. Kraškovič jun., *Die Psychologie der Kollektivitäten* (translated from the Croatian [into German] by Siegmund von Posaveč), Vukovar 1915.
2. See Walter Moede, 'Die Massen- und Sozialpsychologie im kritischen Überblick' ['Mass and social psychology: a critical survey'], in *Zeitschrift für pädagogische Psychologie und experimentelle Pädagogik von Meumann und Scheibner*, XVI, 1915.
3. [Le Bon, *The Crowd*, op. cit., p. 44.]
4. William McDougall, *The Group Mind*, Cambridge 1920.
5. Ibid., p. 22.
6. Ibid., p. 23.
7. Ibid., p. 24.
8. [= emotions. 'Affect' is the technical term used by Freud (*Affekte*) and by psychology generally. It is defined by the *Concise Oxford Dictionary* as 'an emotion, a feeling, or a desire, esp. as leading to action'.]

9. William McDougall, *The Group Mind*, op. cit., p. 25.

10. Ibid., p. 39.

11. Ibid., p. 41.

12. W. Trotter, *Instincts of the Herd in Peace and War*, London 1916.

13. [*Addition, 1923*:] Unlike an otherwise sympathetic and acute critique by Hans Kelsen ('Der Begriff des Staates und die Sozialpsychologie' ['The notion of the state and social psychology'], in *Imago* VIII/2, 1922), I cannot concede that this kind of furnishing of the 'mass mind' with organization means hypostatizing it – that is to say, granting it independence from the mental processes present in the individual.

IV

Suggestion and libido

We started out from the basic fact that an individual within a mass experiences as a result of the influence of the mass what is often a far-reaching change in his mental activity. His affectivity is extraordinarily enhanced while his intellectual performance is noticeably reduced, both processes clearly tending towards an increasing resemblance to the other individuals in the mass – a result that can be achieved only through a lifting of the inhibitions peculiar to each individual and through that individual renouncing his special structures of inclination. We have heard that these often unwanted effects are at least partially held back by a superior 'organization' on the part of masses, but the basic fact of mass psychology, namely the two propositions of affect enhancement and thought inhibition in the primitive mass, is not contradicted thereby. What interests us, though, is finding the psychological explanation for this mental transformation of the individual within the mass.

Rational factors, such as the intimidation of the individual mentioned above, i.e. the action of the individual's self-preservation drive, clearly fail to cover the phenomena to be observed. What we are offered otherwise as an explanation by authors in the fields of sociology and mass psychology is always the same, albeit under different names: the magic word *suggestion*. Tarde called it *imitation*, but we have to agree with the author who tells us that Tarde's 'imitation' comes under the heading of suggestion, being in fact a consequence thereof.[1] With Le Bon, everything alienating in social phenomena is attributed to two factors: reciprocal suggestion by individuals and the prestige of leaders. However, prestige in turn finds expression only in its effect, which is to evoke suggestion. With McDougall, we were able momentarily to gain the impression that his principle of 'primary affective induction' made the assumption of suggestion dispensable. On further consideration, however, we have to recognize that this principle is no different in what it says than the familiar assertions of 'imitation' or 'contagion'; it simply lays greater stress on the affective factor. There is no doubt that such a tendency does exist in us, namely that of succumbing to a particular affect when we become aware of a sign of that affective state in someone else. But how many times do we successfully resist it, repudiating the affect, often reacting in the diametrically opposite fashion? So why do we regularly surrender to that contagion in the mass? Again, we shall have to say: it is the suggestive influence of the mass compelling us to obey this imitative tendency that induces the affect within us. Actually, even apart from this there is no getting round suggestion in McDougall. The message we hear from him, as from others, is: masses are distinguished by especial suggestibility.

This paves the way for the statement that suggestion (more correctly, suggestibility) is in fact something fundamental, something irreducible, a basic fact of human mental life. Such was the view taken by Bernheim, too, whose astonishing skills I witnessed personally in 1889.[2] However, I remember a vague hostility to this tyranny of suggestion even then. If a patient who was not proving submissive was told forcefully: But what are you doing? *Vous vous contre-suggestionnez!* I said to myself that this was a clear case of injustice and an act of violence. The man (I felt) had every right to counter-suggestions if an attempt is being made to subjugate him with suggestions. My resistance subsequently took the form of a rebellion against allowing suggestion, which explained everything, to evade explanation itself. In this connection, I recalled the old riddle:

> Christopher bore Christ,
> But Christ carried the world,
> So tell me: what was Christopher
> Standing on at the time?

Christophorus Christum, sed Christus sustulit orbem:
Constiterit pedibus dic ubi Christophorus?[3]

Approaching the vexed question of suggestion again after avoiding it for some thirty years, I find that nothing has changed. In
saying which, I am in fact able to make one exception (which as
it happens reveals the influence of psychoanalysis). I see that especial efforts have been made to formulate the concept of suggestion correctly – that is to say, to establish conventions for the use
of the term.[4] Nor are such efforts redundant, because the word is
moving in the direction of an ever-wider application with a looser
and looser connotation. Soon it will denote the exerting of any
influence whatever, as it does in English, where 'to suggest' covers
a range of meanings from communicating an idea to stimulating a
reaction.[5] However, as regards the essence of suggestion, i.e. the
conditions under which influence is exerted for no adequate logical reason, no explanation has been produced. I should not be
afraid to back up this assertion by analysing the literature of the
past thirty years; the reason why I refrain from doing so is that I
know a thorough study, setting itself just such a task, is already in
preparation in my vicinity.[6]

Instead, I shall try to shed some light on mass psychology by
using the term *libido*, which has served us so well in our study of
psychoneuroses.

Libido is an expression from affectivity theory. It is how we refer
to the energy (considered as a quantitative value, albeit currently
an unmeasurable one) of those drives having to do with everything
that can be brought together under the heading of love. The core
of what we call love is of course what is generally known as love
and poets sing of, namely sexual love with the goal of sexual union.
However, we do not separate off from that the other things that
share the name of love: self-love, on the one hand, and on the other
hand parental and infant love, friendship, general love of humanity, and even dedication to concrete objects as well as to abstract
ideas. Our justification is that psychoanalytic investigation has taught
us that all these urges are expressions of the same drive-impulses

as push the sexes in the direction of sexual union; and though in other circumstances they may be pushed away from that sexual goal or stayed in its achievement, nevertheless they always preserve enough of their original essence for their identity to remain recognizable (self-sacrifice, striving for greater closeness).

We feel, then, that with the word 'love' in its multiple applications language has effected a wholly justified synopsis and that we cannot do better than place our scientific discussions and descriptions on the same foundation. By taking that decision, psychoanalysis unleashed a storm of indignation – as if it had been guilty of some wanton innovation. Yet with this 'extended' conception of love psychoanalysis was doing nothing original. The philosopher Plato's *'eros'* coincides perfectly, in its origin, action and relationship to sexual love, with the libido of psychoanalysis, as Nachmansohn and Pfister have shown in detail;[7] and if the apostle Paul prized love above all else in his famous First Letter to the Corinthians, he undoubtedly understood it in the same 'extended' sense,[8] which just goes to show that people do not always take their great thinkers seriously, even when they profess great admiration for them.

In psychoanalysis, these love drives (*a potiori* and because of their origin) are referred to as sexual drives. Most 'educated people', finding this choice of name offensive, have taken their revenge by saddling psychoanalysis with the charge of 'pan-sexualism'. Anyone who regards sexuality as something shameful and degrading to human nature is of course at liberty to use the more genteel expressions 'Eros' and 'eroticism'. I could have done so myself from the outset and spared myself much opposition as a result. However, I chose not to, being keen to avoid concessions to feeble-heartedness. There is no knowing where such an avenue will lead; one gives way over words at first and then little by little in deed as well. I cannot see that anything is gained by being ashamed of sexuality; after all, the Greek word *eros*, which apparently softens the offence, is quite simply the translation of our German word *Liebe*,[9] and ultimately, the man who can wait need make no concessions.

So we shall try adopting the premise that love relationships (to use an inert expression, emotional ties) also form part of the essence of the mass mind. Let us remember that the existing literature makes no mention of them. In it, what would constitute their equivalent is obviously hidden from view behind the folding screen of suggestion. We base our expectation initially on two brief thoughts. First, that the mass is obviously held together by some kind of force. But to what force could such an achievement be better ascribed than to Eros, which holds the whole world together? Second, that the impression given when the individual surrenders his uniqueness in the mass and admits the influence of others is that he does so because of an inherent need to be in agreement with those others rather than in opposition to them – so he may in fact be doing it *ihnen zuliebe* ['for their sake'].[10]

Notes

1. [The author referred to is] Brugeilles, 'L'essence du phénomène social: La suggestion', in *Revue philosophique de la France et de l'Étranger*, LXXV, 1913. [Brugeilles is commenting on French sociologist Gabriel Tarde (1843–1904).]

2. [French physician Hippolyte Bernheim (1840–1919), who specialized in hypnotism.]

3. Konrad Richter, *Der deutsche St. Christoph*, Berlin 1896 (*Acta Germanica*, V, I).

4. By McDougall, for instance, in 'A note on suggestion', in *Journal of Neurology and Psychopathology*, vol. 1, no. 1, May 1920.

5. [Freud's original text runs 'und wird bald jede beliebige Beeinflussung bezeichnen wie im Englischen, wo *"to suggest, suggestion"* unserem "Nahelegen", unserer "Anregung" entspricht'.]

6. [*Addition, 1925:*] Unfortunately, this piece of work never materialized.

7. Nachmansohn, 'Freuds Libidotheorie, verglichen mit der Eroslehre Platos' ['Freud's libido theory compared with Plato's eros theory'], in *Internationale Zeitschrift für Psychoanalyse* III, 1915; Pfister, 'Plato als Vorläufer der Psychoanalyse' ['Plato as forerunner of psychoanalysis'], in *Internationale Zeitschrift für Psychoanalyse*, VII, 1921.

8. 'If I speak in the tongues of men and of angels, but have not love, I

am a noisy gong or a clanging cymbal' etc., 1 Cor. 13:1 ff. [Revised Standard Version; the Authorized Version uses the word 'charity'.]

9. [And *our* English word 'love', of course.]

10. [But note the presence of '-*liebe*' in the German expression.]

V

Two artificial masses: church and army

Looking at the morphology of masses, let us not forget that very different types of mass can be distinguished as well as conflicting trends in their formation. There are very short-lived masses and very long-lasting ones; homogeneous ones, comprising individuals of a similar type, and non-homogeneous; natural and artificial masses, the latter also requiring some external compulsion to make them cohere; primitive masses and structured, highly organized masses. However, for reasons that are as yet unclear, we should like to attach particular value to a distinction that the existing literature tends to underrate, namely that between leaderless masses and masses with leaders. And in stark contrast to the usual practice, our study is not going to take a relatively simple process of mass formation as its starting-point but will begin with highly organized, enduring, artificial masses. The most interesting examples of such formations are the church, as the congregation of believers, and the armed forces.

Church and army are artificial masses. That is to say, a certain external compulsion is applied to prevent them from falling apart[1] and to hold back changes in their structure. A person is not usually asked, nor is he at liberty to say whether he wishes to join such a mass; any attempt to leave is usually frowned upon or severely punished, or it is coupled with quite specific conditions. Why these socializations require special safeguards in this way is far removed from our present concern. What interests us is simply the fact that, in these highly organized masses that enjoy such protection against disintegration, certain circumstances are very clearly in evidence that are much more hidden elsewhere.

Widely though the two may differ in other respects, both the

45

church (and it will be to our advantage to take the Catholic church as our model) and the army are governed by the same pretence (illusion) that a supreme head exists (in the Catholic church, Christ; in the army, the commander) who loves every individual in the mass with an identical love. Everything depends on that illusion; were it to be dropped, church and army alike would, in so far as their respective external compulsions permitted, disintegrate immediately. In the case of Christ, that identical love is made explicit: 'as you did it to one of the least of these my brethren, you did it to me'.[2] For individuals within the mass of believers, Christ stands in the relationship of a benevolent elder brother; he is a father-substitute to them. All demands made upon individuals are derived from this love of Christ. A streak of democracy runs through the church – precisely because, before Christ, all are equal, all have the same share in his love. Not without good reason is the similarity of the Christian community to a family evoked, and if believers address one another as brothers in Christ, they mean brothers through the love that Christ has for them. There can be no doubt about it: what binds each individual to Christ is also the cause of what binds those individuals to one another. It is the same with the army: the commander is the father who loves all his soldiers equally, and that is what makes them comrades together. The army differs structurally from the church in that it comprises a stepped pyramid of such masses. Each captain is the commander and father of his unit, so to speak, each sergeant of his platoon. Granted, a similar hierarchy has evolved in the church, but there it does not play the same 'economic' role,[3] since greater knowledge of and concern for individuals may be ascribed to Christ than to the human commander.

Against this view of the libidinal structure of an army, it will rightly be objected that the ideas of country, national glory, and other things that are of such significance for the cohesion of the army have found no place here. The answer to that is: this is a different, rather more complicated case of mass bonding, and as the examples of great military leaders (Caesar, Wallenstein, Napoleon) show, such ideas are not essential for an army to continue to exist. The possibility of the leader being replaced by a guiding idea and the relations between the two are things we shall touch on briefly at a later stage. Neglecting this libidinal factor in the army, even if it is not the only one at work, seems to be not merely a theoretical shortcoming but also a practical risk. Prussian militarism, which was as unpsychological as the German scientific world, may have had to learn this lesson in the Great War. The fact is, the battlefield neuroses that subverted the German army have largely been seen as a protest by the individual against the role imposed on him by the army, and according to E. Simmel the inconsiderate treatment meted out to the common man by his superior officers may be placed at the top of the list of motives behind such indispositions.[4] A better appreciation of this libido requirement might well have prevented the extraordinary promises of the American president's 'Fourteen Points' from finding such ready credence, and a magnificent instrument would not have come apart in the German strategists' hands.

Note that, in these two artificial masses, each individual has this libidinal tie, on the one hand to the leader (Christ, the commander), and on the other to the rest of the individuals in the mass. How these two attachments relate to each other, whether they are of the same kind and the same value, and how they should be described in psychological terms are questions we must reserve for a subsequent investigation. However, we would venture now to level a mild reproach against the authors of the existing literature for having done less than justice to the importance of the leader as regards the psychology of the mass, whereas our choice of the first object of investigation has placed us in a more favourable position. We cannot help feeling that we are on the right track – one capable of shedding light on the principal phenomenon of mass psychology, namely the individual's lack of freedom within the mass. If each individual experiences so substantial an emotional attachment in two directions, we shall not find it hard to trace back to this situation the observed alteration and restriction of that individual's personality.

We receive another hint in this same direction (namely that the essence of a mass consists in the libidinal attachments present within it) in the phenomenon of panic, which can best be studied in military masses. Panic arises when such a mass is subverted. It is in the nature of panic that no order from the superior officer commands obedience any more and that each man looks after himself without regard for the others. The mutual ties have ceased to bind, releasing a vast, senseless fear. Here again, of course, the obvious objection is that it is in fact the other way around: the fear had grown so great that it was able to overcome all regard for others and all attachments. McDougall even uses the case of panic (albeit non-military) as a prime example of what he calls affective enhancement through 'primary induction'.[5] However, this kind of rational explanation misses the point completely. What needs explaining is why the fear has become so vast. The size of the danger cannot be blamed, since the same army as is now a prey to panic may perfectly well have survived similarly great, indeed greater dangers, and it is almost of the essence of panic that it is out of all proportion to the threatened danger, often breaking out for the most trivial of reasons. When the individual, seized with panic fear, proceeds to look after himself, he evinces his understanding that the affective attachments that had hitherto kept the perceived danger in check have ceased to exist. Now, though, facing the danger alone, he may well see it as greater. In other words, it is as if panic fear presupposes a loosening of the libidinal structure of the mass and justifiably reacts to it, rather than the other way around: that the mass's libido attachments are destroyed by the fear of danger.

These remarks in no way contradict the assertion that, within the mass, fear grows to monstrous proportions through induction or contagion. McDougall's view is wholly appropriate in cases where the danger is truly great and where no strong emotional ties exist within the mass – conditions that are met when, for instance, fire breaks out in a theatre or pub. The instructive case, which also serves our purposes, is the one mentioned above: a body of armed men panics when the danger has not risen above the usual level, which has been well tolerated many times. Use of the word 'panic' cannot be expected to be sharply and unambiguously defined. Sometimes it denotes any kind of mass fear; at other times it refers to an individual's fear when this becomes wholly disproportionate. Often the term seems to be reserved for the case where the outbreak of fear is not justified by the occasion. Taking the word 'panic' to mean mass fear enables us to put forward a far-reaching analogy. Fear in the individual is evoked either by the size of the danger or by the cessation of emotional ties (libido charges),[6] the latter case being that of neurotic fear.[7] In the same way, panic arises as a result of an increase in the danger affecting everyone or as a result of the emotional ties that hold the mass together coming to an end, and this latter case is analogous to neurotic fear.[8]

When McDougall describes panic as one of the clearest products of the 'group mind', he gets himself into the paradoxical position of saying that this (we call it the 'mass mind') eliminates itself in one of its most spectacular expressions. There can be no doubt that panic means the subversion of the mass, leading as it does to the cessation of any consideration that the individuals constituting the mass normally show for one another.

The typical occasion for panic breaking out is not unlike that portrayed in Nestroy's *Judith und Holofernes*, a parody of the drama *Judith* by Friedrich Hebbel.[9] In it a soldier shouts: 'The commander has lost his [i.e. Holofernes's] head!', whereupon all the Assyrians take flight. Loss of the leader in any sense, or his becoming insane, finds expression in panic – even when the danger remains the same. When the bond with the leader goes, so (as a rule) do the reciprocal bonds between the individuals making up a mass. The mass dissipates like the contents of a Bologna flask when the top is snapped off.

The disintegration of a religious mass is less easy to observe. Recently a novel of Catholic origin, recommended by the Bishop of London, came into my hands. It is an English novel, entitled *When It Was Dark*, and it depicts such a possibility in a clever and (to my mind) telling fashion.[10] The book narrates, as if from the standpoint of the present day, how a conspiracy of enemies of the person of Christ and the Christian faith successfully arranges to have a tomb discovered in Jerusalem containing an inscription in which Joseph of Arimathea confesses that, for reasons of respect for the dead, he secretly had Christ's body removed from its original tomb on the third day and reinterred in this place. With that, the resurrection of Christ and his divine nature are dismissed, and the consequence of this archaeological discovery is to deliver a shattering blow to European civilization, leading to an extraordinary increase in crime and acts of violence of all kinds, which diminishes only once the forgers' plot has been successfully exposed.

What comes out in the subversion of the religious mass posited in the novel is not fear, for which there is no occasion, but reckless, hostile impulses against other persons that had previously, due to the equal love of Christ, been unable to find expression.[11] Even during Christ's reign, however, those individuals lie outside this bond of attachment who do not belong to the community of believers, who do not love Christ and whom Christ does not love; for that reason a religion, even one calling itself the religion of love, must be hard and unloving towards those who do not belong to it. Ultimately, of course, every religion is such a religion of love for all whom it embraces, and it lies in everyone's nature to be cruel and intolerant towards non-members. One should never, no matter how hard one finds it personally, censure believers too severely for this; unbelievers and the indifferent have it psychologically that much easier in this respect. If nowadays this sort of intolerance no longer finds such violent and cruel expression as in earlier centuries, that hardly justifies the conclusion that mankind's ways have become milder. The reason is far more likely to be found in the undeniable weakening of religious feeling and of the libidinal ties that depend thereon. If another mass attachment takes the place of the religious one, as socialism seems currently to be doing, the same intolerance towards outsiders will ensue as in the era of the Wars of Religion, and if differences of scientific opinion ever managed to attain a similar level of importance for masses, the result would be the same for this motivation as well.

Notes

1. [*Addition, 1923:*] The attributes 'stable' and 'artificial' appear, in the case of masses, to coincide or at least to be closely associated.
2. [Matt. 25:40 (RSV).]
3. [Freud's use of the term *ökonomisch* is rather special. According to J. Laplanche and J.-B. Pontalis, *The Language of Psycho-Analysis* (tr. Donald Nicholson-Smith), London 1973 (reprinted 1988), it 'qualifies everything having to do with the hypothesis that psychical processes consist in the circulation and distribution of an energy (instinctual energy) that can be quantified, i.e. that is capable of increase, decrease and equivalence' (p. 127). To highlight this, wherever the term occurs I have placed it in inverted commas.]
4. E. Simmel, *Kriegsneurosen und 'psychisches Trauma'*, Munich 1918.
5. [W. McDougall, *The Mass Mind*, Cambridge 1920, p. 24.]
6. [*Libidobesetzungen*. Freud eventually settled on the term *Besetzung* in 1895 to embody an idea he had been working towards for some time. The German word possesses a theatrical connotation ('casting', as an action as well as the outcome of that action) and a military connotation ('occupation'). Both suggest 'filling' something (a role or a country) for a purpose. I hope to evoke a similar response in the English reader's mind by extending the analogy into the realm of electricity and rendering *Besetzung* (here and elsewhere in this volume) as 'charge'. Laplanche and Pontalis, in *The Language of Psycho-Analysis* (op. cit., see note 3), define *Besetzung* (James Strachey's 'cathexis') as follows: 'Economic concept: the fact that a certain amount of psychical energy is attached to an idea or to a group of ideas, to a part of the body, to an object, etc.']
7. See [Sigmund] Freud, *Vorlesungen zur Einführung in die Psychoanalyse* [*Introductory Lectures on Psycho-Analysis, Standard Edition*, vols XV–XVI], Lecture XXV.
8. See in this connection the imaginative if somewhat fantastical essay by Béla von Felszeghy, 'Panik und Pan-Komplex', in *Imago* VI, 1920.
9. [Friedrich Hebbel, *Judith*, 1841; Johann Nepomuk Nestroy, *Judith und Holofernes*, 1849.]
10. [Guy Thorne (pseud. of Cyril Arthur Edward Ranger Gull), *When It Was Dark, A Story*, London 1903.]
11. See also, in this connection, the explanation of similar phenomena following the collapse of national authority in P. Federn, *Die vaterlose Gesellschaft* ['The fatherless society'], Vienna 1919.

VI

Other tasks and areas for study

So far we have examined two artificial masses and found that they are dominated by two different sorts of emotional tie, of which the one to the leader appears to have a more determining influence (at least so far as the mass is concerned) than the other, namely the tie that binds the individuals of the mass together.

However, in the morphology of masses there is still much that needs to be examined and described. One would have to take as one's starting-point the observation that a simple crowd of people does not in fact constitute a mass until such ties have become established within it, but one would have to concede that in any large group of people the tendency to form a psychological mass emerges very readily. One would need to note the different kinds of mass (some more durable than others) that occur spontaneously and to study the conditions of their coming into being and their decay. Above all, the difference between masses that have a leader and leaderless masses would occupy our attention; whether masses with leaders are not the more natural, more complete ones, whether in the others the leader may not be replaced by an idea, an abstract concept (to which of course religious masses with their physically intangible head already form the transition), whether such a replacement is not supplied by a collective tendency, a desire in which a great many persons can share. That abstract concept might in turn be embodied more or less fully in the person of a secondary leader, as it were, and the relationship between idea and leader would produce an interesting range of possibilities. The leader or the guiding idea might also become negative, so to speak; aversion to a particular person or institution might have as unifying an effect as positive devotion, evoking similar emotional ties. The question then arises (among others): is the leader truly indispensable so far as the essence of the mass is concerned?

However, all these questions, some of which may well be dealt with in the literature of mass psychology, will be incapable of diverting our interest from the basic psychological problems that present themselves to us in the structure of a mass. To begin with, we are gripped by an observation that promises us, by the shortest route, proof that it is libidinal attachments that characterize a mass.

Take the way people in general behave towards one another emotionally. According to Schopenhauer's famous allegory of the hedgehogs seeking warmth, no one can bear the intimacy of too-close contact with another human being.[1]

On the evidence of psychoanalysis, almost every close emotional relationship of any duration between two people (marriage, friendship, parenthood, childhood[2]) includes a sediment of negative, hostile emotions that escapes perception only because repressed. It is less veiled when partners quarrel, or when subordinates grumble about their superiors. The same thing happens when people congregate in larger entities. Whenever two families join together as a result of a marriage, each considers itself better or more respectable at the expense of the other. Of two nearby towns, each will become the bitter rival of the other; every little parish looks down on its neighbour. Closely related peoples feel a mutual revulsion, south Germans cannot abide north Germans, Englishmen constantly insult Scots, the Spaniard despises the Portuguese. That greater differences result in virtually unbridgeable aversions (Gaul versus Teuton, Aryan versus Semite, white versus black) has ceased to surprise us.

Where the hostility is directed against otherwise loved persons, we talk of emotional ambivalence and explain such a case to ourselves in what is surely too rational a fashion by the many occasions for conflicts of interest that arise in just such intimate relationships. In the unveiled emergence of aversions to and revulsions against close others we recognize the expression of a self-love, a narcissism, that, in seeking to assert itself, behaves as if the occurrence of a departure from its individual manifestations implied some criticism of those manifestations and a call for their reshaping. Why so great a degree of sensitivity should have seized upon these particular details of differentiation we do not know; unmistakably, however, such human behaviour implies a readiness to hate, an aggressiveness whose roots are unknown and that one would be inclined to characterize as elemental.[3]

However, all this intolerance vanishes, temporarily or permanently, as a result of mass formation and in the mass. For as long as the mass endures or as far as it extends, the individuals behave as if they were uniform; they tolerate the other person's individuality, treat that person on an equal footing, and feel no aversion in his regard. That kind of reduction of narcissism can only, according to our theoretical notions, be generated by one factor, by libidinal attachment to other persons. Self-love finds bounds only in love of others, love of objects.[4] The question will immediately be asked whether community of interests alone, without any libidinal contribution, will not in itself inevitably lead to toleration of and consideration for the other. To counter this objection, it will be pointed out that in fact no permanent reduction of narcissism comes about in this way since such toleration lasts no longer than the immediate advantage drawn from the other's co-operation. But the practical value of this dispute is less than one might think; the fact is, experience has shown that, as a rule, where there is co-operation, libidinal bonds are produced between comrades that extend the relationship between them beyond what is advantageous and pin it there. The same thing happens in human social relationships, as psychoanalytical research has found in the process of individual libidinal development. The libido, taking its cue from the satisfaction of the major life requirements, selects the persons involved in that process as its first objects. And, as with the individual, so too in the development of mankind as a whole, only love has had effect as a civilizing factor in the sense of a turning away from egoism towards altruism. And that applies both to sexual love of a woman, with all the compulsions that flow from it in terms of sparing what the woman loved, and to that desexualized, sublimated homosexual love of the other man, which has to do with working together.

So when reductions of narcissistic self-love appear in the mass that have no effect outside it, here is compelling indication that the essence of mass formation consists in new types of libidinal ties among the members thereof.

Now, our interest is going to be very much in knowing what kinds of tie those are within the mass. Up to now, our psychoanalytical theory of neurosis has concerned itself almost exclusively with the attachment of such love drives to their objects as still pursue direct sexual goals. Clearly, in the mass, no such sexual goals can be at issue. We are dealing here with love drives that, without being any less vigorous in their effect, have nevertheless been deflected from their original goals. It so happens that we have already, in the context of ordinary sexual object-charging, observed phenomena that correspond to a deflection of the drive from its sexual goal. These we have described as degrees of being in love, acknowledging that they imply a certain impairment of the 'I'. We shall now be devoting more thorough attention to these phenomena of being in love in the well-founded expectation of finding in them relationships that can be transferred to attachments within masses. But we should also like to know whether the kind of object-charging with which we are familiar from sexual life represents the only avenue of emotional attachment to another person or whether we need to consider other such mechanisms. Psychoanalysis does in fact teach us that there are other mechanisms of emotional attachment, so-called *identifications*. Too little is known about these processes, and they are difficult to describe; in fact, examining them is going to take us away from the subject of mass psychology for quite some time.

Notes

1. 'A family of hedgehogs massed very close together one cold winter's day, hoping to use one another's warmth to protect themselves against the cold. However, they soon felt one another's prickles, which made them draw apart. When the need for warmth brought them closer together once

again, this second evil was repeated, with the result that they were bounced back and forth between the two ills until they had established a moderate degree of distance from one another in which they could best endure their condition' (*Parerga und Paralipomena*, Part II, XXXI, 'Gleichnisse und Parabeln' ['Allegories and fables']).

2. Possibly with the sole exception of the mother–son relationship, which, being based on narcissism, is undisturbed by subsequent rivalry and is strengthened by the first signs of a sexual object-choice.

3. In a recently (1920) published essay, 'Jenseits des Lustprinzips' ['Beyond the Pleasure Principle', *Standard Edition*, vol. XVIII, p. 7; *Beyond the Pleasure Principle and Other Writings*, Penguin 2003, p. 43], I sought to link the polarity of love and hate to a postulated conflict between life and death drives and to present the sex drive as the purest representative of the former, namely the life drive.

4. See *Zur Einführung des Narzissmus* ['On the Introduction of Narcissism', in *Beyond the Pleasure Principle and Other Writings*, Penguin, 2003, p. 1], 1914.

VII

Identification

Identification is known to psychoanalysis as the earliest expression
of an emotional attachment to another person. It plays a part in
the prehistory of the Oedipus complex. The small boy exhibits a
special interest in his father, wanting to become like him, be like
him, take his place in every respect. Not to put too fine a point
on it, he takes his father as his ideal. This behaviour has nothing
to do with a passive or feminine attitude towards the father (and
towards the male sex in general); in fact it is exquisitely masculine. It is wholly consistent with the Oedipus complex, which it
helps to prepare.

At the same time as this identification with his father, possibly
even earlier, the boy has begun to undertake a true object-
charging of his mother in accordance with the support-seeking
type.[1] In other words, he evinces two psychologically different attachments: to his mother, a straightforwardly sexual object-charging;
to his father, an exemplary identification. For a while the two exist
in parallel, without influencing or interfering with each other. In
consequence of the inexorable standardization of mental life, they
eventually meet, and this coming together gives rise to the normal
Oedipus complex. The boy notices that, for him, his father bars
the way to his mother; his identification with his father now assumes
a hostile note and becomes identical with the desire to take his
father's place with his mother too. The fact is, identification is
ambivalent from the outset; it can as easily turn into an expression of tenderness as into a wish to remove. It behaves like a product of the first *oral* stage of libido organization in which the coveted,
treasured object was incorporated by eating and was annihilated

57

as such in the process. The cannibal, as we know, never gets beyond this point; he loves to eat his enemies, and he does not eat those he cannot somehow hold in affection.[2]

The fate of this father-identification is later easily lost from view. It may then happen that the Oedipus complex suffers an inversion, that the father is in a feminine mind-set taken as the object from which the direct sexual drives expect satisfaction, and father-identification has then become the precursor of object-attachment to the father. The same applies, *mutatis mutandis*, with regard to the small daughter.

It is a simple matter to express the difference between this kind of father-identification and choice of the father as an object in a formula. In the former instance the father is what the child wishes to *be*, in the latter what the child wants to *have*. It is the difference, in other words, between whether the attachment fixes on the subject or the object of the 'I'. The former is therefore possible before any sexual object-choice. It is very much harder to illustrate the difference metapsychologically. All that is understood is that identification tries to shape a person's own 'I' along similar lines to the other that the person has taken as his 'example'.

We extract identification from a more intricate context in the case of neurotic symptom-formation. The young girl we should like to dwell on now suffers (she says) from the same symptoms as her mother, for instance the same painful cough. Now, this may happen in various ways. Either the identification is the same as from the Oedipus complex, implying a hostile desire to replace the mother, and the symptom expresses the object-love for the father; it effects the replacement of the mother under the influence of guilt feelings: you wanted to be your mother – now you are, at least in terms of illness. That is then the complete mechanism of hysterical symptom-formation. Or alternatively, the symptom is the same as that of the loved person (as when, for instance, Dora in 'Fragment of an Analysis of Hysteria'[3] imitates her father's coughing); in that case the only way we can describe the facts of the case is by saying *identification has taken the place of choice of object, object-choice has regressed to become identification*. We have heard that identification is the earliest and most natural form of emotional attachment; in the circumstances of symptom-formation, i.e. of repression, and of the dominance of the mechanisms of the unconscious, it often happens that object-choice once again becomes identification – that is to say, the 'I' takes on the qualities of the object. Remarkably, in such identifications the 'I' will on one occasion copy the unloved person, on another the loved person. Another thing that inevitably strikes us is that on both occasions the identification is partial and highly restricted, borrowing only a single feature from the object-person.

A third, particularly frequent and significant case of symptom-formation is when identification wholly disregards the object-relationship to the person copied. If for example one of the girls in a boarding-school has received a letter from her secret lover that provokes her jealousy and to which she reacts with a fit of hysteria, some of her friends who are in the know will adopt the fit, as we say, through the medium of psychical infection. The mechanism is that of identification on the basis of being able to or wanting to put oneself in the same position. The others would also like to have a secret love affair, and under the influence of guilt feelings they also accept the associated illness. It would be wrong to say that they appropriate the symptom out of sympathy. On the contrary, sympathy springs only from identification, and the proof is that such infection or imitation is sometimes also engendered where presumably there was less prior fellow feeling between the two parties than customarily exists among female boarding-school friends. One 'I' has perceived in the other a significant analogy in one point (in our example, in the same emotional readiness), whereupon an identification forms in that point, and under the influence of the pathogenic situation that identification shifts to become a symptom that the first 'I' has produced. Identification through the symptom thus becomes a sign of an overlap between the two 'I's that must be kept repressed.

What we have learned from these three sources can be summed up as follows: firstly, identification is the most natural form of emotional attachment to an object; secondly, through regressive channels it becomes a substitute for a libidinal object-attachment, as it were by introjection of the object into the 'I'; and thirdly, it may arise in connection with every newly perceived instance of having something in common with a person who is not an object of the sex drives. The more significant that 'having something in common', the more successful this partial identification must be capable of becoming, so corresponding to the beginning of a fresh attachment.

We already suspect that the reciprocal attachment of the individuals making up a mass is in the nature of such an identification through their having a great deal in common emotionally, and we may assume that what they have in common consists in the manner of their attachment to the leader. Another suspicion may tell us that we are a long way from having exhausted the problem of identification, that we are faced here with the process that psychology calls 'empathy' and that contributes most towards our understanding of the non-'I' element in other persons. For our present purposes, however, we mean to confine ourselves to the most immediate affective influences of identification and to disregard its importance for our intellectual life.

Psychoanalytical research, which has occasionally also tackled the more difficult problems of psychoses, has also been able to show us identification in a number of other cases not easily amenable to our understanding. I shall deal with two of these cases in detail as material for our further considerations.

The genesis of male homosexuality is in a great many instances as follows. The young man has been fixated on his mother in terms of the Oedipus complex for an unusually long time and with unusual intensity. Finally, with puberty at last complete, the time comes to exchange the mother for a different sex-object. Here an abrupt reversal occurs: instead of leaving his mother, the youth identifies with her, transforming himself into her and henceforth seeking objects capable of taking the place of his 'I' for him, objects that he can love and care for in the way he has learned to do from his mother. This is a frequent occurrence; it can be confirmed any number of times and is of course wholly independent of any assumption that may be made regarding the organic driving-force and the motives behind that sudden change. What is striking about this identification is its extensiveness; it transforms the 'I' in an extremely important respect, in its sexual character, on the model of the existing object. In the process, the object itself is relinquished (whether completely or only in the sense that it is retained in the unconscious is not at issue here). For us, however, identification with the relinquished or lost object as a replacement for the same, [what we call] introjection of that object into the 'I', is no longer anything new. Occasionally, this kind of occurrence can be observed directly in the young child. Just such an observation was recently published in the *International Journal of Psychoanalysis*, where a child, unhappy at the loss of a kitten, announced straight out that he was now the kitten himself and accordingly walked on all fours, refused to sit up at table, etc.[4]

Another example of this kind of introjection of the object was provided by our analysis of melancholy, an affect that of course counts the real or affective loss of the loved object among its most conspicuous occasions. A major characteristic of these cases is cruel self-disparagement of the 'I' in conjunction with unsparing self-criticism and instances of bitter self-reproach. Studies have shown that such evaluation and such reproaches are basically aimed at the object and represent the revenge of the 'I' upon it. The shadow of the object has fallen on the 'I', as the present author has written elsewhere.[5] The introjection of the object is here unmistakably plain.

But such accesses of melancholy show us something else that may be important as regards our subsequent reflections. They show us the 'I' divided, split in two, with one part raging against the other. This other part is the one changed by introjection, the part that includes the lost object. But the part that rages so cruelly is not unknown to us either. It includes the conscience, a critical agency within the 'I', which even in normal times adopted a critical stance vis-à-vis the 'I', only never so implacably and so unfairly. We have already had to make the assumption on previous occasions ('Narcissism', 'Mourning and Melancholia') that such an agency develops within our 'I' that can cut itself off from the other 'I' and come into conflict with it. We called it the '"I"-ideal' and attributed to it such functions as self-observation, moral conscience, dream censorship, and the principal influence in repression. We said it was the heir to the original narcissism in which the infant 'I' was self-sufficient. Little by little (we went on) it takes from the influences of the environment those demands that the environment makes upon the 'I' and that the 'I' is not always able to meet, with the result that, where a person cannot himself be content with his 'I', that person may still find satisfaction in the 'I'-ideal as distinct from the 'I'. In observation mania, we further ascertained, the disintegration of this agency becomes manifest and in the process its derivation from the influences of the authorities, primarily the parents, is exposed.[6] We did not omit to add, however, that the distance between this 'I'-ideal and the actual 'I' varies greatly between individuals and that for many this differentiation within the 'I' goes no further than in the child.

But before we can use this material to help us to understand the libidinal organization of a mass, we need to consider a number of other correlations between object and 'I'.[7]

Notes

1. [*Anlehnungstypus. Anlehnung* is another instance (like *Besetzung*) of Freud's rather special use of an ordinary German word being regularly rendered in English by a learned-looking term derived from the Greek ('anaclisis'; *adj.* 'anaclitic'). For a full exposition the reader is referred to Laplanche and Pontalis, *The Language of Psycho-Analysis*, op. cit., (1998), pp. 29 ff.; all the general reader needs to know is that Freud distinguished two avenues by which the individual selects 'objects' to charge with emotion: the 'narcissistic' (focusing on the self) and what I choose to call the 'support-seeking' (based on a more realistic approach to the future satisfaction of drives).]

2. See *Drei Abhandlungen zur Sexualtheorie*, op. cit. [*Three Essays on Sexual Theory*], and Abraham, 'Untersuchungen über die früheste prägenitale Entwicklungsstufe der Libido' ['Investigations into the earliest pre-genital

stage in the development of the libido'], in *Internationale Zeitschrift für Psychoanalyse*, IV, 1916, reprinted in Abraham, op. cit., *Klinische Beiträge zur Psychoanalyse*, Internationale Psychoanalytische Bibliothek, vol. 10, 1921.

3. ['Fragment of an Analysis of Hysteria', *Standard Edition*, vol. VII, p. 3.]

4. Markuszewicz, 'Beitrag zum autistischen Denken bei Kindern' ['On autistic thinking in children'], in *Internationale Zeitschrift für Psychoanalyse*, VI (1920).

5. 'Trauer und Melancholie' ['Mourning and Melancholia', *Standard Edition*, vol. XIV, p. 239], in *Sammlung kleiner Schriften zur Neurosenlehre* ['A collection of brief essays on the theory of neurosis'], fourth series, 1918.

6. *Zur Einführung des Narzissmus* ['On the Introduction of Narcissism' (1914) – although the *Standard Edition* calls the piece 'On Narcissism: An Introduction', *Standard Edition*, Vol. XIV, p. 69].

7. We are well aware that these examples taken from pathology do not exhaust the nature of identification and that in consequence we have left part of the riddle of mass-formation untouched. A far more thorough and more comprehensive psychological analysis would need to be made here. From identification, one avenue leads via imitation to empathy, i.e. to an understanding of the mechanism whereby we are able to say anything at all about the mental life of another person. Even with regard to the manifestations of an existing identification, much remains to be explained. One consequence of identification is that a person reins in any aggression against the person identified with, sparing that person and coming to that person's aid. Studying such identifications as, for example, underlie the clan led Robertson Smith to the surprising conclusion that they are based on recognition of a common substance (*Kinship and Marriage*, 1885) and can therefore also be created by a shared meal. This trait means that such identification can be brought into association with the primeval history of the human family construed by myself in *Totem und Tabu*.

VIII

Being in love and hypnosis

Even at its most whimsical, linguistic usage remains true to some kind of reality. For instance, although it describes as 'love' a wide variety of emotional relationships that we too, theoretically, group together as love, it questions whether that love is in fact the real, true, proper thing, thus indicating a whole hierarchy of possibilities within the love phenomenon. Nor do we have any difficulty in finding the same in observation.

In a series of cases, being in love is simply object-charging on the part of the sex drives for the purpose of direct sexual satisfaction (in fact, it dies once it has achieved that goal); that is what is referred to as ordinary, sensual love. However, as we know, the libidinal situation seldom remains so simple. The certainty with which the need that had just died could be expected to revive must presumably have been the immediate motive for endowing the sex object with a permanent charge [/casting it in a permanent role] and 'loving' it even during the lust-free interludes.

From the very remarkable developmental history of the human love-life there stems a second factor. In the first stage, usually complete by the age of five, the child had found in one parent an initial love-object on which all its sex drives, thirsting for satisfaction, had focused. The repression that then supervened forced the child to renounce most of those childish sexual goals and left behind a far-reaching modification of the child's relationship to its parents. The child remained attached to its parents, but with drives that have to be called 'goal-inhibited'. The feelings that the child henceforth experiences for these loved persons are described as 'affectionate'. The earlier 'sensual' tendencies are

known to remain more or less strongly preserved in the unconscious, with the result that in a sense the original full current
continues to exist.[1]

We know that, with puberty, fresh and very powerful tendencies towards direct sexual goals set in. In untoward cases they
remain as a sensual current divorced from the continuing 'affectionate' emotional trends. One is then faced with the image whose
twin aspects are so readily idealized by certain schools of thought
in the literature. The man shows infatuated leanings towards highly
respected women who, however, do not attract him sexually; he is
potent only towards other women whom he does not 'love', indeed
whom he thinks little of or even despises.[2] More often, though,
the growing youth achieves a degree of synthesis of non-sensual
or heavenly and sensual or earthly love, while his relationship to
his sex-object is characterized by a combination of uninhibited and
goal-inhibited drives. Depending on the contribution of the goal-
inhibited affection drives, it is possible to gauge the extent of being
in love as opposed to merely sensual desire.

In connection with this kind of being in love, our attention was
drawn from the outset to the phenomenon of sexual overestimation, the fact that the loved object enjoys a certain freedom from
criticism, with all that object's qualities being valued more highly
than those of unloved persons or than at a time when it was not
loved. Even partially effective repression or reduction of sensual
tendencies gives rise to the illusion that it is because of the object's
mental merits that it is also loved sensually, whereas in fact the
reverse is the case: it was sensual attraction that contrived to bestow
those merits on the object in the first place.

The striving that skews judgement here is that of *idealization*.
But this makes it easier for us to find our bearings; we know that
the object is treated in the same way as the person's own 'I' – in
other words, that in the condition of being in love a great deal of
narcissistic libido overflows on to the object. In some forms of love
choice it is even strikingly obvious that the purpose of the object
is to take the place of a person's own unattained 'I'-ideal. The
object is loved because of the perfections that a person has striven

after for his own 'I' and now seeks to acquire in this roundabout way in order to satisfy his narcissism.

If sexual overestimation and the condition of being in love attain even greater proportions, interpreting the image becomes less and less ambiguous. The tendencies pushing the person towards direct sexual satisfaction can now be repressed completely – as, for example, happens regularly in the case of youthful infatuation; the 'I' becomes less and less demanding, the object increasingly splendid and more precious; eventually, the object acquires the whole of the self-love of the 'I', with the result that the latter's self-sacrifice becomes a natural consequence. The object has, as it were, consumed the 'I'. Elements of humility, reduced narcissism, and self-harm are present in every case of being in love; in extreme cases they are merely intensified, and as a result of the withdrawal of sensual demands they alone remain paramount.

This is especially readily the case in connection with unhappy, unfulfillable love, since with each sexual satisfaction what happens is that sexual overestimation suffers a further demotion. At the same time as this 'self-abandonment' of the 'I' to the object, which is in fact indistinguishable from sublimated self-abandonment to an abstract idea, the functions assigned to the 'I'-ideal fail completely. The criticism normally exercised by this agency falls silent; everything the object does and demands is correct and beyond reproach. Conscience is not applied to any occurrence that favours the object; in the blindness of love, the lover becomes an unrepentant criminal. The whole situation can be summed up neatly in the sentence: *The object has usurped the place of the 'I'-ideal.*

The difference between identification and the condition of being in love in its highest forms (called fascination or amorous dependence) is now easy to describe. In the former case the 'I' has enriched itself with the qualities of the object (to use Ferenczi's expression, it has 'introjected' the object into itself); in the latter case the 'I' has become poorer, it has abandoned itself to the object, setting the object in place of its most important constituent. However, closer examination shows that this account erects sham opposites that do not in fact exist. We are not talking about impoverishment or enrichment in 'economic' terms; the condition of being deeply in love can also be described as the 'I' having introjected the object into itself. It may be that another distinction comes closer to the essence here. In the case of identification, the object had become lost or been given up; it is then reinstated in the 'I', with the 'I' undergoing a partial change, modelling itself on the lost object. In the other case, the object is preserved and is as such 'over-charged' by and at the expense of the 'I'. But in this respect too there is some doubt. If it is established that identification presupposes the relinquishment of object-charging, can there be no identification where the object is preserved? And before we allow ourselves to become involved in debating this delicate question, it may already have dawned on us that another alternative captures the essence of this situation, namely *whether the object is set in place of the 'I' or of the 'I'-ideal*.

From being in love it is clearly not a big step to hypnosis. The correspondences between the two are obvious. The same humble subjection, submissiveness, uncritical acceptance of hypnotist and loved object alike. The same soaking up of personal initiative; evidently, the hypnotist has taken the place of the 'I'-ideal. In hypnosis, all relationships only become clearer and more intense, so it would make more sense to explain being in love in terms of hypnosis than the other way around. The hypnotist is the sole object; no other object, apart from the hypnotist, receives any attention. The fact that the 'I' experiences the hypnotist's demands and assertions in a dreamlike state reminds us that we neglected to mention keeping a check on reality as being one of the functions of the 'I'-ideal.[3] No wonder the 'I' deems a perception to be real if the psychical agency charged with the task of examining reality lends its support to that reality. The total absence of tendencies with uninhibited sexual goals further contributes to the extreme purity of the phenomena associated with hypnosis. The hypnotic relationship is an unrestricted amorous surrender that excludes sexual satisfaction, whereas in the condition of being in love such satisfaction is only provisionally deferred and remains in the background as a future potential goal.

On the other hand, we can also say that the hypnotic relationship is (if the expression will be permitted) the formation of a mass of two. Hypnosis offers a good comparison with mass formation, being actually identical with the latter. From the complicated structure of the mass it isolates one element for us, namely the behaviour of the mass individual towards the leader. This numerical restriction distinguishes hypnosis from mass formation, just as the absence of directly sexual tendencies distinguishes it from the condition of being in love. In that respect, it occupies the middle ground between the two.

Interestingly, it is precisely such goal-inhibited sexual tendencies that achieve lasting attachments between people. This is easily explained, however, by the fact that they are incapable of complete satisfaction, whereas uninhibited sexual tendencies find themselves extraordinarily reduced as a result of their removal in the wake of each attainment of the sexual goal. Sensual love is destined to expire in satisfaction; to be capable of lasting it must from the outset have been mixed with purely affectionate, i.e. goal-inhibited constituents, or it must undergo such a conversion.

Hypnosis would provide us with a smooth solution to the riddle of the libidinal constitution of a mass if it did not itself still contain features that elude the rational explanation offered so far, namely that it is like the condition of being in love but with the directly sexual tendencies excluded. Much about it must still be acknowledged as being not understood, as being mysterious. It contains an admixture of paralysis from the relationship of a superior to a powerless inferior – which links up with the fright hypnosis of animals, for instance. The manner in which it is engendered and how it relates to sleep are both obscure, and the puzzling selection of persons who make suitable subjects while others reject it completely points to a factor as yet unknown that becomes effective through it and is perhaps what allows libido attitudes within it to be so pure. Another remarkable feature is the way the moral conscience of the hypnotized person may often prove resistant, even where the person is otherwise wholly suggestible and submissive. However, that may be due to the fact that, in hypnosis as usually practised, an awareness may be retained that this is only a game, an unreal reproduction of a different situation – one of very much greater vital significance.

Our discussions hitherto, however, have fully prepared us to set out the formula for the libidinal constitution of the mass. At least of the kind of mass we have been considering up to now – in other words, one that has a leader and has not been able to acquire secondarily the properties of an individual as a result of having too much 'organization'. *Such a primary mass is a number of individuals who have set one and the same object in place of their 'I'-ideal and who have consequently identified with one another in terms of their 'I'.* The relationship can be illustrated diagrammatically:

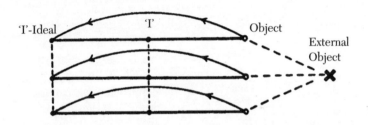

Notes

1. See *Drei Abhandlungen zur Sexualtheorie* [*Three Essays on the Theory of Sexuality* (1905), Standard Edition, vol. VII, p. 125].

2. 'Über die allgemeinste Erniedrigung des Liebeslebens' ('Concerning the most common degradation of love life'), in *Sammlung kleiner Schriften zur Neurosenlehre*, fourth series, 1918.

3. See 'Metapsychologische Ergänzung zur Traumlehre' ['A metapsychological supplement to the theory of dreams'], in *Sammlung kleiner Schriften zur Neurosenlehre*, fourth series, 1918. [*Standard Edition*, vol.

XIV, p. 219. *Addition 1923:*] Some doubt seems to have arisen in the meantime regarding the legitimacy of this attribution. Thorough discussion is called for.

IX

The herd instinct[1]

Only briefly shall we enjoy the illusion that with this formula we have solved the riddle of the mass. Very soon we shall inevitably be troubled by the reminder that what we have done, basically, is posit a referral to the riddle of hypnosis, on which so much work remains to be done. And it is at this point that a further objection shows us the way forward.

We may tell ourselves that the substantial affective ties that we recognize in the mass are quite adequate to explain one of its characteristics – namely the lack of independence and initiative on the part of the individual, the fact that the individual's reaction is the same as everyone else's, the way the individual sinks down, as it were, to become a mass individual. Looked at as a whole, however, the mass shows us more; certain features – a weakening of intellectual performance, uninhibited affectivity, the inability to exercise moderation and postpone things, the tendency to overstep all bounds in the expression of emotion and to observe none whatsoever in action – these and everything like them, such as we find so impressively portrayed in Le Bon, add up to an unmistakable picture of the kind of regression of mental activity to an earlier level that we are not surprised to find among savages or children. Such regression belongs particularly to the nature of ordinary masses,[2] while, as we have heard, it can be largely disregarded in the case of highly organized, artificial masses.

This gives us the impression of a state of affairs in which the individual's isolated stir of emotion and personal intellectual response are too weak to assert themselves on their own and are entirely obliged to await reinforcement through similar reiteration by the rest. We are reminded of how much of such dependence phenomena belongs to the normal constitution of human society, how little originality and personal courage are found therein, how extensively every individual is dominated by the attitudes of a mass mind, which come out as racial characteristics, class prejudices, public opinion, and the like. The riddle of suggestive influence increases for us once we admit that such influence is exercised not only by the leader but also by each individual upon every other individual, and we reproach ourselves with having one-sidedly emphasized the relationship to the leader while improperly repressing the other factor: mutual suggestion.

Thus pointed in the direction of modesty, we shall be inclined to listen to a different voice that promises us enlightenment on simpler foundations. One such voice comes to me from Wilfred Trotter's shrewd book on the herd instinct, about which I have only one regret: that it is not wholly emancipated from the antipathies unleashed by the last great war.[3]

Trotter derives the mental phenomena described in connection with the mass from a herd instinct (he uses the term 'gregarious-ness'), innate in humans as it is in other types of animal. This belonging to a herd is biologically an analogy and almost an exten-sion of multicellularity; in terms of the theory of the libido, it is a further expression of the inclination (proceeding from the libido) of all similar living creatures to unite in ever larger units.[4] The individual feels 'incomplete' when alone. The small child's fear is already an expression of this drive, this herd instinct. Contradiction of the herd is tantamount to separation from it and is therefore anxiously avoided. But the herd rejects everything new, everything unusual. The herd instinct, Trotter tells us, is something primary; it 'cannot be split up'.

Trotter places what he takes to be primary drives (or instincts)[5] in the following order: self-assertion, feeding, sex and herding. The last, he says, often finds itself in conflict with the others. Guilt feelings and a sense of duty are the typical possessions of a 'gregarious animal'. Moreover, Trotter sees the herd instinct as the source not only of the repressive forces that psychoanalysis has demonstrated in the ego but also (as is logically consistent) of the resistance that the physician encounters when administering psychoanalytical treatment. Language, he tells us, owes its importance to its suitability for mutual communication within the herd, providing as it does most of the basis for individuals' identification with one another.

Le Bon was chiefly interested in the characteristically transient nature of mass formation, McDougall in stable socializations; Trotter, for his part, focuses on the most commonplace associations in which man, that ξψου πολιτιχόυ [political animal], lives, explaining them in psychological terms. For Trotter, however, no derivation of the herd instinct (which he describes as primary and irreducible) is required. His comment that Boris Sidis derives the herd instinct from suggestibility is fortunately superfluous so far as he is concerned; it is an explanation following a known, unsatisfactory pattern, and the converse of that proposition, namely that suggestibility is a child of the herd instinct, seems to me far more plausible.

However, with even greater justification than against the others, the objection may be levelled against Trotter's portrayal that it pays too little heed to the role of the leader in the mass. The fact is, we incline towards the opposite view, holding that the nature of the mass is incomprehensible if we ignore the leader. The herd instinct leaves no room for the leader whatsoever; the leader is added to the mass only coincidentally. And in this connection there is the further fact that, starting from this drive, nothing leads to a need for God; the herd, as it were, has no herdsman. But Trotter's portrayal can also be undermined psychologically; in other words, there is at least a case for saying that the herd instinct is not incapable of being broken down further, that it is not primary in the sense that the self-preservation drive and the sex drive are primary.

Of course, it is not easy to trace the ontogenesis of the herd instinct. The small child's fear of being left alone, which Trotter seeks to claim as an early expression of the drive, in fact suggests a different interpretation. It is directed at the mother (and subsequently at other persons in whom the child has confidence), and it expresses an unfilled yearning that the child, not yet knowing what else to do with it, turns into fear.[6] The lonely child's fear is not alleviated by seeing just anybody 'from the herd'; on the contrary, it is the advent of such a 'stranger' that sparks it off. Also, it is a long time before the child reveals anything like a herd instinct or mass sentiment. That emerges only in the multiple nursery; it arises out of the children's relationship to their parents, and it is a reaction against the original envy with which the elder child greets the younger. No doubt the elder child does wish jealously to drive the younger off, keep it away from the parents, and deprive it of every entitlement; however, given that that child too (like every succeeding one) is similarly loved by the parents and in view of the impossibility of maintaining its hostile stance without harming itself, the elder child is forced to identify with the other children, and there emerges within the swarm of siblings a mass or community sentiment that then develops further at school. The first demand of this reaction-forming is for justice and equal treatment for all. Everyone knows how loudly and inexorably that demand finds expression at school. If a child cannot itself become the favourite, then at least (it feels) none of them should receive favour. This transformation and replacement of jealousy by a mass sentiment in nursery and classroom might be thought improbable, were the same process not in evidence again later in different circumstances. Think of the throng of infatuated women and girls who surround the singer or pianist after the performance. Clearly, the obvious thing is for each of them to be jealous of the others; however, in view of their number and the consequent impossibility of attaining the goal of their infatuation, they repudiate envy. Rather than tear one another's hair out, they behave like a uniform mass, paying homage to their hero in joint operations; they would be happy, for instance, to share a lock of his hair. Originally rivals, they have been able, through bestowing equal love upon the same object, to identify one with another. If a drive-situation may (as is indeed usually the case) turn out in various ways, we shall not be surprised to find that the eventual outcome will be the one associated with the possibility of a certain satisfaction, whereas a different one, even a more obvious one, will not ensue because actual circumstances refuse to let it attain that goal.

What is subsequently found to operate in society as community spirit, *esprit de corps*, etc. undeniably springs from an original envy. No one should seek to stand out; all should be and possess the same. The implied meaning of social justice is that a person denies himself much in order that others, too, shall have to deny themselves as much or (which comes to the same thing) be unable to ask for it. This demand for equality is the root of social conscience and the sense of duty. In an unexpected fashion it is revealed in the syphilitic's fear of infection, which psychoanalysis has taught us to understand. The fear exhibited by these poor people corresponds to their violent rejection of an unconscious desire to spread their infection to others (because why should they be the only ones infected; why should they be excluded from so much and the rest not?). The splendid story of the judgement of Solomon has the same core. If one woman has lost her child, the other's should not live either. By that wish the grieving party is identified.

In other words, the social sense is based on reversing an initially hostile emotion to become a positively stressed attachment that has the character of an identification. So far as our current understanding of the process goes, that reversal appears to take place under the influence of a shared tie of affection to a person outside the mass. We do not ourselves regard our analysis of identification as exhaustive, but for our present purposes we need only return to one particular feature, namely that consistent implementation of parity of treatment is demanded. We have heard already, in discussing the two artificial masses of church and army, that a prerequisite of both is that everyone should be loved in the same way by one person, the leader. Let us not forget, however, that the mass's demand for equality applies only to the individuals who make it up, not to the leader. All individuals should be equal with one another, but they all wish to be dominated by one person. Many equals, capable of identifying with one another, and a single person who stands above them all – that is the situation we find realized in the viable mass. So let us venture to correct Trotter's statement that man is a 'herd animal' and suggest instead that he is a 'horde animal', an individual member of a horde headed by a leader.

Notes

1. [*Der Herdentrieb* – literally, the herd 'drive'.]
2. [Or 'crowds', as Le Bon calls them.]
3. W. Trotter, *Instincts of the Herd in Peace and War*, London 1916 (second edition, 1919).
4. See my essay *Jenseits des Lustprinzips* [*Beyond the Pleasure Principle*].
5. [Freud has to give both words here because, where he uses the active *Trieb* (rendered here as 'drive'), authors writing in English once tended to use the passive 'instinct' (for which the German equivalent is *Instinkt*). Freud usually renders Trotter's 'herd instinct' as *Herdentrieb*.]
6. See *Vorlesungen zur Einführung in die Psychoanalyse* [*Introductory Lectures on Psychoanalysis*], Lecture XXV on fear.

X

The mass and the primal horde

In 1912 I took up Charles Darwin's suggestion that the earliest form of human society was the horde under the unrestricted control of one powerful man. I tried to show that what had happened to that horde had left ineradicable traces in the ancestral history of the human race; I specifically suggested that the development of totemism, which bears within it the seeds of religion, morality and social organization, has to do with the brutal murder of the chief and the transformation of the paternal horde into a fraternal community.[1] Granted, this is a mere hypothesis, like so many others with which the student of prehistory seeks to illuminate the darkness of primeval times (a 'Just-so Story', as a rather charming English critic once wittily dubbed it). However, in my view such a hypothesis has merit if it lends itself to creating coherence and comprehension in ever wider fields of enquiry.

Human masses again present us with the same familiar picture of the super-powerful individual amid a throng of equal companions as is contained in our idea of the primal horde. The psychology of the mass, as we know it from the descriptions we have cited repeatedly – the disappearance of the conscious individual personality, the orientation of thoughts and feelings along the same lines, the dominance of affectivity and the unconscious mind, the tendency towards immediate execution of intentions as they arise – all that corresponds to a state of regression to precisely the same kind of primitive mental activity as one would wish to attribute to the primal horde.[2]

The mass thus appears to us as a resurgence of the primal horde. In the same way as primeval man is preserved virtually in every individual, any crowd of people can re-create the primal horde; in so far as mass formation habitually dominates people's lives, we recognize in it the continued existence of the primal horde. We are obliged to conclude that mass psychology is the oldest psychology of the human race; the discipline that, disregarding all the residues of the mass, has been isolated as the psychology of the individual emerged only subsequently, piece by piece and, as it were, always only partially from the old mass psychology. We shall now try to indicate the starting-point of that development.

A moment's thought shows us how, in what respect, this assertion needs to be qualified. Individual psychology must in fact be the same age as mass psychology, since from the outset there were two types of psychology: that of the individuals making up a mass and that of the father, the chief, the leader. The individuals making up the mass were bound in the same way as we find they are today, but the father of the primal horde was free. Despite his isolation his intellectual deeds were powerful and independent, his will required no reinforcement by others. We assume, logically, that his 'I' was less bound libidinally; he loved no one but himself, and others only in so far as they served his requirements. Nothing surplus was surrendered by his 'I' to objects.

At the dawn of human history he was the *superman*, the *Übermensch* whom Nietzsche expected only the future to produce. Even today, mass individuals need the pretence that they are loved by the leader equally and fairly, but the leader himself need love no one else; his may be a *Herrennatur*, a 'master nature' – totally narcissistic, yet self-assured and independent. We know that love holds narcissism in check, and we could show how, in consequence of that effect, it has become a civilizing element.

The primal father of the horde was not at this point immortal, as deification later made him. When he died, he had to be replaced; probably his replacement was one of the younger sons, who until then had been a mass individual like any other. So there has to be a possibility of turning the psychology of the mass into individual psychology; we need to find a set of circumstances in which such a transformation is easily achieved – much as bees are able, when necessary, to turn a female larva into a queen rather than into a worker. We can imagine only one thing here: the primal father had prevented his sons from satisfying their direct sexual tendencies, forcing them into abstinence and consequently into the emotional attachments to himself and to one another that were able to proceed from the tendencies with inhibited sexual goals. He forced them, so to speak, into mass psychology. His sexual jealousy and intolerance ultimately became the ground and reason for mass psychology.[3]

For the one who succeeded him there was also the possibility of sexual satisfaction, and with it a way out of the conditions of mass psychology opened up. Fixation of the libido on woman, the possibility of satisfaction without delay and build-up ended the importance of goal-inhibited sexual tendencies and allowed narcissism always to rise to the same height. We shall be returning to this relationship between love and character formation in a postscript.

Let us highlight as being particularly informative the relationship to the constitution of the primal horde occupied by the organization through which (apart from coercion) an artificial mass is held together. In connection with army and church, we have seen that this is the pretence that the leader loves each and every individual in a fair and equal way. But this is nothing short of an idealistic reworking of the circumstances of the primal horde, in which all the sons were aware of being persecuted by the primal father in the same manner and feared him in the same manner. The next form of human society, the totemistic clan, already had this transformation (on which all social obligations rest) as a prerequisite. The indestructible strength of the family as a natural mass formation rests on the fact that this essential prerequisite of the father's equal love for it really can obtain.

But we expect even more from tracing the mass back to the primal horde. We also want it to give us a clue to the hitherto unplumbed, mysterious element in mass formation hiding behind the enigmatic words hypnosis and suggestion. And I believe it can do that. Remember: hypnosis has something plain uncanny about it; however, that uncanny quality points in the direction of some-thing ancient and familiar that has undergone repression.[4] Think how hypnosis is induced. The hypnotist professes to be in posses-sion of a mysterious power that robs the subject of his own will, or (which comes to the same thing) the subject believes him to be. This mysterious power (still often popularly known as animal magnetism) must be the same as that which, for primitives, consti-tutes the source of the taboo, the same as proceeds from kings and chiefs and makes them dangerous to approach (*mana*). The hypnotist, then, claims to be in possession of this power. And how does he manifest it? By asking the person to look into his eyes; typically, he will hypnotize with his gaze. Now, for primitives it was precisely the sight of the chief that they found dangerous and unbearable, as that of the deity was to be for mortals subsequently. Moses still had to act as middleman between his people and Jehovah, for the people could not bear the sight of God, and when he returned from God's presence his face shone; some of the *mana* had been transferred to him, as in the case of the primitives' medium.[5]

However, hypnosis may be caused in other ways too, which is confusing and has given rise to some unsatisfactory physiological theories. It can result from staring at a shiny object, for instance, or listening to a monotonous sound. The fact is, such procedures serve only to divert and grip the conscious attention. The situa-tion is the same as if the hypnotist had said to the person: I want you now to concern yourself solely with me, the rest of the world is utterly without interest. Of course, it would be technically inap-propriate for the hypnotist to say any such thing; the subject would be wrenched out of his unconscious frame of mind by it and provoked into conscious contradiction. But so long as the hypno-tist avoids directing the subject's conscious mind towards his inten-tions and the subject immerses himself in an activity in connection with which the world inevitably does appear uninteresting to him, a situation arises in which the subject really does concen-trate entirely on the hypnotist, falling into the attitude of rapport, of transference, vis-à-vis the hypnotist. In other words, the hypnotist's indirect methods, much like many techniques of joking, have the effect of holding back certain distributions of mental energy that would disturb the course of the unconscious process, and they lead ultimately to the same goal as direct influencing by staring or stroking.[6]

Ferenczi rightly discovered that with the sleep command often given to induce hypnosis the hypnotist is putting himself in the place of the subject's parents. Ferenczi believed two types of hypnosis should be distinguished: an unctuously appeasing type, which he ascribed to the mother image, and a threatening one, which he ascribed to the father.[7] In hypnosis, the order to go to sleep implies nothing more nor less than an invitation to withdraw all interest from the world and concentrate it on the person of the hypnotist; that is how the subject sees it too, because it is this withdrawal of interest from the outside world that constitutes the psychological definition of sleep and the foundation on which the affinity between sleep and the hypnotic state is based.

In other words, by his actions the hypnotist awakens in the subject part of the latter's archaic inheritance that also concerned the subject's parents and that in relation to the subject's father experienced an individual revival, the idea of an overpowering and dangerous personality in the face of whom the only possible attitude was one of passive masochism, to whom one must inevitably lose one's will, and being alone with whom ('coming under his gaze') looked very risky. That is about the only way that we can imagine the relationship between an individual member of the primal horde and the primal father. We know from other reactions that the individual has retained a variable amount of personal aptitude for reviving such ancient situations. However, an awareness that hypnosis is after all only a game, a false renewal of those old impressions, may remain and may provide resistance against any excessively serious consequences of the hypnotic removal of the will.

So the uncanny, compulsive nature of mass formation evident in its suggestion phenomena can no doubt rightly be traced to the fact that it has its origin in the primal horde. The leader of the

81

mass is still the feared primal father, the mass still wishes to be dominated by absolute power, it is in the highest degree addicted to authority (in Le Bon's expression, it has a thirst for subordination). The primal father is the mass ideal that dominates the 'I' in place of the 'I'-ideal. Hypnosis has every right to be described as a 'mass of two'. There is no further need to define suggestion as a conviction based not on perception and thinking but on erotic attachment.[8]

Notes

1. *Totem und Tabu* [*Totem and Taboo*], 1912–13, in *Imago* ('Einige Übereinstimmungen im Seelenleben der Wilden und der Neurotiker' ['Some correspondences in the mental lives of savages and neurotics']); published in volume form 1913, fourth edition 1925 [*Standard Edition*, vol. XIII, p. 1].

2. What we were saying before about the general characteristics of humanity must particularly apply to the primal horde. The individual's will was too weak; he lacked the courage to act. No other impulses arose but collective ones; only a joint will existed, no single will. The idea did not dare become will unless backed by the perception that it was widely shared. This weakness of the imagination is explained by the strength of the emotional attachment felt jointly by all, but similarity of circumstances and the absence of private property help to determine the uniformity of individual mental acts. Not even excremental needs rule out mutuality, as may be noted among children and soldiers. The only major exception is the sexual act, in which a third person is at best superfluous and at worst condemned to an awkward wait. On how the sexual need (genital satisfaction) reacts against everything associated with the herd, see below.

3. It can further be assumed, for instance, that the banished sons, separated from their father, progressed from identification with one another to homosexual object love, thus gaining the freedom to kill their father.

4. 'Das Unheimliche', in *Imago*, V (1919) [translated into English as 'The Uncanny', *Standard Edition*, vol. XVII, p. 219].

5. See *Totem und Tabu* and the sources cited therein.

6. The situation in which a person is unconsciously focused on the hypnotist while consciously occupied with a constant stream of uninteresting perceptions has its counterpart in the events of psychoanalytical treatment,

which merits a mention here. It happens at least once in every analysis that the patient stubbornly maintains that just now he quite definitely cannot think of anything. The patient's free associations falter, and the usual promptings to set them going remain ineffectual. Further urging will eventually elicit the admission that the patient is thinking about the view from the window of the consulting-room, the pattern on the wall-paper he sees before him, or the gas-lamp hanging from the ceiling. One then knows immediately that the patient has gone into transference, that he is preoccupied by as yet unconscious thoughts relating to the doctor, and one sees the faltering in the patient's ideas disappear as soon as he is offered this explanation.

7. Ferenczi, 'Introjektion und Übertragung' ['Introjection and transference'], in *Jahrbuch für psychoanalytische und psychopathologische Forschungen*, I, 1909.

8. It strikes me as worth stressing that what we have said in this section means we have to abandon the Bernheim view of hypnosis and fall back on the naive older view. According to Bernheim, all hypnotic phenomena are to be derived from the suggestion factor, which requires no further explanation. Our conclusion is that suggestion is a partial phenomenon of the hypnotic state that is grounded quite adequately in an unconsciously preserved disposition from the prehistory of the human family.

XI

A level within the ego

If, bearing in mind the mutually supplementary descriptions of authors writing about mass psychology, one casts a general look at the life of the individual person today, one may, faced with the complications that emerge here, be discouraged from offering a comprehensive account. Each individual is a component of many masses, has ties in many directions as a result of identification, and has built up his 'I'-ideal on the basis of a wide variety of models. Each individual thus has a share in many mass minds (those of his race, his class, his religious community, his nationality, etc.) and may also, beyond that, rise to a certain amount of independence and originality. With their steady continuity of effect, these constant, long-lasting mass formations are less in evidence than the rapidly formed, transitory masses on the basis of which Le Bon outlined his brilliant psychological description of the mass mind. Yet it is in these noisy, ephemeral masses that are, so to speak, superimposed on the others that the miracle occurs whereby what we have just acknowledged as individual development disappears without trace, albeit only temporarily.

Our understanding of that miracle is that the individual surrenders his 'I'-ideal, exchanging it for the mass-ideal embodied in the leader. The miracle (we might add by way of qualification) is not equally great in every case. In many individuals, separation of 'I' and 'I'-ideal is not very far advanced, the two can still easily coincide, the 'I' has often retained its earlier narcissistic satisfaction with itself. The choice of leader is greatly facilitated by this circumstance. Often the leader need only possess the typical properties of such individuals in a particularly pure and well-defined form and give an impression of greater strength and libidinal freedom; the need for a powerful head will then do the rest, investing the leader with the superior might to which he would perhaps not normally be entitled. Others whose respective 'I'-ideals would otherwise not have found embodiment in his person uncorrected are then swept along 'by suggestion' – that is to say, as a result of identification.

We realize that the contribution we have been able to make towards explaining the libidinal structure of the mass comes down to drawing a distinction between 'I' and 'I'-ideal and to the dual type of attachment (identification and insertion of the object in place of the 'I'-ideal) made possible as a result. The assumption of such a level in the 'I' as a first step in analysing the 'I' must eventually demonstrate its justification in the most varied areas of psychology. In my essay 'On the Introduction of Narcissism',[1] I collected together all the pathological material that, at the time, could be used in support of such a separation. However, its importance may be expected to turn out to be very much greater the more work is done on the psychology of psychoses. Let us not forget that the 'I' now enters into the relationship of an object to the 'I'-ideal that has developed from it, and that possibly all the interactions between external object and 'total-I'[2] with which we have become familiar in neurosis theory are repeated on this new stage within the 'I'.

Here I want to look into only one of the conclusions possible from this standpoint and thus continue discussing a problem that I had to leave unresolved elsewhere.[3] Each of the mental distinctions that have become known to us has the effect of making the mental function more difficult, increasing its fragility and potentially triggering a failure of that function, i.e. an illness. Thus in being born we took the step from utterly self-sufficient narcissism to perception of a changeable outside world and the beginning of object-finding, and associated with that is the fact that we do not permanently tolerate the new state, that we periodically undo it and in sleep return to the previous state of dullness and object-avoidance. In this we are of course obeying a hint from the outside world, which through the periodic change from day to night temporarily deprives us of most of the stimuli affecting us. The second example (of greater importance to pathology) is subject to no such restriction. In the course of our development we have separated our mental stock into a coherent 'I' and an unconscious, repressed part left outside the 'I', and we are aware that the stability of this fresh acquisition is exposed to constant bombardment. In dream and in neurosis this excluded part knocks at the gates guarded by inhibitions, asking to be admitted, and in wakeful health we make use of special tricks to bypass those inhibitions and, experiencing pleasure, temporarily admit that repressed part into our 'I'. Jesting and humour (and to some extent the comic generally) may be seen in this light. Similar instances of lesser consequence will occur to every expert on the psychology of neuroses, but I want to move on swiftly to the desired application.

It would be quite conceivable that separation of the 'I'-ideal from the 'I' is also not tolerated on a permanent basis and must occasionally regress. Despite all the renunciations and restrictions placed upon the 'I', periodic breaching of the bans is the rule. This is shown by the institution of feasts. Originally, feasts were quite simply excesses ordained by law; in fact, they owe their joyful character to this liberation.[4] The Romans' Saturnalia and our present-day carnival[5] have this key feature in common with the feasts of primitives (which tend to result in every kind of dissipation, with what are normally the most sacred rules being flouted). But the 'I'-ideal comprises the sum total of all the restrictions that the 'I' should observe, so retraction of the ideal would inevitably be a splendid celebration for the 'I', which might then once again be happy with itself.[6]

There is invariably a feeling of triumph when something in the 'I' coincides with the 'I'-ideal. Guilt feelings (and the sense of inferiority) can also be seen as expressions of the tension between 'I' and ideal.

There are people, as everyone knows, whose general mood fluctuates periodically from excessive dejection through a certain in-between condition to an exalted sense of well-being, such fluctuations occurring in very different degrees of amplitude from the barely noticeable to the sorts of extreme that as melancholia and mania constitute very painful or disturbing intrusions in the life of the person concerned. In typical cases of such cyclical depression, external causes do not appear to play a decisive role, while internal motives are found in no greater number and in no different a form in such patients than in anyone else. It has therefore become customary to assess such cases as non-psychogenic. We shall be looking later at other very similar cases of cyclical depression that, however, can easily be traced back to mental traumas.

In other words, the reason for these spontaneous fluctuations of mood is not known; we lack an understanding of the mechanism by which melancholia is replaced by mania. That would make these the patients for whom our supposition might hold good, namely that their 'I'-ideal has temporarily disappeared into the 'I', having previously ruled with especial severity.

Let us be quite clear about this: there is no doubt, on the basis of our analysis of the 'I', that, in the manic, 'I' and 'I'-ideal have come together, with the result that the person, in a mood of triumph and self-satisfaction untroubled by self-criticism, is able to delight in the removal of inhibitions, consideration for others and self-reproach. It is less evident but none the less highly probable that the misery of the melancholic expresses a sharp conflict between the two authorities within the 'I' in which the over-sensitive ideal bluntly exposes its condemnation of the 'I' in delusions of insignificance and in self-abasement. The only question is whether the cause of these altered relations between 'I' and 'I'-ideal should be sought in the periodic rebellions against the new institution postulated above or whether different circumstances should be held responsible.

The abrupt switch to mania does not inevitably feature among the symptoms of melancholy depression. There are simple single and also regularly recurring melancholias that never suffer such a fate. On the other hand there are melancholias in which the occasion clearly plays an aetiological role. These are the ones following the loss of a loved object, whether through the death of the same or as a result of circumstances necessitating the withdrawal of libido from the object. Such a psychogenic melancholia can equally well turn into mania and this cycle be repeated a number of times, as is the case with an apparently spontaneous one. In other words, the circumstances are somewhat obscure, particularly since only a few forms and cases of melancholia have hitherto been subjected to psychoanalytical investigation.[7] Up to now we understand only those cases in which the object has been abandoned after showing itself unworthy of love. It is then re-erected in the 'I' through identification and judged severely by the 'I'-ideal. Reproaches and aggression against the object come to light as melancholy self-reproach.[8]

The descent into mania can follow this kind of melancholia, too; this eventuality constitutes a trait that owes nothing to the other characteristics of the syndrome.

However, I see no difficulty in having the fact of the periodic rebellion of 'I' against 'I'-ideal taken into consideration in respect of both types of melancholia, the psychogenic and the spontaneous. In the latter case it can be assumed that the 'I'-ideal tends to display especial severity, which then automatically leads to its temporary neutralization. In psychogenic melancholia, the 'I' would be prompted to rebel as a result of the sort of ill-treatment on the part of its ideal that it experiences in the event of identification with a discarded object.

Notes

1. ['Zur Einführung des Narzissmus' ('On the Introduction of Narcissism'), op cit.]
2. [Freud's *Gesamt-Ich*.]
3. 'Trauer und Melancholie' ['Mourning and Melancholia'], op. cit.
4. *Totem und Tabu* [*Totem and Taboo*], op. cit.
5. [Freud is undoubtedly referring to the pre-Lenten celebrations characteristic of Catholic Europe.]
6. Trotter has repression proceed from the herd instinct. It is more a translation into a different mode of expression than a contradiction if I

say in my 'On the Introduction of Narcissism' that, from the standpoint of the 'I', formation of the ideal is the precondition for repression.

7. See also Abraham, 'Ansätze zur psychoanalytischen Erforschung und Behandlung des manisch-depressiven Irreseins usw.' ['Approaches to the psychoanalytical study and treatment of manic-depressive psychosis etc.'], 1912, in *Klinische Beiträge zur Psychoanalyse* (1921).

8. To be more precise, they hide behind the reproaches directed at the person's own 'I', giving them the solidity, tenacity and irrefutability that characterize the self-reproaches of melancholics.

XII

Postscript

During the investigation that has now reached a provisional conclusion, we were offered various side-turnings that we avoided initially but down which many a clearer insight beckoned. Let us now make up for some of those deferments.

A) The distinction between 'I'-identification and replacement of the 'I'-ideal by the object finds intriguing clarification in the two large artificial masses we examined at the outset, namely the army and the Christian church.

Obviously, the soldier takes his superior (in reality, the army commander) as his ideal, whereas he identifies with his peers and from that shared 'I'-dom derives the obligations of comradeship as regards mutual support and sharing of property. He becomes ridiculous, however, if he seeks to identify with the commander. The rifleman in *Wallenstein's Camp* pokes fun at the sergeant on that account:

> *Wie er raüspert und wie er spuckt,*
> *Das habt ihr ihm glücklich abgeguckt . . .*

> [The way he clears his throat and spits, That you've really got off pat . . .][1]

In the Catholic church it is different. Every Christian loves Christ as his ideal and feels attached to other Christians through identification. The church, however, requires more. The Christian should further identify with Christ and love other Christians as

Christ loved them. At both points, in other words, the church calls for supplementation of the libido position resulting from formation of the mass. Identification is to be added where object-choice has taken place, and object-love where there is identification. This increase clearly goes beyond the constitution of the mass. A person may be a good Christian and yet have no thought of setting himself in Christ's place and, like him, embracing all humanity in his love. There is in fact no need for him to believe that he, a weak human being, possesses the Saviour's breadth of mind and strength of love. But this further development of libido distribution within the mass is probably the element on which Christianity bases its claim to have attained a higher morality.

B) We said that it would be possible to indicate where in the mental development of humanity the step forward from mass to individual psychology occurred for the individual as well.[2]

For this purpose we must briefly return to the scientific myth of the father of the primal horde. He was later elevated to the position of creator of the world – rightly so, since he had fathered all the sons who made up the first mass. He was the ideal of each one of them, simultaneously feared and worshipped, which for a later age gave rise to the notion of taboo. That plurality came together one day, killing and dismembering him. None of the mass victors was able to take his place, or if one of them did so the fighting resumed until they realized that they must all renounce their father's inheritance. They then formed the totemic brotherhood, all enjoying equal rights and bound together by the totem bans that were to keep the memory of the murder alive and atone for it. However, dissatisfaction with what had been achieved remained and became the source of fresh developments. Gradually those who had united in the fraternal mass drew closer to a restoration of the old state of affairs at a new level, and the husband once again became head of a family, breaking the prerogatives of the matriarchy that had become established during the fatherless period. By way of indemnification, he may at that time have acknowledged the mother goddesses, whose priests were castrated to safeguard the mother in accordance with the example provided by the father of the primal horde. Nevertheless, the new family was but a shadow of the old; its fathers were many, and each was restricted by the other's rights.

At that time nostalgic deprivation may have prompted one individual to detach himself from the mass and adopt the role of the father. The man who did this was the first epic poet, the step forward was taken in his imagination. The poet rearranged reality to suit his nostalgia. He invented the heroic myth. The hero was the man who had single-handedly struck the father dead, the father who still figured in myth as a totemic monster. As the father had been the boy's first ideal, the poet now created the first 'I'-ideal in the hero who seeks to take the father's place. The link to the hero probably sprang from the youngest son, the mother's darling, whom she had shielded against his father's jealousy and who in primal horde times had become the father's successor. In the made-up reworking of primeval times woman, who had been the prize and the enticement to murder, no doubt became a temptress and the instigator of the atrocity.

The hero claims to have performed single-handed the deed that surely only the horde as a whole would have dared accomplish. Nevertheless, as Rank remarks, traditional tales retain clear traces of a denial of the facts of the case. In such tales, it often happens that the hero who has to discharge a difficult task (usually a younger son, not infrequently one who has presented himself to the surrogate father as stupid, i.e. not a threat) is in fact only able to solve that task with the help of a swarm of tiny animals (bees, ants). These, according to Rank, are the brothers of the primal horde, just as in dream symbolism insects and vermin denote siblings (disparagingly, as little children). Moreover, each of the tasks in myth and fairy tale is easily recognizable as a substitute for the heroic deed.

Myth, in other words, is the step by which the individual exits from mass psychology. The first myth was undoubtedly psychological, the hero myth; the explanatory nature myth must have emerged much later. The poet who, having taken that step, has in imagination detached himself from the mass is nevertheless, as

Rank further observes, able in reality to find his way back to it. Because he goes to that mass and tells it of his hero's deeds, which he has made up. Basically that hero is none other than himself. He thus drops down to the level of reality and lifts his audience up to the level of imagination. His audience, however, understand the poet; they are able, on the basis of the same nostalgic relationship to the primal father, to identify with the hero.[3]

The lie of the heroic myth culminates in deification of the hero. Possibly the deified hero came before the father-god, precursor of the return of the primal father as deity. The chronological sequence of deities would thus be: mother-god – hero – father-god. But it was only with the elevation of the never-forgotten primal father that the deity received the features we still recognize today.[4]

C) We have talked a lot in this essay about direct and goal-inhibited sex drives and may hope, perhaps, that such a distinction will meet with no great resistance. Nevertheless a detailed discussion of the subject will not be unwelcome, even if it simply echoes what to a large extent has been said before.

The first but also the finest example of goal-inhibited sex drives was the one to which the libidinal development of the child introduced us. All the feelings that the child experiences for its parents and nursemaids live on without restriction in the desires that give expression to the child's sexual aspiration. The child demands from these loved persons all the caresses with which it is familiar, it wishes to kiss them, touch them, inspect them, it is curious to see their genitalia and to be present at their private excretory routines, it vows to marry its mother or nursemaid, whatever it may understand by that, imagines bearing its father's child, etc. Direct observation as well as subsequent analytical investigation of the residues of childhood leave us in no doubt about the immediate confluence of tender and jealous feelings and sexual intentions and tell us how thoroughly the child makes the loved person the object of all its not yet properly centred sexual tendencies. (See [my] *Three Essays on Sexual Theory*.)

This initial love-structuring by the child, which is typically assigned to the Oedipus complex, is known to suffer a repressive phase from the beginning of the latency period. What is left of it presents itself to us as a purely affectionate emotional attachment directed towards the same people but no longer to be described as 'sexual'. Psychoanalysis, which probes the depths of mental life, has no difficulty in showing that the sexual attachments of earliest infancy also remain in existence, albeit repressed and unconscious. It encourages us to claim that, wherever we come across a feeling of affection, that feeling is the successor to a fully 'sensual' object-attachment to the person concerned or to that person's example (*imago*). It is not of course capable of telling us without separate examination whether in a given instance what was once a sexual torrent still exists in a repressed form or whether it is already exhausted. To be more precise, we know for a fact that it is still present as form and possibility and may at any time, as a result of regression, be reoccupied and reactivated; the question is only (and this cannot always be determined) what charge and what effectiveness it currently still possesses. We need to guard equally against two sources of error here: against the Scylla of underestimating the repressed unconscious and against the Charybdis of tending to gauge the normal entirely against the criterion of the pathological.

Psychology, which is unwilling or unable to penetrate the depths of what is repressed, sees every affectionate emotional attachment as expressing tendencies not directed at the sexual, despite the fact that they proceed from tendencies that were so aimed.[5]

We are justified in saying that they have been diverted from these sexual goals, even if there are difficulties in the way of portraying such a diversion in accordance with the requirements of metapsychology. Moreover, these goal-inhibited drives still retain some of the original sexual objectives; the affectionately clinging character, the friend, the admirer also seek out the physical proximity and sight of the person henceforth loved only in the '*Pauline*' sense. If we are so inclined, we can see this diversion from the goal as a first step towards *sublimation* of the sex drives, or alternatively we can set the limits for the latter at an even greater distance. Goal-inhibited sex drives have one major functional advantage over uninhibited ones. Being incapable of full satisfaction, properly speaking, they are particularly suited to creating lasting attachments, whereas straight sex drives lose energy each time they are satisfied and must wait to be renewed by another build-up of sexual libido, with the possibility that the object may be changed in the mean time. Inhibited drives are capable of any amount of mixing with uninhibited drives; they can turn back into them as they once proceeded from them. It is a well-known fact that emotional relationships of a friendly nature based on respect and admiration (between master and pupil, say, or performer and captivated listener, particularly if she is female) can easily develop into erotic desires (Molière's *'Embrassez-moi pour l'amour du Grec'*).[6] Indeed, the emergence of such initially purposeless emotional ties provides a direct and often-trodden path to choice of sex object. In *Die Frömmigkeit des Grafen von Zinsendorf* ['The Devoutness of Count Zinsendorf'], Pfister illustrates an all too obvious and surely not isolated instance of how easily even intense religious commitment may revert to ardent sexual arousal. On the other hand, it is also very common for direct, inherently short-lived sexual tendencies to become transformed into permanent, purely affectionate attachments. Indeed, the consolidation of a marriage sealed in amorous passion largely rests on this process.

It will of course not surprise us to hear that goal-inhibited sexual tendencies ensue from direct sexual tendencies when internal or external obstacles block the attainment of sexual objectives. The repression of the latency period is just such an internal (or rather, internalized) obstacle. We assumed in connection with the father of the primal horde that it is through his sexual intolerance that he coerces all his sons into abstinence, forcing them into goal-inhibited attachments while he reserves free sexual pleasure for himself and so remains unattached. All the attachments on which the mass is based are in the nature of goal-inhibited drives. But that is our lead-in to discussion of a fresh topic dealing with the relationship of the direct sex drives to mass formation.

D) The last two observations have already prepared us to find the direct sexual tendencies unfavourable to mass formation. The evolutionary history of the family has of course also known mass relationships of sexual love (group marriage), but the more important sexual love became for the 'I' (in other words, the more 'being in love' it developed) the more urgently it demanded to be restricted to two people (*una cum uno*), as indicated by the nature of the genital goal. Polygamous tendencies had to find satisfaction in successive changes of object.

The two people reliant on each other for the purpose of sexual satisfaction demonstrate against the herd instinct, against mass feeling, by seeking to be alone. The more deeply they are in love, the more perfectly they are content with each other. Their rejection of the influence of the mass finds expression as a sense of shame. The extremely intense emotions of jealousy are mustered to shield the choice of sexual object against damage by any mass attachment. Only if the affectionate, personal element in the relationship is wholly subordinate to the sensual element does sexual intercourse by one couple in the presence of others or do simultaneous sex acts within a group (as in an orgy) become possible. That, however, implies a regression to an earlier state of sexual relations in which 'being in love' played no role as yet and sexual objects were seen as being of equal value – rather in the spirit of Bernard Shaw's malicious quip to the effect that to be in love is inordinately to exaggerate the difference between one woman and another.

There exist a great many indications that the condition of being in love only entered into sexual relations between man and woman at a late stage, so that the opposition between sexual love and mass attachment was also late in developing. Now it may seem that this assumption is incompatible with our myth of the primal family. The band of brothers is supposed, after all, to have been driven to parricide by love for their mothers and sisters, and it is hard to imagine that love otherwise than as an unbroken, primitive one – in other words, as a deeply felt combination of the affectionate and the sensual. However, on closer examination this objection fades into a confirmation. The fact is, one of the reactions to the parricide was the establishment of totemic exogamy, the banning of any sexual relationship with the women of the family who had been loved tenderly since childhood. This drove a wedge between the affectionate and sensual impulses of the man, which sits fast in his love-life to this day.[7] Because of that exogamy, men's sensual needs had to make do with unknown, unloved women.

In the large artificial masses that are church and army there is no room for woman as sexual object. The sexual relationship between man and woman remains outside such organizations. Even where masses form that contain a mixture of men and women, gender difference plays no part. It makes little sense to ask whether the libido that holds masses together is homosexual or heterosexual in character, it is not differentiated by gender, and it wholly disregards particularly the libido's goals of genital organization.

The direct sexual tendencies preserve a measure of personal activation even for the individual who otherwise disappears in the mass. Where they become too powerful, they subvert any kind of mass-formation. The Catholic church had the best of motives in advising the faithful to remain unmarried and imposing celibacy on its clergy, but being in love has often driven even priests out of the church. Similarly, love of women breaks through the mass attachments of race, national segregation and social class, thus making important contributions to cultural development. It seems established that homosexual love tolerates mass attachments much better, even where it surfaces as an uninhibited sexual tendency – a remarkable fact, elucidating which may well take us far.

Psychoanalytical examination of psychoneuroses has taught us that the symptoms of such neuroses are traceable to repressed but still active direct sexual tendencies. The formula may be completed by adding: or to goal-inhibited sexual tendencies in which the inhibition is not entirely successful or has given way to a return to the repressed sexual goal. In line with this circumstance is the fact that neurosis renders a person asocial, lifting those affected out of the usual mass-formations. In fact, neurosis may be said to have a similarly subversive effect on the mass as the condition of being in love. Conversely it can be observed that, wherever there has been a powerful thrust towards mass-formation, neuroses diminish and may, at least for a time, disappear completely. Attempts have also quite rightly been made to turn this conflict between neurosis and mass-formation to therapeutic advantage. Even one who does not regret the disappearance of religious illusions in today's cultural climate will concede that, while they still held sway, they afforded those in thrall to them their strongest protection against the threat of neurosis. Nor is it difficult to see all attachments to mystical religious or philosophical sects and communities as cures-gone-awry for a wide variety of neuroses. All this has to do with the difference between direct and goal-inhibited sexual tendencies.

Left to himself, the neurotic is obliged to replace the large mass formations from which he is excluded with symptomatic substitutes. The neurotic creates his own fantasy world, religion, and system of delusion, echoing the institutions of humanity in a distorted form that clearly attests the overwhelming contribution of the direct sexual tendencies.[8]

E) Let us end with a comparative appreciation of the conditions that we have been considering from the standpoint of libido theory: being in love, hypnosis, mass formation and neurosis.

The condition of *being in love* rests on the simultaneous presence of direct and goal-inhibited sexual tendencies, with the object attracting to itself part of the narcissistic 'I'-libido. It has room only for the 'I' and the object.

Hypnosis shares with the condition of being in love this restriction to the two persons, 'I' and object, but it rests entirely on goal-inhibited sexual tendencies and sets the object in place of the 'I'-ideal.

The *mass* reproduces this process, coinciding with hypnosis in the nature of the drives holding it together and in replacing 'I'-ideal by object, but it adds identification with other individuals, which may originally have been made possible by the same relationship to the object.

Both conditions, hypnosis and mass formation, are hereditary deposits from the phylogenesis of the human libido – hypnosis as susceptibility, the mass moreover as direct survival. Replacing direct sexual tendencies by goal-inhibited ones furthers in both of them the separation of 'I' from 'I'-ideal on which a start has already been made in the case of being in love.

Neurosis is different. It too rests on a peculiarity of human libidinal development, namely the dual beginning of the direct sexual function, interrupted by the latency period.[9] To that extent it shares with hypnosis and mass formation the character of a regression, which being in love lacks. It appears wherever the advance from direct to goal-inhibited sex drives has not been wholly successful, and it corresponds to a *conflict* between the drives taken up into the 'I', which have undergone such a development, and the parts of the same drives that (like the other, wholly repressed drives) are striving to emerge from the repressed unconscious to achieve direct satisfaction. In terms of content, neurosis is immensely rich, comprising as it does every possible relationship between 'I' and object, not only those in which the object is preserved but also others in which it has been abandoned or set up within the 'I' itself – as well as the conflict relations between the 'I' and its 'I'-ideal.

(1921)

Notes

1. [*Wallensteins Lager* is the first of Schiller's trilogy of plays about the seventeenth-century German general. In portraying the habits of Wallenstein's soldiers, the play highlights their devotion to and confidence in their leader.]

2. What follows was influenced by an exchange of ideas with Otto Rank. [*Addition 1923:*] (See 'Die Don Juan-Gestalt' in *Imago*, VIII, 1922). The essay appeared in volume form in 1924.

3. See also Hanns Sachs, 'Gemeinsame Tagetträume: Autoreferat eines Vortrages auf den VI. Psychoanalytischen Kongress im Haag', 1920, in *Internationale Zeitschrift für Psychoanalyse*, VI (1920); also now available in volume form (Imago-Bücher, vol. 3).

4. This abbreviated account has taken no material from saga, myth, fairy tale, history of manners, etc. to support the construction.

5. The hostile emotions are of course rather more complicated in structure.

6. [This literary allusion is actually a misquotation; Molière's text (*Les Femmes savantes*, III, 5) reads:

> Quoi! monsieur sait du grec! Ah! Permettez, de grâce,
> Que, pour l'amour du grec, on vous embrasse.

And here is an interesting possibility: was a *Fehlleistung* (what is usually called a 'Freudian slip') responsible for Freud's faulty memory capitalizing *Grec*, thus substituting a male person for the language?]

7. See 'Über die allgemeinste Erniedrigung des Liebeslebens', op. cit. ['Concerning the most common degradation of love life'].

8. See *Totem und Tabu* [*Totem and Taboo.*], end of Section II: 'Taboo and ambivalence'.

9. See *Drei Abhandlungen zur Sexualtheorie*, op. cit. [*Three Essays on Sexual Theory*].

A Religious Experience

In the autumn of 1927 a German-American journalist whom I had been delighted to receive (G. S. Viereck) published an interview with me in which there was talk, among other things, of my lack of religious faith and my indifference to a continuance after death. The so-called interview was widely read and brought me a number of letters, including this one from an American physician:

The thing that struck me most was your answer to the question as to whether you believe in a continuance of the personality after death. You apparently answered: That makes no sense to me.

I write to you today to tell you of an experience I had in the year in which I completed my medical course at the University of X. One afternoon I happened to be in the dissecting-room when the corpse of an old woman was brought in and laid on a dissecting-table. This sweet-faced woman made a great impression on me. A thought flashed across my mind: no, there is no God; if there were, he would never have allowed this dear old woman to enter the dissecting-room.

When I returned home that afternoon, I had formed an inner resolve, under the impression of what I had glimpsed in the dissecting-room, not to enter a church again. Even before this, the teachings of Christianity had been an object of doubt for me.

However, while I was still thinking about this, a voice spoke in my soul, saying that I should reconsider my decision carefully. My spirit[1] answered this inner voice: If I am given certain knowledge that Christian teaching is true and the Bible is the word of God, I shall accept it.

Over the next few days God made it clear to my soul that the Bible is God's word, that everything taught about Jesus Christ is true, and that

Jesus is our only hope. After so clear a revelation, I accepted the Bible as the word of God and Jesus Christ as my Redeemer. Since then God has revealed himself to me through many unmistakable signs.

As a brother physician I ask you to focus your thoughts on this important matter and assure you that, if you approach it with an open mind, God will reveal the truth to your soul, too, as he has to me and to so many others . . .

I replied courteously that I was delighted to hear that it had become possible for him, as a result of such an experience, to retain his faith. For me [I went on] God had not done as much, he had never caused me to hear such an inner voice and if (in view of my age) he did not hurry up it would not be my fault if I remained to the end what I am now – 'an infidel Jew'.

My colleague's charming rejoinder contained the assurance that Jewishness was no obstacle on the way to orthodoxy and demonstrated this by various examples. It culminated in the announcement that zealous prayers would be offered to God, asking him to give me the 'faith to believe'.

Such intercession has yet to show success. Meanwhile, my colleague's religious experience makes me wonder. I am inclined to say that it asks for an attempt to interpret it by affective motives, because as it stands it is disconcerting and particularly ill-founded in logic. God notoriously allows far worse horrors to happen than that the corpse of an old lady with a nice face should be laid on a dissecting-table. It was ever thus, and at the time when my American colleague was completing his studies it cannot have been otherwise. Nor, as a would-be doctor, can he have been so unworldly as to be ignorant of all such disasters. So why should his indignation against God have burst out over that particular impression received in the dissecting-room?

For someone used to looking at people's inner experiences and actions analytically, the explanation is obvious – so obvious that in my memory it directly infiltrated the facts of the case. When I mentioned my pious colleague's letter in discussion on some occasion, I said he had written that the female corpse's face had put him in mind of his own mother. In fact, the letter said no such thing (and a moment's consideration tells me it cannot possibly have done so), but that is the explanation that irresistibly imposes itself under the impression of the affectionate terms in which the old woman is remembered ('sweet-faced . . . dear old woman'). The affect aroused by the young doctor's remembrance of his mother can thus be blamed for his lapse of judgement. And one who is unable to shake off the psychoanalyst's bad habit of adducing in evidence petty details that also admit of a different, less radical explanation will be reminded of the fact that the colleague later addresses me as 'brother physician'.[2]

The course of events, then, may be pictured as follows. The sight of the naked body of a woman (or one destined to be stripped), who reminds the young man of his mother, arouses in him the yearning for the mother that derives from the Oedipus complex. This is immediately complemented by an access of rebellion against the father. Father and God are not yet, in his case, very far apart. The wish to exterminate the father may reach consciousness in the form of doubt about the existence of God; it may seek to justify itself rationally as anger at mistreatment of the mother-object. The fact is, the child typically considers what the father does to the mother in sexual intercourse to constitute mistreatment. The new impulse, displaced into the religious sphere, is simply a repetition of the Oedipus situation and as such soon meets with the same fate. It succumbs to a powerful counter-current. During the conflict the level of displacement is not maintained, there is no mention of arguments to justify God, nor is it said by what unmistakable signs God has proved his existence to the doubter. The conflict appears to have been played out in the form of a hallucinatory psychosis; inner voices are heard, warning against resistance to God. The issue of the struggle again manifests itself in the religious sphere. It is the one preordained by the fate of the Oedipus complex: total subjection to the will of God the father; the young man became a believer, accepting everything that he had been taught about God and Jesus Christ since childhood. He had a religious experience, he underwent conversion.

All that is so simple and so transparent that one cannot avoid asking whether, as a result of understanding this case, anything at all has been gained as regards the psychology of religious conversion. I refer to an excellent work by Sante de Sanctis (*La conversione religiosa*, Bologna 1924)[3] that also makes use of all the findings of psychoanalysis. Reading this book, one is confirmed in one's expectation that by no means all cases of conversion can be seen through as easily as the one narrated here, but that in no point does our case contradict the views that modern research has formed concerning this matter. What marks out our observation is the association with a particular occasion, which made disbelief flare up once again before finally, so far as this individual was concerned, being overcome.

(1927)

Notes

1. [Elsewhere in this volume I have rendered *Seele* as 'mind' (as being truer to Freud's rejection of the metaphysical), but here I have no hesitation in (re-)translating Freud's *Seele* as 'soul' and *Geist* as 'spirit'; the author of the letter is clearly at home with 'religious' terminology.]

2. [Freud adds: '. . . as I have managed only imperfectly to convey in translation'. He had written *ein wohlwollender Kollege* ('a well-meaning colleague') before quoting the English phrase in parentheses. Other phrases quoted by Freud in the original English appear between inverted commas.]

3. [An English edition was published three years later: Sante de Sanctis, *Religious Conversion* (translated by Helen Augur), London 1927.]

The Future of an Illusion

I

Having lived for quite some time within a specific culture and tried repeatedly to study the nature of its origins and the path of its development, one also feels tempted just occasionally to turn and look in the other direction and ask what fate has in store for that culture and what changes it is destined to undergo. One quickly becomes aware, however, that any such venture is invalidated from the outset by several factors, chief among which is that only a few individuals are capable of commanding an overview of human activity in all its ramifications. Most people have found it necessary to concentrate on one or a small number of fields; yet the less a person knows about past and present, the shakier that person's judgement will inevitably be with regard to the future. Another factor is that, in this judgement in particular, the subjective expectations of the individual play a role that is hard to assess; yet those expectations turn out to depend on purely personal elements in an individual's own experience, his or her more or less hopeful attitude to life, as dictated by temperament and by degree of success or lack of it. Lastly, there is the effect of the remarkable fact that people in general experience their present almost naively, unable to appreciate what it holds; they must first put some distance between it and them – in other words, the present must first have become the past before it will furnish clues for assessing what is to come.

So anyone yielding to the temptation to pronounce on the probable future of our culture will do well to bear in mind the reservations outlined above – likewise the uncertainly that, as a general rule, attaches to any prediction. The consequence for me is that, in my haste to flee this excessive task, I shall swiftly resort to the smaller, more restricted area on which my attention has been focused hitherto, having first determined where that area lies in relation to the larger picture.

We know that human culture, by which I mean everything in which human life has risen above its animal circumstances and in which it distinguishes itself from animal life (and I refuse to separate culture and civilization), shows the observer two sides. It includes on the one hand all the knowledge and skill that humanity has acquired in order to control the forces of nature and obtain from it goods to satisfy human needs, and on the other hand all the institutions that are required to govern the relations of human beings one to another and in particular the distribution of such goods as can be obtained. The two directions of culture are not independent of each other, firstly because the mutual relations of human beings are extensively influenced by the amount of drive-satisfaction made possible by the commodities available, secondly because the individual human being can himself,[1] vis-à-vis another person, assume the relationship of a commodity in so far as that other person makes use of the said individual's labour or takes the individual as sexual object, but thirdly because every individual is, in virtual terms, an enemy of culture, which is in fact supposed to constitute a universal human interest. It is a curious fact that human beings, incapable of living in individual isolation, nevertheless find the sacrifices that culture asks of them in order to make human coexistence possible a heavy load to bear. Culture, in other words, needs to be defended against the individual, and its arrangements, institutions and decrees all serve that end. Their purpose is not only to put in place a certain distribution of goods but also to maintain it; there is a need, in fact, for them to protect against the hostile impulses of humanity everything that serves to tame nature and generate commodities. Human creations are easily destroyed, and science and technology, having built them up, can also be used to tear them down.

This gives the impression that culture is something imposed on a reluctant majority by a minority that has managed to gain possession of the instruments of power and coercion. The natural assumption is of course that these difficulties are not of the essence of culture itself but spring from the imperfections of the forms of culture developed hitherto. Indeed, it is not hard to demonstrate such shortcomings. Whereas humanity has made continuous advances in controlling nature and can expect to make even greater ones, similar progress in the government of human affairs cannot be ascertained with any certainty, and it has doubtless always been the case (as it is again today) that many people wonder whether this bit of their cultural inheritance is in fact worth defending. One would think that some rearrangement of human relationships must be possible such as would cause the sources of dissatisfaction with culture to dry up by renouncing coercion and the suppression of drives and allowing people to devote themselves to acquiring and enjoying commodities undisturbed by inner discord. That would be the Golden Age, except that one wonders whether such a condition can ever be realized. It seems instead that every culture must be based on coercion and drive renunciation; it does not even appear certain that, with coercion removed, the majority of human beings will be prepared to take upon themselves the labour that must be performed if greater quantities of essential commodities are to be obtained. We need in my view to accept that destructive (i.e. anti-social and anti-cultural) tendencies are present in all human beings and that in a large proportion of people such tendencies are powerful enough to dictate their behaviour within human society.

This psychological fact assumes crucial importance as regards assessing human culture. Whereas our first impression was that the key thing about culture was the conquest of nature in order to obtain the commodities essential to life and that the dangers threatening culture could be removed by effective distribution of such goods among human beings, the emphasis now seems to have shifted away from the material towards the mental.[2] It becomes crucial whether and to what extent the burden of the libidinal sacrifices imposed on human beings can be successfully lightened and human beings reconciled to and compensated for the part of that burden that inevitably remains. Domination of the mass by a minority can no more be dispensed with than coercion to perform cultural work, because masses are lethargic and unreasonable, they are averse to renouncing their drives, they cannot be persuaded by arguments that this is unavoidable, and individuals within masses reinforce one another in giving free rein to their lack of restraint. Only the influence of exemplary individuals whom they accept as their leaders will induce them to perform the labour and suffer the voluntary privations on which the continued existence of culture depends. It is all very well, such leaders being persons with a superior understanding of the necessities of life who have brought themselves under control so far as their own libidinal desires are concerned. However, there is a risk so far as they are concerned that, in order to retain their influence, they will yield to the mass more than the mass yields to them, which is why it seems necessary for them to have access to instruments of power making them independent of the mass. In short, two very common properties of human beings are to blame for the fact that only through a measure of coercion can cultural institutions be upheld: humans are not, of their own volition, keen on work, and arguments are powerless against their passions.

I know what will be said against these remarks. The objection will be raised that the character of human masses as portrayed here, which supposedly proves the indispensability of coercion for cultural activity, is itself simply the result of defective cultural institutions that have made human beings bitter, vindictive and unapproachable. Fresh generations, full of love and brought up to respect intellectual achievement, having early experience of the benefits of culture, will also have a different attitude towards it; they will see it as their very own possession, and they will be prepared to offer it the sacrifices of labour and libidinal satisfaction required for its preservation. They will be able to dispense with coercion and will differ little from their leaders. If human masses of such quality have not existed in any culture hitherto, the reason is that no culture has yet hit upon the institutions that will influence people in such a way – and do so from childhood on.

One may doubt whether it is at all or indeed already (given the present state of our control over nature) possible to produce such cultural institutions, one may wonder where they are to come from, this body of superior, rock-steady, selfless leaders who will need to educate future generations, one may shrink from the appalling amount of coercion that will become unavoidable if such plans are ever to be implemented. The splendour of the intention and its importance for the future of human culture are beyond dispute. It rests securely on the psychological insight that humans are equipped with the most diverse libidinal predispositions, which the experiences of early childhood point in their final direction. The limits of human educability will therefore also define the effectiveness of any such cultural change. It may be doubted whether and to what extent a different cultural environment will be capable of erasing the two qualities of human masses that make leadership of human affairs so difficult. The experiment has never been made. In all probability, a certain percentage of human beings will always (because of morbid predispositions or excessively powerful drives) remain asocial, but even if we simply manage to bring today's anti-cultural majority down to a minority we shall have achieved a great deal – possibly all that can be achieved.

I do not want to give the impression that I have wandered a long way from the path of my investigation, as announced above. So let me say expressly that I have no intention of passing judgement on the great cultural experiment currently being conducted in the stretch of land between Europe and Asia. I have neither the knowledge nor the ability to pronounce on its feasibility, to examine the suitability of the methods being applied, or to measure the inevitable gulf between plan and execution. What is happening there, being incomplete, does not allow of the kind of consideration for which our long-consolidated culture presents the material.

Notes

1. [Or of course 'herself'; may I again ask the reader to allow that 'human beings', etc. may be of either sex?]

2. [. . . *aufs Seelische*. I choose 'mental' (as meaning 'of the mind') to reflect the 'one-ness' of the human person that Freud consistently propounded – as opposed to the 'other' dimension suggested by a word such as 'spiritual'. When Bruno Bettelheim called his book *Freud and Man's Soul*, I believe he was unduly influenced by (among other things) the consonance of the two words *Seele* and 'soul' in his native and adopted tongues.]

II

Suddenly, we have slipped out of the economic sphere and into the psychological. We were tempted at first to look for the content of culture in terms of the commodities available and the institutions set up to distribute them. With the recognition that every culture rests on an obligation to work and on a renunciation of drives and therefore inevitably evokes opposition in the person to whom those demands apply, it became clear that commodities themselves, the means of obtaining them, and the arrangements for their distribution cannot be the essential or sole constituent of culture. The reason is that they are under threat from the rebelliousness and addiction to destruction of culture's co-owners. In addition to commodities we now have the means that can serve to defend the culture, the instruments of coercion and other instruments charged with the task of reconciling people to it and compensating them for their sacrifices. The latter, however, may be described as the mental property of culture.

In the interests of a uniform mode of expression, let us call the fact that a drive cannot be satisfied 'denial', the institution that lays down that denial a 'ban', and the state that the ban brings about 'privation'.[1] The next step is then to distinguish between privations that affect everyone and privations that do not affect everyone but only groups,[2] classes, or even individuals. The former are the oldest: with the bans that they imposed, culture began the process of separation from the brutish primal state, no one knows how many thousands of years ago. To our surprise, we found that they are still influential, still form the nucleus of hostility to culture. The libidinal desires that suffer thereunder are reborn with every child;

there is a class of people, namely neurotics, who react even to these denials with anti-social behaviour. Such libidinal desires are those of incest, cannibalism and bloodlust. It sounds strange that these desires, condemnation of which appears to attract universal agreement, should be bracketed together with others, the granting or denial of which is so vehemently fought over in our culture, yet in psychological terms this is justified. Nor is the cultural stance adopted towards these earliest libidinal desires by any means uniform: only cannibalism seems universally frowned on and beyond all non-analytical examination, while the strength of incestuous desires may still be sensed behind the ban, and murder is under certain circumstances still practised (indeed, preached) in our culture. The future may well hold in store for us cultural developments in which other, currently quite possible satisfactions of desire will seem as unacceptable as that of cannibalism does today.

Even in connection with these oldest drive-renunciations, a psychological factor comes into consideration that retains its significance for all the rest as well. It is not true that the human mind had undergone no development since the earliest times and in contrast to the advances made by science and technology is the same today as at the beginning of history. One such mental advance can be demonstrated here. It lies in the direction of our evolution that external coercion is gradually internalized in that a specific mental agency, namely the human Above-'I', takes it under its command. Every child acts out for us the process of such a change; in fact, it is what makes the child a moral and social being. This strengthening of the Above-'I' is an extremely valuable psychological piece of cultural content. The persons in whom it has occurred turn from being enemies of culture to being upholders of culture. The more numerous they are in a given cultural environment, the more secure that culture will be and the more likely it is to be able to dispense with external instruments of coercion. Now, the degree of such internalization varies widely so far as individual libidinal bans are concerned. As regards the oldest cultural requirements mentioned above, internalization (leaving aside the unwelcome exception of neurotics) seems largely complete. The situation changes when one turns to the other libidinal demands. One then notices with surprise and concern that a majority of people will heed the relevant cultural bans only under pressure from external coercion – in other words, only where such pressure is able to make itself felt and so long as it inspires fear. The same applies with regard to those so-called 'moral' cultural requirements that are set for everyone similarly. Most of what is said about the moral unreliability of human beings belongs here. Untold numbers of civilized human beings who would recoil from murder or incest do not deny themselves satisfaction of their greed, aggression or sexual desires and will not hesitate to harm others through lying, cheating and calumny, if they can get away with it, and this has doubtless always been the case, through many cultural epochs.

As regards restrictions that relate only to specific classes of society, the circumstances encountered are obvious as well as being never missed. It is to be expected that these neglected classes will envy the privileged their prerogatives and do everything to be rid of their own greater degree of privation. Where this is not possible, a permanent measure of dissatisfaction will assert itself within that culture that may lead to dangerous rebellions. However, if a culture has not got beyond the point where the satisfaction of some participants requires the oppression of others, maybe the majority (and this is the case with all contemporary cultures), then, understandably, the oppressed will develop a deep hostility towards a culture that their labour makes possible but in whose commodities they have too small a share. In that case, no internalization of cultural bans can be expected among the oppressed; indeed, they will be loath to acknowledge those bans, striving instead to destroy the culture itself, and in the end abolishing its very premises. The anti-cultural stance of such classes is so evident that what tends to be the latent hostility of the better-served strata of society has been overlooked on that account. It goes without saying that a culture that fails to satisfy so many participants, driving them to rebellion, has no chance of lasting for any length of time, nor does it deserve one.

The degree of internalization of cultural precepts (to use a popular, non-psychological phrase: the moral level of participants) is not the only mental asset to be taken into consideration when it comes to appraising a culture. There is also its wealth of ideals and artistic creations – that is to say, the satisfactions derived from both.

People are over-inclined to place the ideals of a culture (i.e. its judgements as to which are the supreme achievements, those most worth striving for) among its psychological assets. It seems at first as if such ideals determine the achievements of the culture group; what actually happens, though, is probably that the ideals emerge in line with the earliest achievements made possible by the combined effects of a culture's inner aptitude and external circumstances, and that those earliest achievements are then captured by the ideal for continuation. In other words, the satisfaction that the ideal gives to those involved in a culture is narcissistic in nature, being based on pride in what has already been achieved. For it to be complete, it requires comparison with other cultures that have plumped for different achievements and evolved different ideals. On the strength of those differences, every culture gives itself the right to look down on the others. This is how cultural ideals occasion rupture and hostility between different culture groups – most obviously amongst nations.

Narcissistic satisfaction arising out of the cultural ideal is also one of the forces successfully countering cultural hostility within the culture group. Not only do the privileged classes, who enjoy the benefits of that culture, share in it; the oppressed may share in it, too, in that the right to despise outsiders is their compensation for the restrictions placed on them in their own circle. A person may be a poor plebeian, burdened by debts and compulsory military service, yet that person is a Roman and as such involved in the task of ruling over other nations and writing their laws. However, this identification of the oppressed with the class that controls and exploits them is only part of a larger context. On the other hand, the former may be emotionally bound to the latter; their hostility notwithstanding, they may see their masters as embodying their ideals. Without such basically satisfactory relationships, it would be a mystery why certain cultures survived for so long, despite justified hostility on the part of large sections of the population.

Different again is the satisfaction that art gives those involved in a culture group, though as a rule this remains beyond the reach of the masses, who are preoccupied by exhausting labour and have received no personal education. Art, as we learned long ago, offers substitute satisfactions for the oldest, still most deeply felt cultural renunciations and therefore has a uniquely reconciling effect with the sacrifices made for it. On the other hand, its creations boost the identification feelings of which every culture group stands in such need by fostering impressions that are experienced jointly and held in high esteem; but they also contribute to narcissistic satisfaction if they represent the achievements of the particular culture, offering impressive reminders of its ideals.

Possibly the most important item in the psychical inventory of a culture has yet to be mentioned. This is what in the broadest sense constitutes its ideas about religion – in other words (words that will require justification at a later stage), that culture's illusions.

Notes

1. [In Freud's terminology, *Versagung* ('denial'), *Verbot* ('ban'), and *Entbehrung* (privation) respectively.]
2. [Here Freud uses the word *Gruppen* (rather than *Masse/Massen*, which I have consistently translated as 'mass/masses').]

III

What constitutes the special value of religious ideas?

We have spoken of hostility to culture, engendered by the pressure that a culture exerts, the libidinal renunciations that it demands. Imagining its bans lifted, a man is free to choose any woman he wishes as sexual object; he may without compunction strike his rivals for the woman dead or kill anyone else who stands in his way, and he may help himself to any of his neighbour's goods without asking permission. How splendid, what a string of satisfactions life would then have to offer! Before long, of course, the next problem emerges. Everyone else has precisely the same desires as myself and will give me no more quarter than I give him. Basically, this means that only a single individual can derive unrestricted happiness from such a removal of cultural restrictions, a tyrant, a dictator who has grabbed all the instruments of power for himself, and even he has every reason to hope that others will respect at least one cultural ban: the one saying 'you shall not kill'.

But how ungrateful (how short-sighted, in fact) to strive for an abolition of culture! What is left then is the state of nature, and that is far harder to bear. Granted, nature would demand no drive-restrictions of us, it would leave us be, but nature has its own particularly effective way of placing restrictions on us: it kills us – coldly, cruelly, without a qualm, it seems to us – perhaps on the very occasions of our satisfaction. It was precisely because of the perils with which nature threatens us that we got together in the first place and created culture, which is meant among other things to enable us to live together. Indeed, the main function of culture, the real reason for its existence, is to shield us against nature.

As we know, it already does a pretty good job of that now in many respects and will one day, clearly, do a far better one. But no one succumbs to the deluded belief that nature has already been conquered; few dare hope that it will one day be wholly subject to the human race. There are the elements, which appear to mock any kind of human constraint: earth, which heaves and splits open, burying all things human and all the works of humankind; water, which when in tumult swamps and drowns everything; storms, which blow everything away; there are diseases, which we have only recently come to recognize as attacks by other living creatures, and finally there is the painful riddle of death, against which no remedy has yet been found, nor probably ever will. These powers nature lines up against us, magnificent, cruel, relentless, reminding us of our weakness and of the helplessness we had thought our cultural activities would overcome. One of the few pleasing and uplifting impressions furnished by the human race is when, faced with an elemental disaster, it forgets its cultural muddle-headedness and all its internal problems and enmities and recalls the great common task of preserving itself against the superior might of nature.

As for humanity as a whole, so too for the individual human, life is hard to bear. A certain amount of privation is imposed on him by the culture to which he belongs, some suffering is heaped on him by other people, either despite the rules laid down by that culture or because of that culture's imperfection. In addition, there is what untamed nature (he calls it fate) does him in the way of harm. A constant state of fearful expectation and some severe injury to natural narcissism should follow from such a condition. We already know how the individual reacts to the damage inflicted on him by culture and by other people: he develops a corresponding degree of resistance to the institutions of that culture, of hostility to culture. But how does he defend himself against the superior forces of nature, of fate, which threaten him like everyone else?

Culture does the job for him; it does it for everyone in the same way; in fact, remarkably, more or less all cultures are alike in this. For instance, culture does not cease to operate once it has performed its task of defending the individual human against nature; it simply continues that task by other means. In this case, the task is a multiple one: man's badly threatened self-esteem craves consolation, the world and life need to lose their terror, and at the same time humanity's thirst for knowledge, which is of course driven by the strongest practical interest, craves an answer.

With the first step, much is already gained. And that is to humanize nature. Impersonal forces and fates are unapproachable, they remain forever alien. But if passions rage in the elements as they do in the human heart, if even death is not something spontaneous but an act of violence perpetrated by an evil will, if everywhere in nature a person is surrounded by beings like those he knows from his own society, then he will breathe easier, feel at home in quite unfamiliar surroundings, be able, mentally, to deal with his irrational fears; a person may still be defenceless but he is not helpless any longer, not paralysed, he can at least react. In fact, he may not even be defenceless: he can deploy against those violent supermen out there the same resources as he uses in his society. He can try beseeching them, appeasing them, bribing them; by exerting such influence, he will rob them of some of their power. That kind of replacement of a natural science by psychology not only brings immediate relief; it also points the way towards further coping with the situation.

Because there is nothing new about this situation, it has its model in infancy, it is simply a continuation of an earlier situation, in fact; one had experienced this kind of helplessness back then, as a small child facing parents whom one had reason to fear (particularly the male parent), but of whose protection one was also confident in the face of the dangers one was aware of at the time. So the obvious thing was to compare the two situations. Also, as in dream life, wish then got its money's worth, so to speak. A premonition of death assails the sleeper, wanting to put him in the grave, but dream work is able to select the condition in which even this feared event becomes wish-fulfilment; the dreamer sees himself in an ancient Etruscan tomb into which, happy to have his archaeological interests catered to, he had descended. Similarly, a person does not simply turn the forces of nature into people among whom he is able to move as amongst his peers; that would not do justice, in fact, to the overpowering impression he has of them. Instead, he invests them with a paternal character, turning them into gods, and in the process following not only an infantile model but also, as I have tried to show, a phylogenetic model.

In time, the first observations of regularity in natural phenomena are made; they are found to conform to laws, and the forces of nature lose their human traits as a result. However, the helplessness felt by human beings remains, as do their paternal yearnings and the gods. The latter retain their triple function of warding off the terrors of nature, reconciling humans to the cruelty of fate, notably as revealed in death, and compensating them for the sufferings and privations imposed upon them by living together in a culture group.

Little by little, though, the emphasis within the exercise of those functions shifts. People notice that natural phenomena develop spontaneously in accordance with inner necessities; the gods are still the lords of nature, they set nature up in a certain way and they can now leave it to itself. Only occasionally do they intervene in its course, working what are called miracles, as if to affirm that they have surrendered none of their original power. As regards the distribution of fates, there remains an uncomfortable suspicion that the bewilderment and helplessness of the human race is beyond remedy. This is where the gods fail most; if they themselves create fate, it has to be said that their ways are mysterious; the most gifted nation in the ancient world glimpsed dimly that *Moira* stands above the gods and that the gods themselves have their fates. And the more nature becomes autonomous, with the gods withdrawing from it, the more earnestly all expectations focus on the third function attributed to them and the more the moral sphere becomes their proper domain. The task of the gods now becomes to make good the ills and short-comings of culture, to heed the sufferings that people inflict on one another in living together, and to supervise implementation of the rules of culture with which humans find it so hard to comply. The rules of culture are themselves deemed to be of divine provenance; exalted above human society, they are extended to nature and world events.

In this way a treasury of ideas is created, born of the need to make human helplessness bearable, its building materials memories of everyone's own helplessness and that of the childhood of the human race. Quite obviously, this possession shields man in two directions: against the perils of nature and fate and against the damage inflicted by human society itself. In context, the message is: life in this world serves a higher purpose, one not easy to guess, admittedly, but without doubt implying a perfection of human nature. Probably the spiritual side of humanity, the soul,[1] which has slowly and reluctantly separated from the body down the ages, is the intended object of such elevation and enhancement. Everything that happens in this world does so in execution of the intentions of a higher intelligence that, albeit in ways (including some roundabout ways) that are hard to follow, ultimately steers it all in the direction of the good, i.e. that which is gratifying to ourselves. A benevolent and only apparently strict Providence watches over us all, not permitting us to become the plaything of all-powerful, pitiless natural forces; death itself is no destruction, no return to inorganic lifelessness, but the start of a new kind of existence situated on the path to higher development. Conversely, the same moral laws as our cultures have drawn up also govern all that happens in the world, the only difference being that a supreme judicial instance watches over them with incomparably greater might and rigour. In the end, everything good will find its reward, everything evil its punishment, if not in this form of life then in later existences that start after death. This means that all life's terrors, sufferings and hardships are destined to be obliterated; life after death, which extends our earthly existence just as the invisible part of the spectrum is appended to the visible, will bring all the perfection that we may have missed here. And the superior wisdom that guides this process, the universal goodness that finds expression in it, the justice that finds implementation through it – these are the properties of the divine beings that also created ourselves and the world as a whole. Or rather, of the one divine being into which in our culture all the gods of earlier times have become compressed. The people that first achieved this concentration of divine properties was not a little proud of such progress. It had exposed the paternal core that had always lain hidden behind every god figure; basically, this was a return to the historical beginnings of the god idea. With God now a single being, relations towards him could recover the intimacy and intensity of the child's relationship with its father. But having done so much for their father, folk wanted to be rewarded, they wanted at least to become the only beloved child, the chosen people. Many centuries later, a pious America claimed to be 'God's own country', and for one of the forms in which humans worship the deity that is indeed true.

The religious ideas summarized above naturally went through a lengthy development, and different cultures captured them in different phases. I have extracted a single such phase of development, corresponding approximately to the end result in our present-day white Christian culture. It is easy to see that not all pieces of that entity fit equally well together, that not all pressing questions are answered, that the inconsistency of everyday experience can be dismissed only with difficulty. But such as they are these ideas (religious in the broadest sense) are reckoned the most precious possession of culture, the most valuable thing it has to offer its participants, held in far higher esteem than all the skills of parting the earth from its treasures, feeding humanity, fending off disease, etc. People think life is unbearable unless they attach to such ideas the value that is claimed for them. The question is: what are these ideas in the light of psychology, why are they held in such high esteem, and (venturing shyly on) what are they actually worth?

Notes

1. [Here I happily render *Seele* as 'soul', because the context makes clear that Freud *is* talking about something separate.]

IV

An investigation that proceeds smoothly in the style of a monologue is not wholly risk-free. One is too tempted to brush aside ideas that would interrupt it, and in return one gets a feeling of uncertainty that one seeks in the end to drown out by being overly decisive. So I shall imagine an opponent who follows my remarks mistrustfully, and from time to time I shall give him the floor.

I hear him say: *'You have repeatedly used the expressions: culture creates these religious ideas, culture makes them available to its participants, there's something disconcerting about that; I couldn't say why myself, it doesn't sound as self-evident as that culture has made arrangements regarding the distribution of the product of labour or regarding rights to woman and child.'*

My view, however, is that one is entitled to use such expressions. I was trying to show that religious ideas sprang from the same necessity as all the other attainments of culture, from the need to mount a defence against the oppressive dominance of nature. There was a second motive, too, namely the urge to correct the painfully felt imperfections of culture. It is also particularly apt to say that culture bestows such ideas upon the individual, because the individual discovers them, they are brought to him complete, he would be incapable of finding them on his own. It is the legacy of many generations he is entering upon, taking it over like his multiplication tables, like geometry, etc. There is a difference here, of course, but it lies elsewhere and cannot yet be examined. You mention the sense of being disconcerted: that may have something to do with the fact that this body of religious ideas is usually presented to us as divine revelation. However, that is itself part of the religious system, it completely ignores what we know to have been the historical emergence of those ideas and the way they differed in different eras and cultures.

'*Another point – more important, it seems to me. You make the humanization of nature proceed from the need to put an end to human bewilderment and helplessness in the face of its dreaded forces, establish a relationship with it, and eventually gain some influence over it. But that kind of motive seems superfluous. Primitive man, after all, has no choice, no other way of thinking. It is natural for him (innate, so to speak) to project his being out into the world and to regard every process that he observes as springing from beings basically similar to himself. That is the only way he can understand things. And it is by no means self-explanatory, in fact it is a remarkable coincidence, if by thus giving free rein to his natural disposition he should succeed in meeting one of his major needs.*'

I do not find that so extraordinary. Do you believe, then, that a person's thinking has no practical motives, that it simply expresses a selfless curiosity? Surely that is highly unlikely? I take the view that, even when personifying the forces of nature, the human being is conforming to an infant model. Having learned from the people who made up his earliest environment that, if he established a relationship with them, that was the way to influence them, he subsequently, with the same intention, treated everything else he encounted in the same way as he had treated them. So I do not disagree with your descriptive comment, it really is natural to man to personify everything he seeks to understand with a view to controlling it afterwards (mental coping as preparation for physical), but I also provide the motive and genesis of that peculiarity of human thinking.

'*And now a third thing. You dealt with the origins of religion before, in your book* Totem and Taboo. *But there the picture is different. Everything is the father–son relationship, God is the exalted father, yearning for a father is the root of religious need. Since then, apparently, you have discovered the element of human powerlessness and helplessness, to which the biggest role in the formation of religion is in fact generally ascribed, and now you shift on to helplessness everything that was once the father complex. Could you please tell me about this change?'*

Willingly, I was just waiting for the challenge. If it really is a change. *Totem and Taboo* was meant to throw light not on the emergence of religions but only on that of totemism. Can you explain, from any of the standpoints known to you, why the first form in which protective divinity revealed itself to man was animal, why there was a ban on killing and eating that animal, and why it was nevertheless the solemn custom, once a year, to come together to kill and eat it? That is exactly what happens in totemism. And there is little point in arguing about whether totemism should be described as a religion. It is intimately related to the later divine religions, with the totem animals becoming the sacred animals of the gods. And the earliest but most deep-rooted moral restrictions (the bans on murder and incest) spring from the soil of totemism. Now, whether or not you accept the conclusions of *Totem and Taboo*, I hope you will concede that, in the book, a number of very remarkable scattered facts are brought together into a consistent whole.

Why the animal god was inadequate in the long run and was replaced by the human form is scarcely touched on in *Totem and Taboo*, while other problems of how religion took shape are not mentioned at all. In your eyes, is such a restriction tantamount to a denial? My work is a good example of strict isolation of the part that psychoanalytical examination can play in solving the problem of religion. If I now attempt to add the other, less deeply concealed part, you ought not to accuse me of contradiction – any more than of one-sidedness previously. It is my job (of course it is) to demonstrate the links between what I said earlier and what I am submitting now, between the underlying and the manifest motivation, between the father complex and human helplessness and need for protection.

Those links are not difficult to find. They are the connections between the helplessness of the child and that (perpetuating it) of the adult, with the result that, as was to be expected, the psychoanalytical motivation behind the formation of religion becomes the infantile contribution to its manifest motivation. Let us place ourselves in the inner life of the small child. You remember the choice of object in accordance with the support-seeking type[1] that analysis talks about? The libido, following the paths of the narcissistic needs, attaches itself to the objects that promise to satisfy those needs. For example, the child's mother, who stills its hunger, becomes its first love-object and undoubtedly also its first protection against all the vague dangers that threaten it from the outside world – the child's first fear shield, we might say.

The mother is soon supplanted in this function by the stronger father, with whom it then remains right throughout childhood. However, the child's relationship to its father is burdened with a curious ambivalence. The father was himself a danger, possibly because of the earlier relationship to the mother. As a result, the child fears him no less than it yearns for and admires him. The signs of this ambivalence in the father relationship are deeply embedded in all religions, as is also explained in *Totem and Taboo*. If as a person grows older he realizes that he is destined to remain a child for ever, that he can never manage without protection against alien superior powers, he invests those powers with the traits of the father-figure, creating for himself gods of whom he is afraid, whom he seeks to win over, and to whom he nevertheless assigns his protection. The motif of yearning for the father is thus identical with the need for protection against the consequences of human powerlessness; the defence provided against infant helplessness gives the reaction to the helplessness that the young adult is forced to acknowledge (i.e. the formation of religion) its characteristic features. However, it is not our intention to explore the development of the God notion any further; what concerns us here is the complete treasury of religious ideas as transmitted to the individual by his culture.

Notes

1. [*Anlehnungstypus* – known to most psychoanalysts in the English-speaking world by the neologistic 'anaclitic type'. See above, p. 62, note 1.]

V

To resume the thread of our investigation – what, then, is the psychological significance of religious ideas, how are we to classify them? The question is by no means easy to answer at first. After rejecting various formulations, we are left with one only: they are dogmas, statements about facts and circumstances of external (or internal) reality that convey something we have not discovered for ourselves and that demand to be believed. Since they impart information about what is most important and most interesting for us in life, they are valued particularly highly. Whoever knows nothing of them is deeply ignorant; whoever has taken them on board as knowledge may consider himself greatly enriched.

Of course, there are many such dogmas regarding a wide variety of things in this world. Every school lesson is full of them. Take geography, for instance. There we are told: Constance lies on the Bodensee.[1] As the German student song says: 'If you don't believe it, go and see!' I do happen to have been there and can confirm that that beautiful city does indeed lie on the shore of a broad stretch of water that all who live around it call 'the Bodensee'. I too am now wholly convinced of the correctness of that geographical assertion. I am reminded of another, very remarkable experience in this connection. It was as a grown-up man that I first stood on the hill of the Athenian Acropolis, surrounded by ruined temples, gazing out over the blue sea. Mingled with my happiness was a sense of astonishment that came to me as: so it really is true, what we were taught at school! How shallow, how feeble must have been the belief I had acquired then in the actual truth of what I was being told for me to feel such surprise now! Yet I am reluctant to over-stress the significance of that experience; a different explanation for my astonishment is possible – one that did not occur to me at the time, is thoroughly subjective in character, and has to do with the exceptional nature of the place.

Thus all such dogmas demand belief in their content, though not without justifying their claim. They present themselves as the abbreviated outcome of a longer thought process based on observation as well as, no doubt, on inference; if a person means to go through the process for himself rather than accept the result, they show that person how. And invariably one is also told where the knowledge that the dogma proclaims comes from, unless, as with geographical assertions, that goes without saying. For example, the earth is in the shape of a ball; proofs advanced are Foucault's pendulum, the behaviour of the horizon, and the possibility of sailing around the world. Since all concerned agree that it is not feasible to send all schoolchildren off on voyages of circumnavigation, it is felt sufficient to have the teaching of the classroom accepted 'in good faith' – but in the knowledge that the path to personal conviction remains open.

Let us try gauging the dogmas of religion by the same measure. When we ask what their claim to be believed is based on, we receive three answers that are oddly out of harmony with one another. Firstly, they are worthy of belief because our forefathers believed in them back then; secondly, we possess proof handed down to us from that same dim and distant time; and thirdly, it is forbidden to ask for such authentication anyway. This kind of undertaking was once punished with the utmost severity, and even today society frowns on anyone trying it again.

This third point inevitably arouses our strongest misgivings. There can only ever be one motive for such a ban, namely that society is well aware of the shakiness of the claim it makes for its religious teachings. Otherwise it would surely have no hesitation in providing anyone who wished to form his own conviction with the necessary means. So it is with a mistrust that will not be easy to assuage that we set about examining the other two arguments. We are asked to believe because our forefathers believed. Yet those ancestors of ours were far less knowledgeable than ourselves, they believed in things that we, today, cannot anyhow accept. It is at least possible that religious teachings, too, might be of such a kind. The proofs they bequeath to us are enshrined in writings that themselves bear all the signs of unreliability. They are full of contradictions and have been reworked and adulterated; where they speak of actual attestations they are themselves unattested. It is not much help if, for their wording or even simply for their content, the provenance of divine revelation is asserted, since that assertion itself forms part of the teachings that are to be examined as to their credibility – and no proposition, as we know, can prove itself.

This leads us to the odd conclusion that precisely those pronouncements from our cultural inheritance that might be of the greatest significance so far as we are concerned, communications whose allotted function is to explain to us the mysteries of the world and reconcile us to the tribulations of existence – precisely they have the feeblest authentication of all. We could never agree to accept a fact of such indifference to us as that whales give birth to young rather than lay eggs, were there no better proof of it than that.

This state of affairs constitutes a very remarkable psychological problem in itself. Nor should anyone think that the foregoing remarks about the unverifiable nature of religious teachings contain anything new. People have always been aware that they defy proof – as were, surely, the forefathers who bequeathed such an inheritance. Probably many of them harboured the same scepticism as we have ourselves, but the pressure on them was too great for them to dare voice their misgivings. And countless men and women have tormented themselves with identical doubts ever since, trying to suppress them because they felt under an obligation to believe; many brilliant intellects have met with defeat in this conflict, many individuals have been damaged by the compromises in which they sought a way out.

If all the proofs that are advanced for the credibility of religious doctrines stem from the past, the obvious course is to examine whether the present, which can be better assessed, is also capable of furnishing such proofs. If one single component of the religious system could successfully be removed from doubt in this way, the whole would gain exceptionally in credibility. This is where the activities of spiritualists come in; convinced that the individual soul[2] lives on, they seek to put this one proposition of religious teaching beyond doubt so far as we are concerned. Sadly, they cannot disprove that, when their spirits appear and say things, these are simply products of their own mental activity. They have cited the spirits of the greatest men, the most outstanding thinkers, but all the pronouncements and messages received from them have been so silly, so wretchedly uninformative, that we can find nothing that merits belief beyond the ability of such spirits to adapt themselves to the group invoking them.

At this point we must look at two tests that give the impression of making strenuous efforts to avoid the problem. One of these, violent in nature, is ancient, the other subtle and modern. The first is the Church Father's *credo quia absurdum*. This is supposed to mean that religious teachings escape the requirements of reason, they are above reason. Their truth must be felt inwardly, it need not be understood. However, this *credo* is interesting only as confession, as claim to power it is without obligation. Am I to be obliged to believe every absurdity? And if not, why this one in particular? There is no authority higher than reason. If the truth of religious teachings depends upon an inward experience attesting that truth, what about the many people who do not have so rare an experience? Everyone can be required to use the gift of reason that they possess, but an obligation that applies to all cannot be based on a motive that exists only for very few. If an individual has drawn from a deeply personal state of ecstasy the unshakeable conviction that the teachings of religion represent the real truth, what is that to the next man?

The second test is the 'as if' philosophy. This says that there are plenty of assumptions in our intellectual activity that we quite agree are unfounded, even absurd. They are called fictions, but for a variety of reasons we allegedly have to act 'as if' we believed those fictions. This (we are told) applies with regard to the teachings of religion because of their incomparable importance as regards sustaining human society.[3] This line of argument is not far removed from the *credo quia absurdum*. However, in my opinion the 'as if' demand is one that only a philosopher can make. Anyone whose thinking is not influenced by the arts of philosophy will never be able to accept it; so far as he is concerned the admission of absurdity, of being contrary to reason, is the end of the matter. Such a person cannot, particularly as regards treating his most important interests, be made to sacrifice the certainties that he otherwise requires for all his everyday activities. I remember how one of my children distinguished himself at an early age by attaching particular importance to objectivity. When the children were being told a story, to which they were listening with rapt attention, he would come up and ask: 'Is that a true story?' When this was denied, he assumed a scornful expression and withdrew. People can be expected before long to react to the 'story' of religion in a similar way, the 'as if' recommendation notwithstanding.

At present, however, they are still behaving quite otherwise, and back in past times religious ideas, for all their indisputable lack of attestation, exerted the most powerful influence on people. This is a new psychological problem. The question must be asked: wherein lies the inner strength of those teachings, to what do they owe an effectiveness that does not depend on acceptance by reason?

Notes

1. [In fact, the usual English name for this large body of water bordering Germany, Austria and Switzerland is 'Lake Constance'.]

2. ['Soul' again, because of the connotation of separateness, but remember that German does not distinguish verbally between 'mind' and 'soul'; *Seele* covers the whole spectrum.]

3. I hope [Freud writes in an original note] I am not being unjust in having the 'as if' philosopher support a view that is not unknown to other thinkers. See Hans Vaihinger, *Die Philosophie des Als ob*, seventh and eighth editions, 1922, p. 68: 'We include under the heading of fiction not

only trivial, theoretical operations but concepts devised by the noblest of men, concepts to which the hearts of the nobler portion of humanity are attached and from which they refuse to be torn. Nor is that what we are trying to do – as *practical fiction* we allow all that to remain in existence; as *theoretical truth*, however, it fades away.'

VI

We have made adequate preparations, I think, to answer both questions. The answer emerges if we examine the psychical genesis of religious ideas. Such ideas, which put themselves forward as dogmas, are not deposits from experience or end products of cogitation, they are illusions, fulfilling the oldest, most powerful, most pressing desires of the human race; the secret of their strength is the strength of those desires. We have seen already how the terrifying impression of helplessness in childhood awakened the need for protection (protection by love), which the father provided, and how awareness of the continuance of that helplessness throughout life prompted the adult to cling to the existence of another (this time mightier) father. Through the gracious action of divine providence fear of the perils of life is allayed, the appointment of a moral world order guarantees fulfilment of the demand for justice that has so often remained unfulfilled within human culture, while prolonging earthly existence by means of a future life provides the spatial and temporal framework within which such wish-fulfilment shall occur. Answers to riddles posed by man's thirst for knowledge, such as how the world came into being and the nature of the relationship between body and mind, are developed in accordance with the premises of this system; it represents a wonderful relief for the individual psyche when the never entirely surmounted conflicts of childhood arising out of the father complex are lifted from its shoulders, so to speak, and fed into a solution that is accepted by everyone.

If I say they are all illusions, I must define the meaning of the word. An illusion is not the same as an error, nor is it necessarily an error. Aristotle's view that filth engenders vermin (which the ignorant masses entertain to this day) was an error, as was that of an earlier medical generation that *Tabes dorsalis*[1] resulted from sexual excess. It would be incorrect to call such errors illusions. On the other hand, it was an illusion on Columbus's part that he had discovered a new sea route to India. How much what he wished for contributed to that error is very clear. It is possible to describe as an illusion the assertion made by certain nationalists that the Indo-Germanic race is the only one capable of culture, or the belief (which only psychoanalysis has demolished) that the child is a being without sexuality. Typically, the illusion is derived from human desires; in this respect it resembles the psychiatric delusion,[2] though it also differs from it, quite apart from the more complicated structure of the latter. As the key feature of the delusion, we would stress its inconsistency with reality, while the illusion is not necessarily false, i.e. unrealizable or in conflict with reality. For example, a middle-class girl may entertain the illusion that a prince will come to carry her off to his home. It is possible, cases of the sort have occurred. That the Messiah will come and establish a new golden age is far less likely; depending on the personal stance of the person assessing it, he will classify this belief as an illusion or as analogous to a delusion. Instances of illusions that have proved true are not normally easy to find. However, the alchemists' illusion (that they could turn all metals into gold) may be such a one. The desire to have a great deal of gold, as much gold as possible, has been much muted by our modern understanding of the conditions of wealth, yet chemistry no longer considers it impossible to turn metals into gold. In other words, we refer to a belief as an illusion when wish-fulfilment plays a prominent part in its motivation, and in the process we disregard its relationship to reality, just as the illusion itself dispenses with accreditations.

If, armed with this information, we return to the teachings of religion, we may say again: they are all illusions, unverifiable, no one should be forced to regard them as true, to believe in them. Some of them are so improbable, so contrary to everything that we have laboriously learned about the reality of the world, that (making due allowance for the psychological differences) they can be likened to delusions. The reality value of most of them cannot be assessed. Just as they are unverifiable, they are also irrefutable. Too little is known as yet to bring them into closer critical focus. The world's riddles unveil themselves only slowly to our researches, there are many questions science cannot yet answer. However, as we see it, scientific work is the sole avenue that can lead to knowledge of the reality outside ourselves. Again, it is simply an illusion to expect anything of intuition and immersion in the self; that can give us nothing but (highly ambiguous) indications regarding our own inner life, never information about the questions religious dogma finds it so easy to answer. To stick one's own caprice in the gap and use private judgement to pronounce this or that bit of the religious system more or less acceptable would be a wanton undertaking. Such questions are too significant for that – too holy, one might almost say.

At this point, prepare for the objection: '*All right, if even hardened sceptics admit that the claims of religion cannot be refuted by reasoning, why should I not then believe those claims on the grounds that they have so much in their favour: tradition, popular agreement, and all the consolation that they bring?*' Why not, indeed? Just as no one can be forced into belief, nor can anyone be forced into disbelief. However, let no one fall into the trap of assuming that such arguments point the way to right thinking. If there was ever a place for the 'feeble excuse' verdict, this is it. Ignorance is ignorance; no right to believe something can ever flow from it. No rational person will conduct himself so frivolously in other matters and be content with such miserable justifications of his judgements, his partisanship; only in the highest and holiest matters does anyone permit himself that. In reality, he is merely trying to pretend to himself or others that he still holds fast to religion, whereas he detached himself from it a while back. When questions of religion are at issue, people commit all kinds of insincerity, slip into all sorts of intellectual bad habits. Philosophers stretch the meanings of words until scarcely anything of the original sense of those words is left; they call some vague abstraction of their own invention 'God' and now they too are deists, trumpeting their belief in God abroad, able to pride themselves on having discerned a higher, purer concept of God, despite the fact that their God is no more than an insubstantial shadow, no longer the mighty figure of religious teaching. Critics insist on describing as 'deeply religious' a person who admits to a feeling of human smallness and impotence in the face of the totality of the world, although it is not that feeling that constitutes religiousness but in fact the next step, the reaction to it: seeking a remedy for the feeling. The person who does not take that step but instead humbly accepts the minor role of humanity in the wider world – that is the person who is irreligious in the true sense of the word.

It forms no part of the intention of this study to comment on the truth-value of religious teachings. We are content to recognize that, psychologically speaking, they are illusions. However, we need not conceal the fact that this discovery will also greatly influence our attitude towards the question that many must regard as the one that matters most. We know approximately when the teachings of religion were created and by what kinds of people. If we go on to uncover the motives that prompted this, our standpoint on the problem of religion will undergo a marked shift. We tell ourselves how lovely it would be, would it not, if there were a God who created the universe and benign Providence, a moral world order, and life beyond the grave, yet it is very evident, is it not, that all of this is the way we should inevitably wish it to be. And it would be even more remarkable if our poor, ignorant bondsman ancestors had managed to solve all these difficult cosmic questions.

Notes

1. [A disease of the nervous system caused by advanced syphilis.]
2. [*Wahnidee*, whereas 'illusion' is *Illusion*.]

VII

Having acknowledged that the teachings of religion are illusions, the further question immediately arises: are not other parts of our cultural inheritance, parts that we hold in high esteem and allow to dominate our lives, of a similar nature? Could it be that the premises governing our state institutions must likewise be termed illusions, could it be that relations between the genders in our culture are clouded by one or a number of erotic illusions? Our misgivings once aroused, we shall not even shrink from asking whether our own conviction (that by applying observation and thinking in scientific work we can learn something of external reality) is any more firmly grounded. Nothing must be allowed to prevent us from approving the application of observation to our own being and the use of thinking in the service of its own critique. A series of investigations opens up here, the outcome of which would inevitably have a crucial effect on the structure of a 'way of viewing the world'.[1] We also sense that the effort will not be wasted and that it will at least partially justify our suspicion. However, the author's competence balks at so huge a task; he has no choice but to confine his essay to tracing just one of those illusions – that of religion.

Here our opponent shouts 'Stop!' We are about to be called to account for our forbidden conduct. This is what he tells us: 'Archaeological interests are entirely laudable, no doubt, but no one starts an excavation if it is going to undermine the dwellings of the living, making them collapse and burying people under the rubble. The teachings of religion are not just another object to be pored over. Our culture is based on them, it is a condition of the preservation of human society that the vast majority of people* *believes in the truth of those teachings. If people are taught that there is no all-powerful, all-righteous God, no divine world order, and no life after death, they will feel under no obligation to obey the rules of culture. Everyone will follow his anti-social, egoistical drives without fear or inhibition, seeking to assert his power; the chaos that we banished through many millennia of cultural endeavour will return. Even if it were known and could be proved that religion is not in possession of the truth, nothing must be said and people should behave in the way that the 'as if' philosophy requires. In the interests of everyone's preservation! Also, apart from the danger of the enterprise, it constitutes pointless cruelty. Innumerable human beings find no other consolation than the teachings of religion; only with their aid do such folk find life bearable. An attempt is being made to rob them of that support without giving them anything better in its place. Admittedly, science has not come up with much so far, but even if it was a great deal more advanced it would not satisfy the human race. A person has other imperative needs that cold science can never meet, and it is a very strange thing (indeed, the pinnacle of inconsistency) that a psychologist who has always stressed by how much, in human existence, intelligence takes second place to the driven life, should now proceed to deprive people of a precious piece of wish-fulfilment and seek to compensate them with intellectual fare instead.'*

So many accusations, one on top of another! However, I am ready to rebut them all, added to which I shall be putting forward the view that culture is at greater risk if its present attitude towards religion is maintained than if that attitude is abandoned. The trouble is, I hardly know where to begin with my refutation.

Possibly with the assurance that I myself see my undertaking as entirely harmless and risk-free. Overrating the intellect is not on my side this time. If people are as my opponent describes them (and I have no wish to disagree), there is no danger of a pious believer, overwhelmed by my arguments, allowing his faith to be wrested from him. Furthermore, I have said nothing that other, better men have not said far more comprehensively, powerfully and impressively before me. The names of those men are well known;

I shall not cite them lest I make it look as if I am trying to place myself in their line of descent. All I have done (this is the only new element in my account) is to add a certain amount of psychological justification to the criticisms put forward by my great predecessors. This particular addition can scarcely be expected to force an issue that earlier writers failed to effect. I could of course be asked at this point: why write such things when you are confident they will achieve nothing? But we shall come back to that later.

The only person this publication may harm is myself. I shall be treated to the most unpleasant accusations of shallowness, bigotry, lack of idealism and want of sympathy for the highest interests of the human race. However, on the one hand such reproaches are nothing new so far as I am concerned; on the other, when a man has already risen above the displeasure of his contemporaries in younger years, why should it bother him in extreme old age,[2] when he is sure of soon being beyond all favour and disfavour? In the past it was different, such remarks were certain to earn one a curtailment of one's earthly existence and a greatly accelerated opportunity of gaining personal experience of the afterlife. I repeat, however: those times are gone, and today writing such things entails no danger, even so far as the author is concerned. The worst that can happen is that the book is not translated and may not be distributed in one country or another.[3] Not of course in a country that feels confident of the high standing of its culture. But if, in general, one is advocating wish-renunciation and surrender to one's fate, even these losses must be borne.

It then occurred to me to wonder whether publication of this essay might not after all do some damage. Not to a person, granted, but to a thing – namely, the cause of psychoanalysis. The fact is, there is no denying that it is my creation, people have shown plenty of mistrust and ill-will towards it; if I now come out with such unwelcome remarks, they will be only too ready to make the shift, the 'displacement', from my person to psychoanalysis. Now, they will say, we see what psychoanalysis leads to. The mask is off; to a denial of God and the moral ideal, just as we always suspected. To stop us finding out, we were offered the pretence that psychoanalysis, allegedly, has no particular world-view, nor is it capable of forming one.

Such an outcry will be genuinely regrettable so far as I am concerned, because of my many colleagues, some of whom do not begin to share my stance on religious problems. However, psychoanalysis has already withstood many storms and must weather this new one too. In reality, psychoanalysis is a method of research, an impartial tool – like, say, infinitesimal calculus. If a physicist should use the latter to work out that, after a certain time, the earth will perish, people will nevertheless hesitate to ascribe destructive tendencies to the calculus itself and outlaw it accordingly. Everything I have said here against the truth-value of religions did not need psychoanalysis, it had been said by others long before psychoanalysis came about. If applying psychoanalytic method can furnish a fresh argument against the truth content of religion, *tant pis* for religion,[4] but defenders of religion are equally entitled to use psychoanalysis to do full justice to the affective significance of religious doctrine.

Right, to proceed with the defence: religion has clearly done human culture great services, it has contributed much to taming anti-social drives, but not enough. For many thousands of years it has dominated human society; it has had time to show what it can do. Had it succeeded in making the majority of human beings happy, in comforting them, reconciling them to life, turning them into upholders of culture, no one would even think of trying to change the way things are. What do we see instead? That an alarmingly large number of people are dissatisfied with culture and unhappy within it, they experience it as a yoke that needs to be thrown off, we see that those people either devote their whole strength to changing that culture or take their hostility to it to such lengths as to refuse to have anything at all to do with culture and the curbing of drives. Here it will be objected that this state of affairs in fact came about because religion had lost some of its influence over the mass of the people – precisely because of the regrettable effect of scientific advances. We shall note the admission, together with the reasons given for it, and use it later for our own purposes, but the objection itself has no force.

It is doubtful whether, at the time when religious teachings held unrestricted sway, the human race was happier, by and large, than it is today; it certainly no more moral. People have always known how to trivialize the rules of religion, thereby thwarting their intention. Priests, whose role it was to monitor obedience to religion, helped them in this. God's goodness inevitably spiked the guns of his righteousness, as it were: people sinned, then they made sacrifice or did penance, then they were free to sin again. Russian inwardness contrived to reach the conclusion that sin was indispensable to an enjoyment of all the blessings of God's grace; at bottom, therefore, it was pleasing in the sight of God. Obviously the only way priests could keep the bulk of the people submissive to religion was by making such vast concessions to human libidinal nature. The fact remained: God alone is strong and good; humans, by contrast, are weak and sinful. Immorality has always, in every age, found quite as much support in religion as has morality. If the achievements of religion in relation to making people happy, fitting them to culture, and reining them in morally are not better than they are, then surely we must ask: do we overrate its essentialness for humanity and are we wise to base our cultural requirements on it?

Consider the situation that unmistakably obtains today. We heard the admission that religion no longer has the same influence over people as was once the case. (The culture at issue here is European Christendom.) Not because its promises have become more modest but because people find those promises less credible. Let us concede that the reason for the change is the strengthening of the scientific mind in the upper strata of human society. (This may not be the only reason.) Criticism has nibbled away at the evidential value of religious documents, the natural sciences have exposed the errors they contain, comparative research has noticed an embarrassing similarity between the religious ideas to which we pay tribute and the spiritual productions of primitive peoples and eras.

The scientific mind generates a specific way of approaching the things of this world; faced with the things of religion, it pauses, hesitates, and finally here too steps over the threshold. The process is unstoppable, the more people have access to the treasures of our knowledge, the more widespread the severance from religious belief – at first only from the outdated, offensive fashions in which it is kitted out, but then also from its fundamental premises. The Americans who conducted the monkey trial in Dayton are the only ones who have shown consistency.[5] Usually, the inevitable transition takes place through the medium of half-truths and insincerities.

Culture has little to fear from educated persons and those who work with their intellect. The replacement of religious motives for cultural behaviour by other, secular ones would in their case proceed in silence; moreover, they are themselves for the most part upholders of culture. It is different with the great mass of the uneducated and oppressed, who have every reason to be hostile to culture. Provided they do not find out that God is no longer believed in, all is well. But they will find out, they are bound to, even if this essay of mine remains unpublished. And they are ready to accept the results of scientific thinking without there having taken place within them the change that scientific thinking occasions in people. When they do, is there not a risk that the hostility of those masses to culture will pounce on the weak point that they have spotted in the system that keeps them in check?[6] If your only reason for not striking your neighbour dead is that the good Lord forbade it and will punish it severely in this life or the next, but you then learn that there is no good Lord and no need to fear his chastisement, you are going to strike him or her dead without scruple, and only some earthly power will be able to prevent you from doing so. In which case the alternatives are: unrelenting oppression of those dangerous masses, coupled with very careful blocking of all opportunities for intellectual awakening, or a thorough review of the relationship between culture and religion.

Notes

1. [*Weltanschauung.*]
2. [Freud was perhaps seventy when writing this; the cancer that was eventually to cause his death had been diagnosed four years earlier.]

3. [Freud was of course to have his books burned in Berlin in 1933.]

4. [The French phrase is Freud's own.]

5. [Two years earlier (1925), in Dayton, Tennessee, a biology teacher had been found guilty of teaching evolution. The so-called 'Monkey Trial' of 1925 focused opposition between those who accepted the ideas of Charles Darwin and the 'Creationists' of Christian fundamentalism.]

6. [I reluctantly render Freud's colourful *Zwangsherrin* – literally 'dictatrix' (*Kultur* being feminine) – by means of a circumlocution.]

VIII

One would think that no particular difficulties stood in the way of implementing this latter proposal. Granted, it means giving something up, but the gain may be greater and a big risk is avoided. However, people shrink from such a step, as if culture would be exposed to an even bigger risk. When St Boniface chopped down the tree that the Saxons worshipped as sacred, onlookers expected some dreadful event to follow the crime. It did not supervene, and the Saxons accepted baptism.

When culture established the ban on killing the neighbour whom one dislikes personally, who is in the way, or whose goods arouse envy, clearly this occurred in the interests of human coexistence, which would not otherwise be feasible. The reason for this is that the murderer would attract the vengeance of the relatives of the murdered person and the vague jealousy of others who felt an equal inner inclination to commit such violence; in other words, he would not enjoy his revenge or his robbery for long but would have every prospect of soon being done to death in his turn. Even were he to protect himself against the individual enemy by exceptional strength and wariness, he would inevitably be subdued by a league of weaker foes. If no such league emerged, the killing would continue unchecked with the end result that the human race wiped itself out. The same state of affairs would exist between individuals as still exists between families in Corsica but elsewhere only between nations. The risk of physical insecurity, which is the same for all, has the effect of uniting human beings in a society that forbids the individual to kill and reserves the right collectively to kill whoever violates the ban. It is called justice and punishment.

However, this rational explanation of the ban on murder is not the one we give; we claim that God enacted the ban. In other words, we dare to guess his intentions, and we find that he too does not want human beings to wipe one another out. In acting in this way, we clothe the cultural ban in very special solemnity, yet in the process we risk making observance of it dependent on belief in God. If we undo that step, no longer shifting what we want on to God but contenting ourselves with the social explanation, we shall have abandoned that transfiguration of the cultural ban, true, but we shall also have avoided placing it at risk. However, we make another gain as well. Through a kind of diffusion or infection, the character of holiness or inviolability (otherworldliness, one might almost say) has spread from a few major bans to all other cultural institutions, laws and ordinances. On these, however, a halo often does not sit well. It is not simply that they devalue one another by reaching conflicting decisions at different times and in different places; they also display every sign of human inadequacy. It is easy to recognize among them what may simply be a product of a myopic anxiety, the expression of petty interests, or a conclusion drawn from inadequate premises. The criticism to which they will inevitably be subjected also (and to an undesirable extent) reduces respect for other, more justified cultural requirements. It is a difficult task, deciding what God himself required and what is more likely to stem from the authority of an all-powerful parliament or lofty magistrate. So it would be an undoubted advantage to leave God out of it altogether and frankly concede the purely human origin of all cultural institutions and rules. Along with the holiness to which they lay claim, the rigidity and immutability of such commandments and laws would also fall away. People would be able to understand that such precepts had been created not so much to keep them under control, rather to serve their interests; they would gain a more cordial attitude towards them, seeking less to overturn them, more to improve them. This would be an important step along the road leading to a reconciliation with the pressures of culture.

At this point, however, our plea in favour of basing rules of culture on purely rational grounds, i.e. tracing them back to social necessity, is cut short by a scruple. We took as our example the origin of the ban on murder. In which case, does our account match the historical truth? We fear it does not; it appears to be a mere intellectual construct. Having made a particular study of this part of human cultural history with the aid of psychoanalysis, on the basis of that endeavour we are obliged to say that in reality things were different. Purely rational motives achieve little against passionate impulses, even in people nowadays; how much less effective must they have been in connection with the human animal of primeval times! Possibly the latter's descendants would still be uninhibitedly mowing one another down had there not, amongst those murderous deeds, been one, namely the striking dead of the primal father, that had elicited an irresistible emotional reaction involving momentous consequences. That is the origin of the 'you shall not kill' commandment, which in totemism was confined to the father-substitute; extended subsequently to include others, it is still not universally enforced today.

However, as I explain elsewhere (so there is no need for me to repeat those remarks here), that primal father was the primitive image of God, the model on which subsequent generations based the figure of the deity. So the religious account is correct: God really was involved in the origin of the ban; it was his influence, not any understanding of social necessity, that created it. And the displacement of human will on to God is wholly legitimate; men knew that they had violently removed their father, and in reaction to the crime they resolved henceforth to respect his will. Religious teaching is telling us the historical truth, albeit with an element of distortion and disguise; our rational account is a denial of it.

Here we become aware that the treasure-house of religious ideas does not contain wish-fulfilments alone but also significant historical reminiscences. What matchless power it must bestow upon religion, combining the forces of past and future in this way! But possibly, with the aid of an analogy, we can glimpse a different view. It is not a good idea to transplant concepts a long way away from the soil in which they have grown, but this correspondence must be voiced.

We know that the human child has difficulty in making the transformation to culture without passing through a more or less clear period of neurosis. The reason for this is that the child is unable to suppress many of the subsequently unusable drive-demands by rational intellectual effort but must curb them through acts of repression, the usual motive behind which is fear. Most of these childhood neuroses are spontaneously overcome as the child grows up; this is particularly the fate of the obsessional neuroses of childhood. As for the rest, psychoanalytical treatment in later life is supposed to clear those up too. In an entirely analogous manner, one might assume that, during its centuries-long evolution, the human race as a whole gets into states that are like neuroses – and for the same reasons, namely because in the eras when it languished in ignorance and was intellectually weak it produced the drive-renunciations essential to human coexistence through purely affective forces alone. The fall-out from quasi-repressive processes occurring in primeval times clung to culture for a long time to come. Religion, in this reading, is the universal human obsessional neurosis; like the child's, it stemmed from the Oedipus complex, the relationship to the father. Accordingly, a turning away from religion must be expected to occur with the fateful inexorability of a growth process, and we (in this view) are in the throes of that phase of evolution right now.

So our behaviour should be modelled on that of an understanding teacher, who rather than resisting an imminent transformation seeks to promote it while curbing the violence of its breakthrough. However, the analogy does not exhaust the essence of religion. If on the one hand it brings obsessional restrictions such as only an individual obsessional neurosis can do, on the other hand it contains a system of wish-illusions coupled with a denial of reality such as we find in isolation only in amentia, a happy state of hallucinatory confusion. The fact is, these are only comparisons, with the aid of which we are struggling to understand the social phenomenon; the pathology of the individual provides us with no fully adequate equivalent.

It has been pointed out repeatedly (by myself and in particular by Theodor Reik) to what level of detail analogies of religion with obsessional neurosis can be pursued and how much of the particularities and destinies of the emergence of religion can be understood in this way. Another good thing is that the devout believer is to a great extent protected from the risk of certain neurotic ailments; adoption of the universal neurosis relieves him of the task of cultivating a personal neurosis.

Acknowledging the historical value of certain religious teachings increases our respect for them but does not invalidate our proposal to remove them as a motivating force behind the rules of culture. Quite the contrary! It is thanks to these historical residues, in fact, that our view of religious dogmas as quasi-neurotic relics has arisen, and now we can say that it is probably time, as in the analytic treatment of the neurotic, for the results of repression to be replaced by the outcomes of ratiocination. That such reworking will not stop at renunciation of the solemn transfiguration of the rules of culture, that a general revision of the same will inevitably, for many people, lead to their being repealed – these things are to be expected but scarcely to be regretted. That is how our appointed task (that of reconciling people with culture) will to a great extent be resolved. We need make no apology for departing from historical truth in providing a rational motivation for the rules of culture. The truths contained in the teachings of religion are so distorted and systematically dressed up that the mass of humanity is incapable of recognizing them as truth. It is not unlike the way we tell children that babies are brought by the stork. That too is a way of telling the truth in symbolic disguise, because we know what the big bird stands for. But the child does not know, all it hears is the element of distortion, it feels cheated, and we know how often children's distrust of adults and the child's contrariness spring from just such an impression. We have reached the conclusion that it is better to stop handing down such symbolic obfuscations of the truth and refusing to provide the child, in a manner appropriate to its stage of intellectual development, with a knowledge of the way things really are.

IX

'You indulge yourself in contradictions that are difficult to reconcile. First you claim that an essay such as yours is entirely harmless. No one is going to let himself be robbed of his religious belief by such remarks. But since, as we shall see, you do in fact mean to shake that belief, the question legitimately arises: so why publish it? Elsewhere, however, you concede that some harm (much harm, even) may indeed be done if someone discovers that God is no longer believed in. Hitherto obedient, that person will now cast obedience to the rules of culture aside. The fact is, your whole argument that the religious motivation of cultural commands constitutes a danger to culture depends on the assumption that the believer can be turned into a non-believer, and that, surely, is a complete contradiction?

'Another contradiction is when you concede on the one hand that human beings cannot be guided by intelligence, they are in thrall to their passions and libidinal demands, but propose on the other hand that the affective foundations of their cultural obedience be replaced by rational ones. What is that all about? To my mind, it is either one thing or the other.

'Anyway, have you learned nothing from history? A similar attempt to have reason supersede religion has been made before – officially and on a grand scale. Don't you remember the French Revolution and Robespierre? And don't you also remember how ephemeral and miserably unsuccessful the experiment was? It is currently being repeated in Russia, no need to ask how it will turn out this time. Surely we can assume that human beings cannot get by without religion?

'You say yourself that religion is more than an obsessional neurosis. Yet you do not discuss this other aspect. You are content to run
through the analogy with neurosis. It is a neurosis that humanity
needs freeing from. You are not bothered what else gets lost in the
process.'

Probably the appearance of contradiction came about because
I was dealing with complicated matters in too great a hurry. Some
things we can go over again. I still maintain that in one respect
my essay is quite harmless. No believer is going to allow his faith
to be shaken by these or similar arguments. A believer has specific
emotional attachments to the content of religion. There are doubtless innumerable others who do not believe in the same way. They
obey the rules of culture because they let themselves be intimidated by the threats of religion, and they fear religion all the while
they are required to treat it as part of the reality placing restrictions upon them. These are the people who break out as soon as
they are allowed to stop believing in the reality-value of religion,
but again this is something that arguments do not influence. Such
people cease to fear religion once they become aware that others
too are not afraid of it, and they were the object of my claim that
the decline of religious influence would come to their attention
even were I not to publish my essay.

However, I believe you yourself attach greater importance to the
other contradiction with which you reproach me. Humans, you say,
are scarcely amenable to rational motives, they are wholly in thrall
to their libidinal desires. So why deprive them of a libidinal satisfaction and seek to replace it with rational motives? Granted,
humans are like that, but have you ever asked yourself whether
they need to be, whether their innermost nature demands it? Is
the anthropologist able to supply the cranial index of a tribe that
practises the custom of deforming its children's little heads with
bandages from an early age? Think of the distressing contrast
between the radiant intelligence of a healthy child and the intellectual feebleness of the average adult. Is it not at least possible that
in fact religious education is largely to blame for this relative atrophy? I believe it would be a very long time before an uninfluenced

child began spontaneously to have thoughts about God and matters beyond this world. It could be that such thoughts would then follow the same path as in the case of the child's ancestors. Yet no one waits for this to happen; the child is fed the teachings of religion at a time when it is neither interested in them nor able to grasp their scope. Pushing back sexual development and bringing forward the influence of religion – those are the top two programmatic aims of modern pedagogics, are they not? So when the child's mind awakes, the teachings of religion have already become untouchable. But do you suppose it is particularly conducive to strengthening the intellectual function that so important an area should be closed off to it by the threat of hellfire? Once a person has persuaded himself to accept uncritically all the absurdities that the teachings of religion heap upon him and even to overlook the contradictions between them, we need not be too surprised to find him intellectually enfeebled. But we have no means of controlling our libidinal nature apart from our intelligence. How can people dominated by intellectual prohibitions be expected to attain the psychological ideal of the primacy of the intelligence? You will also be aware that women in general are accused of so-called 'physiological feebleness of mind', i.e. of being less intelligent than men. The fact itself is in dispute and its interpretation questionable, but one argument for the secondary nature of such intellectual atrophy is that women suffer from the harshness of the early ban on directing their thoughts towards what they would have been most interested in, namely the problems of sex life. As long as, in addition to the sexual mental block, the religious mental block and the loyal block derived therefrom[1] operate on a person's early years, we really cannot say what that person is really like.

However, I am prepared to moderate my zeal and admit the possibility that I too am chasing an illusion. Maybe the effect of the religious ban on thought is not as bad as I am assuming; it may turn out that human nature remains the same even if education is not abused to induce subservience to religion. I do not know, nor can you know that yourself. Not only do the greatest problems of this life currently seem insoluble; many lesser questions are also difficult to decide. But grant me this much: there are grounds for hope here as regards the future, a treasure may lie buried here by which culture may be enriched, it is worth the effort of experimenting with a non-religious education.[2] If the outcome is unsatisfactory, I am prepared to abandon reform and go back to the earlier, purely descriptive verdict: humans are creatures of feeble intelligence, dominated by their libidinal desires.

On another point I agree with you wholeheartedly. It is certainly a nonsensical plan to seek to abolish religion by force and at a stroke. Principally because there is no chance of its succeeding. The believer will not allow his faith to be taken from him – not by arguments and not by bans. If in a few cases this was in fact achieved, it would be an act of cruelty. A person who has for decades taken a sleeping draught will of course be unable to sleep when deprived of the draught. That the effect of the consolations of religion can be likened to that of a narcotic is neatly illustrated by something happening in America. There an attempt is currently being made (clearly under the influence of matriarchy) to deprive people of all stimulants, drugs and semi-luxuries and sate them, by way of recompense, with the fear of God. The outcome of this experiment is another thing over which we need squander no curiosity.

So I take issue with you when you go on to infer that people cannot do without the consolation of the religious illusion at all, that without it they could not bear the burden of life, could not tolerate cruel reality. No, they could not – those to whom you have been administering the sweet (or bittersweet) poison since childhood. But what about the others, who have been brought up rationally? Perhaps a person not suffering from the neurosis needs no intoxicant to ease it. Granted, such a person will then be in a difficult position, he will have to admit that he is completely helpless, insignificant amid the world's bustle, no longer the mid-point of creation, no longer the object of tender care on the part of a benign Providence. He will be in the same situation as the child who has left the home where it had felt so warm and cosy. But surely infantilism is something that is meant to be overcome? A person cannot remain a child for ever; eventually the child must go out into what

157

has been called 'hostile life'. The process might be termed '*education for reality*'. Do you still need me to make plain to you that the sole object of my essay is to draw attention to the necessity for this step forward?

You are afraid, probably, that people will not survive the ordeal. Well, we can only hope they will. It certainly makes a difference, knowing that one is dependent on one's own strength. A person learns, then, to make proper use of that strength. Humans are not entirely without succour, their science has taught them much since the ice age and will extend their power even further. And as for the great exigencies of fate, against which there is no recourse, they will simply learn to bear them with humility. Of what use to them is the pretence of some great estate on the moon, from the yield of which no one has actually seen a penny as yet? An honest peasant here on this earth will know how to farm his patch in such a way that it feeds him. By withdrawing his expectations from the beyond and concentrating all the forces thus released on earthly existence, he will doubtless manage to make life bearable for all and ensure that culture quite ceases to oppress. Then he will be able, without regret, to echo the words of one of our fellow unbelievers:[3]

> *Den Himmel überlassen wir*
> *Den Engeln und den Spatzen.*

[Let us leave the heavens to angels and to sparrows.]

Notes

1. [Presumably, loyalty to the state in the person of its monarch.]
2. [Freud's phrase is 'den Versuch einer irreligiösen Erziehung zu unternehmen', but the German *irreligiös* lacks the connotation of hostility to religion that the *OED* attributes to 'irreligious'.]
3. [The couplet is from the poem *Deutschland* (Caput 1) by Heinrich Heine.]

X

'That sounds splendid, I have to say. A human race that, having dispensed with all illusions, has become capable of managing tolerably on earth! However, I cannot share your expectations. Not because I am the stubborn reactionary for whom you perhaps take me. No, from level-headedness. I believe we have exchanged roles: you now come across as the enthusiast who allows himself to be carried away by illusions, while I represent the claims of reason, the right to scepticism. What you have been saying seems to me to be based on errors that, following your own procedure, I may term illusions because they so clearly reveal the influence of your desires. You set your hopes on generations uninfluenced by religious teachings in early childhood easily attaining your longed-for goal of the primacy of intelligence over the libidinal life. That is an illusion if ever there was one; on this crucial point human nature is unlikely to change. If I am not mistaken (one knows so little about other cultures), even today there are nations that do not grow up under the pressure of a religious system, and they come no closer to your ideal than do others. If you want to abolish religion from our European culture, that can only happen as a result of a different doctrinal system, and from the outset that system would assume, in its own defence, all the psychological characteristics of religion, the same sanctity, rigidity, intolerance, the same ban on thought. You have to have something of the kind to meet the requirements of education. Education itself is something you cannot dispense with. The road from infant to civilized being is a long one; too many of our weaker brethren would lose their way along it and fail to accomplish their life's work in time if left to *develop on their own, without guidance. The teachings employed in their education will always set limits to the thinking of their more mature years, precisely as you accuse religion of doing today. Can you not see that it is the irredeemable congenital defect of our culture, of every culture, that it asks the compulsive, intellectually feeble child to make decisions that only the mature intelligence of the adult can justify? Yet it cannot do otherwise, given the condensation of centuries of human development into a few childhood years, and only affective forces can make the child cope with its appointed task. That is what your 'primacy of the intelligence' can look forward to.*

'*So you should not be surprised if I speak up for retaining the system of religious teaching as basis for education and human coexistence. It is a practical problem, not a question of reality-value. Since, in the interests of preserving our culture, we cannot put off influencing the individual until he has become culturally mature (many individuals would never be that), since we are compelled to impose on the younger generation some system of teachings aimed at having upon them the effect of a premise that is beyond criticism, the religious system strikes me as being by far the most suitable one for the job. Precisely, of course, because of its wish-fulfilling, consoling power, which you claim to have recognized as an "illusion". Given the problems associated with discerning something of reality (indeed, the doubtfulness of our being able to do so at all), let us not forget that human needs, too, form part of reality – and an important part at that, one that is of particular concern to us.*

'*I find a further advantage of religious doctrine in a feature of it that appears to cause you especial offence. It permits a conceptual purification and sublimation that make it possible to strip away most of what bears traces of primitive and infantile thinking. We are left with a body of ideas that science no longer contradicts and is unable to refute. These rearrangements of religious doctrine, which you condemn as half-measures and compromises, make it possible to avoid a split between the uneducated mass and the philosophical thinker; they preserve the common ground between them that is so important as regards safeguarding culture. There is then no fear of the man in the street discovering that the upper strata of society "no longer believe in God". I think I have demonstrated now that your efforts boil down to an attempt to replace one tried and tested, affectively precious illusion by another that is untried and unsophisticated.'*

I would not have you think I am deaf to your criticisms. I know how hard it is to avoid illusions; the hopes I have professed may indeed themselves be illusory in nature. But one difference I insist on. My illusions (apart from the fact that no punishment attaches to not sharing them) are not unalterable, as are those of religion, they lack that manic character. Should experience reveal (not to me but to others after me who think as I do) that we have made a mistake, we shall drop our expectations. Please, take my attempt for what it is. A psychologist who is well aware of how difficult it is to cope with life in this world is endeavouring to assess the development of humanity on the basis of the scrap of understanding that he has acquired from studying the mental processes of the individual as that individual evolves from being a child to being an adult. In the process, the view forces itself upon him that religion is like a childhood neurosis, and he is optimistic enough to assume that the human race will conquer this neurotic phase, as so many children outgrow their similar neurosis. These insights from individual psychology may be inadequate, transferring them to the human race as a whole may be unjustified, such optimism may be baseless; I own up to all these uncertainties. But one often cannot help saying what one thinks, one's excuse being that no more is claimed for the pronouncement than it is worth.

And there are two points I need to dwell on a little. Firstly, the weakness of my position in no way implies a strengthening of your own. I believe you to be defending a lost cause. Never mind how often we repeat (and rightly so) that the human intellect is powerless in comparison with human drives, there remains something special about that weakness; the voice of the intellect is a low one, yet it does not cease until it has gained a hearing. In the end, after countless rejections, it does so. This is one of the few respects in which one may be optimistic for the future of the human race, but as such it is not without importance. Other hopes can be hitched to it. The primacy of the intellect undoubtedly lies in the far, far distant but probably not infinitely distant future. And since it may be expected to set itself the same goals as you expect your God to realize (on a reduced, human scale, of course, i.e. so far as external reality or Ἀνάγκη allows), namely human love and the limitation of suffering, we can tell each other that our opposition is only temporary; it is not irreconcilable. We hope for the same things, but you are in more of a hurry, are more demanding, and (why not come out with it?) more self-interested than myself and my associates. You want to have bliss begin immediately after death, you demand the impossible of it, you refuse to surrender the claims of the individual. Of those desires, our god Λόγος ['reason']¹ will grant what nature (apart from ourselves) permits, but very gradually, only in the unforeseeable future and for fresh generations. A reward for ourselves, who suffer grievously from life, is not among his promises. On the way to that distant goal your religious teachings will have to be dropped, regardless of whether the first experiments miscarry, regardless of whether the first substitutions prove unfounded. You know why; ultimately, nothing can withstand reason and experience, and the fact that religion contradicts both is all too tangible. Not even reformed religious ideas, where they nevertheless seek to salvage something of religion's consolation content, can escape this fate. Of course, if they confine themselves to proclaiming a superior spiritual essence whose properties are indeterminable and whose purposes are unknowable, they will be safe from the objections of science, but they will also, in that case, be abandoned by the interest of humankind.

And secondly: look at the difference between our respective attitudes to illusion. You need to defend the religious illusion with all your might; if it is invalidated (and it really is pretty much under threat), your world collapses and you are left with no alternative but to despair of everything, of culture and of the future of the human race. I – we – know no such thraldom. Being ready to relinquish a large part of our infantile desires, we can stand it if a few of our expectations turn out to be illusions.

Freed from the pressure of religious teachings, education may not do much to change people's psychological value. Our god Λόγος may not be particularly omnipotent, not able to perform more than a fraction of what his predecessors promised. If we have to concede this, we shall do so with humility. It is not going to make us lose interest in the world and in life, because at one point we have a solid underpinning that you lack. We believe it is possible for the work of science to discover something of the reality of the world, as a result of which we shall be able to increase our power and in accordance with which we shall be able to arrange our lives. If that belief is an illusion, then we are in the same position as yourself, but science has given us proof, in the shape of a great many significant successes, that it is no illusion. Science has numerous overt and even more covert enemies among those who cannot forgive it for having weakened religious faith and for threatening to overthrow it. Those enemies say accusingly how little science has taught us and how very much more (incomparably more) it has shed no light on whatsoever. But they forget how young it is, how difficult were its beginnings, and for how immeasurably brief a time the human intellect has possessed the strength for the tasks of science. Do we not all make the mistake of basing our judgements on time-spans that are too short? We should follow the geologists' example. People complain of the uncertainty of science, pointing to the fact that today it promulgates as law something that the next generation acknowledges to have been an error, substituting a fresh law, which then enjoys an equally brief period of validity. But that is unfair and in part untrue. Changes of scientific opinion constitute development and progress, not upheaval. A law that was initially seen as having total validity turns out to be a special case of a more comprehensive regularity or is curbed by a different law that is discovered only later; a rough approximation to the truth is replaced by one that is more precisely adapted – which in turn looks forward to a more perfect adjustment. In various fields, a research phase has yet to be outgrown in which assumptions are tested that soon need to be rejected as inadequate; in others, an assured and virtually unalterable core of knowledge already exists. Endless attempts have been made radically to devalue the scientific endeavour by suggesting that, because it is tied to the conditions of our own organization, it cannot help but furnish only subjective findings, while the real nature of things outside ourselves remains beyond its reach. However, this is to disregard a number of factors crucial to the perception of scientific work: that our organization (i.e. our mental apparatus) was in fact developed in the effort to map the outside world, so must have realized a certain amount of expediency in its structure; that that apparatus is itself a part of the world we set out to investigate and very much admits such investigation; that the task of science is described in full if we limit it to showing how, because of our unique organization, the world must inevitably appear to us; that the eventual results of science, precisely because of the manner of their acquisition, are conditioned not only by our organization but also by what influenced that organization; and lastly that the problem of a world constitution that takes no account of the mental apparatus by which we perceive it is an empty abstraction, of no practical interest.

No, our science is not an illusion. What would be an illusion would be to think we might obtain elsewhere that which science cannot give us.

(1927)

Notes

1. The divine couple Λόγος-᾽Ανάγκη of the Dutchman Multatuli.

*Moses the Man and
Monotheistic Religion*

I

Moses an Egyptian

Robbing a popular tradition of the man it regards as its greatest son is not an undertaking one will embark on lightly or with enthusiasm – especially if one is oneself a member of the people in question. But one is not going to let an exemplar make one neglect the truth in favour of supposed national interests, and besides, clarifying a particular context may even, one hopes, benefit our understanding.

The man Moses, who gave the Jewish people their liberty, their law and their religion, belongs to so remote an era that the first question, inevitably, is: are we dealing with a historical figure here or with a product of myth? If he lived, it was in the thirteenth (though possibly in the fourteenth) century before our way of calculating time; we have no other testimony to his existence than that contained in the holy books and in the written traditions of the Jews. If that also means that the answer lacks ultimate certainty, the overwhelming majority of historians have pronounced that Moses really existed and that the exodus from Egypt associated with him did actually take place. It is claimed with good reason that the subsequent history of the people of Israel would be incomprehensible if this concession were not made. The fact is, modern scholarship has become much more circumspect, treating traditions in a far gentler way than in the early days of historical criticism.

The first thing about Moses' person that attracts our interest is his name, which in Hebrew is *Moshe*. Where, one may ask, does it come from? What does it mean? As we know, the account in the second chapter of the Book of Exodus supplies an answer.

There we are told that the Egyptian princess who rescued the little boy abandoned in the Nile gave him this name with the etymological justification: 'Because I drew him out of the water.'[1] However, this explanation is clearly inadequate. 'The biblical interpretation of the name "he who was drawn out of the water",' says an author in the *Jewish Lexicon*,[2] 'is popular etymology, with which the active Hebrew form (*moshe* can at best mean no more than "he who draws out") cannot be brought into agreement.' Two further reasons may be given in support of this rejection: first, it makes no sense to attribute to an Egyptian princess a derivation of the name from the Hebrew; secondly, the water out of which the child was drawn was in all probability not the water of the Nile.

On the other hand, for a long time now and from various quarters the supposition has been voiced that the name Moses stems from the Egyptian vocabulary. Rather than list all the authors who have expressed this view, let me interpolate the relevant passage from a recent book by J. H. Breasted, an author whose *History of Egypt* (1906) is regarded as the standard work on the subject. Breasted writes:

It is important to notice that his [this leader's] name, Moses, was Egyptian. It is simply the Egyptian word 'mose' meaning 'child' and is an abridgement of a fuller form of such names as 'Amon-mose' meaning 'Amon-a-child' or 'Ptah-mose', meaning 'Ptah-a-child', these forms themselves being likewise abbreviations for the complete form 'Amon-(has given)-a-child' or 'Ptah-(has given)-a-child'. The abbreviation 'child' early became a convenient rapid form for the cumbrous full name, and the name Mose, 'child', is not uncommon on the Egyptian monuments. The father of Moses without doubt prefixed to his son's name that of an Egyptian god like Amon or Ptah, and this divine name was gradually lost in current usage, till the boy was called 'Mose'.[3]

I quote the whole passage verbatim and am in no way prepared to share responsibility for the details. Also, I am a little surprised that Breasted's list in fact passes over the similar theophoric names found in the catalogue of Egyptian kings, such as *Ah-mose, Thut-mose* (Thothmes), and *Ra-mose* (Ramses).

One would expect one of the many persons who have recognized the name Moses as Egyptian to have gone on to draw the conclusion or at least consider the possibility that the bearer of this Egyptian name was himself an Egyptian. With regard to modern times, we permit ourselves such conclusions without hesitation, although nowadays a person has not one name but two (surname and given name) and despite the fact that changes of name and adjustments to fresh conditions are not out of the question. Consequently, we are not at all surprised to find confirmation that the writer Chamisso was of French extraction, while Napoleon Bonaparte was originally Italian, and that Benjamin Disraeli was indeed an Italian Jew, as his name suggests. And for ancient and early times one would think that such a deduction from name to nationality should be far more reliable still and in fact appear conclusive. Nevertheless, so far as I am aware, in the case of Moses no historian has drawn such a conclusion, not even one who, like Breasted himself, is prepared to accept that Moses was familiar 'with all the wisdom of the Egyptians'.[4]

What stopped them is something we cannot guess for certain. Possibly respect for biblical tradition proved insurmountable. Possibly the idea seemed too monstrous that Moses the man may have been something other than a Hebrew. At any rate, the fact is that acknowledging the Egyptian name is not deemed decisive as regards assessing where Moses came from; no further deduction is made as a result. If the question of the nationality of this great man is considered important, it would presumably be no bad thing to adduce fresh material with which to answer it.

This my modest treatise seeks to do. Its claim to a place in the magazine *Imago* is based on the fact that the substance of what it contributes is an application of psychoanalysis. The argument thus adduced will no doubt impress only that minority of readers who are familiar with psychoanalytical thinking and capable of assessing its findings. To them, however, I hope it will appear significant.

In 1909 Otto Rank, who was then still under my influence, published at my suggestion an essay entitled 'The myth of the birth of the hero'.[5] It deals with the fact that

nearly all major civilized peoples [. . .] magnified their heroes, mythic kings and rulers, inaugurators of religion, founders of dynasties, empires and cities (their national pantheon, in short) in early poems and legends. [. . .] In particular, they clothed the birth and childhood narratives of such persons in fantastical features, the amazing similarity, indeed occasional verbal identity of which (as between different, sometimes widely separate and quite independent peoples) has been known about for a long time and has struck many researchers.

If, using Rank's procedure (the Galton technique, for instance),[6] we construct an 'average saga' that picks out the key features of all such narratives, we obtain the following picture:

The hero is the child of *very exalted* parents, usually a king's son.

His coming into being is preceded by difficulties such as abstinence or prolonged infertility or secret intercourse between the parents because of external bans or obstacles. During the pregnancy or earlier, a warning of his birth is contained in a prophecy (dream, oracle), usually threatening the father with danger.

In consequence, the newborn child, usually at the instigation of *the father or the person representing him*, is condemned to killing or *exposure*; as a rule, the infant is placed in *water* in a small container.

It is then *rescued* by animals or *lowborn folk (shepherds)* and suckled by a *female animal* or *lowborn woman*.

As a man, the hero passes through many vicissitudes, eventually finding his way back to his exalted parents. He then *avenges himself* on his *father* on the one hand, while on the other he is *acknowledged* and achieves greatness and fame.

The earliest historical figure with whom this nativity myth is associated is Sargon of Akkad, founder of Babylon (*c.* 2800 BC). It is not without interest, particularly for our purposes, to reproduce here the account he is said to have given of himself:

I am Sargon, the mighty king, King of Akkad. My mother was a vestal, my father I did not know, while my father's brother lived in the mountains. In my city of Azupirani, which lies on the banks of the Euphrates, my mother, the vestal, did conceive me. *She gave birth to me in secret. She laid me in a vessel of reeds*, sealed my doorway with pitch, *and lowered me into the river*, which did not drown me. The river brought me to Akki, creator of water. Akki, creator of water, did in the goodness of his heart lift me out. Akki, creator of water, *brought me up as his own son*. Akki, creator of water, made me his gardener. In my office as gardener Istar took me to her heart, I became king, and for forty-five years I exercised kingship.

The names with which we are most familiar in the list, beginning with Sargon of Akkad, are Moses, Cyrus and Romulus. However, Rank also compiled a long list of hero-figures from literature or legend to whom the same childhood narrative (either in its entirety or in easily recognizable portions) is attributed. They include Oedipus, Carna, Paris, Telephus, Perseus, Heracles, Gilgamesh, Amphion and Zethus, among others.

The source and slant of this myth are familiar to us from Rank's investigations. I need allude to them only briefly. A hero is someone who boldly rebelled against his father and ultimately vanquished him. Our myth traces that struggle back to the primal age of the individual in that it has the child born against the father's wishes and rescued from his evil intentions. Exposure in a small container is an unmistakable symbolic representation of birth, with the container standing for the womb and water for the amniotic fluid. In countless dreams the parent–child relationship is represented as a being drawn out of water or being rescued from water. Where the popular imagination attaches the nativity myth discussed here to an outstanding figure, it is seeking thereby to acknowledge the person concerned as a hero, proclaiming that that person has fulfilled the pattern of a hero's life. The source of the whole fiction, however, is the 'saga'[7] of the child, in which the son reacts to his changing emotional relationships with his parents, notably with his father. The earliest childhood years are dominated by a sublime over-rating of the father, just as in dream and fairy tale the king and queen always only stand for the parents, whereas later on, under the influence of rivalry and real disappointment, the processes of detachment from the parents and the adoption of a critical attitude towards the father set in.[8] The two families of the myth, the exalted and the lowborn, are accordingly both reflections of the child's own family, as it appears to the child in successive periods of its life.

Such explanations might be said to make both the wide currency and the homogeneity of the myth of the hero's birth wholly comprehensible. It is all the more remarkable that the story of the birth and exposure of Moses occupies a special position – even, in one essential respect, conflicting with the others.

We take as our starting-point the two families between which legend has the child's fate find its course. We know that in the analytical interpretation they coincide, being separate only in terms of time. In the typical form of the legend the first family, into which the child is born, is the exalted one, usually belonging to royalty; the second family, in which the child grows up, is the lowly or demeaned one – in line, in fact, with the circumstances on which the interpretation is based. Only in the Oedipus legend is this distinction blurred. The child exposed by one royal family is adopted by another royal couple. One tells oneself it is hardly an accident if in this particular example the original identity of the two families shows through even in the legend. The social contrast between the two families enables myth, which as we know is supposed to highlight the heroic nature of the great man, to perform a second function, one that will assume especial significance with regard to historical figures. It can also be used to give the hero a patent of nobility, elevating him socially. Cyrus, for example, a foreign conqueror so far as the Medes were concerned, became through the medium of the exposition legend the grandson of the Mede king. Similarly with Romulus: if any such person existed, he was an itinerant adventurer, an upstart; legend made him a descendant and heir of the royal house of Alba Longa.

The case of Moses is entirely different. Here the first family, usually the exalted one, is fairly modest. He is the child of Jewish Levites. But the second, poor family in which the hero normally grows up has been replaced by the royal house of Egypt; the princess brings him up as her own son. This deviation from type came as a surprise to many. Eduard Meyer (and others after him) assumed that the legend had originally been different.[9] The pharaoh, he said, had been warned in a prophetic dream[10] that a son of his daughter would bring danger upon him [the pharaoh] and the kingdom. He therefore had the child, after its birth, exposed on the River Nile. However, it was rescued by Jewish folk and brought up as their child. In consequence of 'nationalist motives', as Rank puts it,[11] the legend was reworked into the form in which we know it.

However, a moment's reflection will show that such an original Moses legend, no longer deviating from the others, cannot have existed. The fact is, the legend is either Egyptian or Jewish in origin. The former case rules itself out: Egyptians had no motive for magnifying Moses; he was not a hero for them. So the legend, apparently, was created within the Jewish people, i.e. coupled in its familiar form with the person of the leader. The trouble was, for that purpose it was quite unsuitable, because how were the [Jewish] people going to be served by a legend that made their great man out to be a foreigner?

In the form in which the Moses legend presents itself to us today, it falls short – quite remarkably – of its secret intentions. If Moses is not a royal scion, legend cannot stamp him a hero; if he remains a Jewish child, it had done nothing to exalt him. Only a scrap of the whole legend remains in effect, namely the assurance that, powerful external forces notwithstanding, the child survived, and this feature was then echoed in the childhood narrative of Jesus, with King Herod taking on the role of the pharaoh. This really does leave us free to assume that some subsequent, clumsy editor of the legendary material felt compelled to insert into the story of his hero Moses something akin to the classical, hero-denoting exposition legend that, because of the special circumstances of the case, could not possibly fit there.

With this unsatisfactory and moreover uncertain conclusion our investigation would have to be content, nor would it have done anything to help answer the question of whether Moses was an Egyptian. However, there is another, possibly more promising approach to doing justice to the exposition legend.

Let us go back to the two families of the myth. We know that at the level of analytical exegesis they are identical, at the mythic level they are distinct: one exalted, the other humble. But when it is a historical figure with whom the myth is coupled, there is a third level: that of reality. One family is the real context in which the person, the great man, was actually born and grew up; the other is fictional, concocted by myth in the pursuit of its ends. As a rule, the actual family coincides with the humble, the concocted family with the exalted one. In the case of Moses, there seems to have been something else going on. Now, it may be that the new viewpoint helps to clarify that the first family, the one from which the child is exposed, is in every instance that can be evaluated the invented one, whereas the subsequent family, into which the child is received and in which it grows up, is the real one. If we dare to accept this proposition as a generality to which we also subject the Moses legend, suddenly it becomes clear: Moses is an Egyptian (probably a member of the nobility) whom legend sets out to turn into a Jew. And that would be our result! Exposure in water was in the right position; to match the new tendency, its purpose had (not without some violence) to be diverted: from being a surrender, it became a means of salvation.

However, the divergence of the Moses legend from all others of its kind could be traced to a particular feature of the Moses story. Whereas usually, over the course of his life, a hero raises himself above his humble origins, the man Moses began his hero's existence by stepping down from his elevated position and lowering himself to the children of Israel.

We undertook this small study in the hope that it would supply us with a second, fresh argument for the conjecture that Moses was an Egyptian. As we heard, the first argument (that from the name) has failed to make a decisive impression on many people.[12] The fresh argument (from analysis of the exposition legend) must not necessarily be expected to meet with any better fortune. The objections will no doubt be to the effect that the circumstances of the formation and transformation of legends are indeed too obscure to justify a conclusion such as ours, and that the traditions regarding the heroic figure of Moses will inevitably, in their intricacy, in their contradictions, and with their unmistakable signs of centuries of sustained tendentious reworking and overlaying, thwart all efforts to throw light on the kernel of historical truth behind them. I do not personally share this negative attitude, but nor am I in a position to refute it.

If no greater certainty could be achieved, why have I brought this investigation to the attention of the public in the first place? I am sorry that my justification can likewise do no more than offer pointers. The fact is, if one allows oneself to be carried along by the two arguments set out above and attempts to take seriously the supposition that Moses was a distinguished Egyptian, some very interesting and far-reaching possibilities emerge. With the help of certain by no means fanciful assumptions, one feels one understands the motives that guided Moses in taking his unusual step, and, closely connected with that, one grasps the reasons that may have underlain many of the traits and peculiarities of the legislation and of the religion he gave to the Jewish people and will even be prompted to adopt significant views regarding the emergence of monotheistic religions in general. The trouble is, deductions of such importance cannot be based on psychological probabilities alone. If the Egyptianness of Moses is posited as one historical landmark, at least one other fixed bearing is necessary if the flood of possibilities that emerge are to be shielded from the criticism that they are a product of fantasy and too far removed from reality. Objective proof of the period in which the life of Moses and hence the exodus from Egypt fell might have satisfied that requirement. No such proof has been found, however, so all further conclusions drawn from the view that Moses was an Egyptian had best remain unvoiced.

Notes

1. [This and other quotations from the Book of Exodus are as rendered in the Revised Standard Version (RSV) of the Christian Bible. A recommended (though less accessible) Jewish English translation of the Jewish scriptures, by Rabbi Avraham J. Rosenberg, is published by the Judaica Press in their Tanach Series.]

2. *Jüdisches Lexikon*, founded by Herlitz and Kirschner, vol. IV, Jüdischer Verlag, Berlin 1930.

3. J. H. Breasted, *The Dawn of Conscience*, New York, London, 1933, p. 350. [Freud adds in parenthesis at the end of the quotation: 'The "s" at the end of the name Moses derives from the Greek translation of the Old Testament. It does not belong to the Hebrew, either, where the name is "Moshe".']

4. Ibid., p. 354 [as alleged in Acts 7:22]. Although the conjecture that Moses was an Egyptian has from the earliest times to the present been quite often voiced without reference to the name.

5. ['Der Mythus von der Geburt des Helden']; Issue 5 in the series 'Schriften zur angewandten Seelenkunde' ['Essays in applied psychology'], Fr. Deuticke, Vienna. I have no intention of belittling the value of Rank's independent contributions to this work.

6. [The reference is to the archaeologist Sir Francis Galton and his use of 'composite photographs'.]

7. [*Familienroman*; literally, 'family fiction'.]

8. [I can only conclude (and Strachey seems to agree) that, unusually for Freud, in the original text this sentence contains grammatical errors. Rather than burden the reader with what would here seem to be a somewhat fussy application of the principle of transparency, I adopt a 'reasonable' reading.]

9. [Eduard Meyer, *Die Israeliten und ihre Nachbarstämme* ('The Israelites and their neighbour tribes'), Halle 1906.]

10. Also mentioned in the account by Flavius Josephus.

11. Op. cit. [see note 5 above], p. 80, note.

12. Eduard Meyer, for example, says: 'The name Moses is probably, the name *Pinchas* in the priestly line of Silo [. . .] undoubtedly Egyptian. That

does not of course prove that these lines were of Egyptian descent, but it presumably does prove that they were related to Egypt' (*idem, Die Mosessagen und die Leviten* ['The Moses legends and the Levites'], Berliner Sitzber., 1905, p. 651). The question, of course, is: what kind of relatedness should one be thinking of here?

II

If Moses was an Egyptian . . .

In an earlier article in this journal,[1] I advanced a fresh argument in an attempt to strengthen the supposition that the man Moses, liberator and law-giver of the Jewish people, was not a Jew but an Egyptian. The fact that his name sprang from the Egyptian vocabulary had long been acknowledged, even if it had yet to receive due appreciation; I added that interpretation of the exposition myth associated with Moses imposed the inference that he was an Egyptian whom the requirements of a people sought to turn into a Jew. At the end of my essay I said that significant, far-reaching conclusions followed from the assumption that Moses had been an Egyptian; however, I also said that I was not prepared to champion those conclusions in public since they are based only on psychological probabilities and lack objective proof. The more important the insights gained in this way, I said, the more one is aware of the danger of exposing them to the critical assaults of the outside world without a sure foundation – like a cast-iron figure resting on feet of clay. No probability, however seductive, is proof against error; even if all the parts of a problem appear to fall into place like the pieces of a jigsaw puzzle, it is important to remember that what is probable is not necessarily true and that the truth is not always probable. And anyway, I thought, it was not an inviting prospect to be likened to the Scholastics and Talmudists, who are content to give free rein to their acumen, regardless of how remote their assertions may be from reality.

Despite these misgivings (which weigh as heavily today as they did then), my conflicting motives have made me decide to add this sequel to the original communication. Again, however, this is not the whole picture, nor is it the most important part of the whole picture.

(1)

If, then, Moses was an Egyptian – the first positive thing to proceed from that assumption is a fresh riddle, and one that is not easy to answer. When a people or a tribe² prepares for a major undertaking, the expectation is of course that one of its members will set him or herself up as leader or be elected to fill that role. But it is not easy to guess what appears to have prompted a distinguished Egyptian (a prince, possibly, or a priest, or a high-ranking civil servant) to place himself at the head of a bunch of culturally backward foreign immigrants and with them leave the country. The Egyptian's notorious scorn for what to him was an alien people makes such a process particularly improbable. In fact, I am inclined to believe that this is precisely why even historians who have acknowledged the name to be Egyptian and attributed to the man all the wisdom of Egypt are reluctant to accept the obvious possibility that Moses was an Egyptian.

This first problem is soon joined by a second. Moses, remember, was not only the political leader of the Jews living in Egypt; he was also their law-giver and educator, and he made them serve a new religion – one that bears his name to this day. But is it so easy for an individual to create a new religion? And if someone wishes to influence another person's religion, surely the most natural thing is for him to convert that other person to his own religion? The Jewish people in Egypt were undoubtedly not without some form of religion, and if Moses, who gave them a new one, was an Egyptian, the suspicion is unavoidable that the other, new religion was that of Egypt.

There is one obstacle to that possibility: the fact of the diametrical contrast between the Jewish religion as traced back to Moses and the religion of Egypt. The former [is] a splendidly rigid monotheism; there is but one god,[3] he is unique, all-powerful, inaccessible; humans cannot withstand the sight of him, may make no image of him, may not even speak his name. In the Egyptian religion, [there is] an almost countless host of deities of varying degrees of merit and diverse origins, some of them personifications of great natural powers such as sky and earth, sun and moon, even the occasional abstraction such as *ma'at* (truth, righteousness), or a caricature such as the dwarfish *Bes*, but most of them local deities dating from the time when the land had been split into numerous tribal districts, gods in the form of animals as if they had yet to accomplish the development from the old totem animals, only vaguely distinguished from one another, with few having special functions attributed to them. The hymns in honour of such gods say more or less the same about each, unreflectingly identifying them with one another in a way that we should find hopelessly confusing. Names of gods are used in combinations, with one almost sinking to the status of an adjective of the other; at the height of the 'New Kingdom', for example, the chief god of the city of Thebes was Amon-re, a compound appellation in which the first part stands for the ram-headed god of the city, while Re is the name of the sparrowhawk-headed sun god of On. Magic, ritual acts, spells and amulets dominated the service of these gods as they dominated the daily life of the Egyptian.

Quite a number of these dissimilarities can easily be put down to the conflict of principle between a rigid monotheism and an unbounded polytheism. Others clearly result from the difference in spiritual level, one religion being very close to primitive phases, the other having raised itself up to the heights of sublime abstraction. It may be because of these two factors that the conflict between the Mosaic and Egyptian religions sometimes seems deliberate, as if it has been intentionally heightened; e.g. when the one condemns every kind of magic and magical being with the utmost rigour, while in the other they proliferate with great luxuriance. Or when the Egyptians' insatiable desire to embody their gods in clay, stone and bronze, for which our present-day museums have such cause to be thankful, is contrasted with the harsh ban on portraying any being, living or imagined. But there is yet another difference between the two religions not touched on by the explanations we have floated. No other people in the ancient world did so much to deny the existence of death or took such meticulous care to make an afterlife possible, which is why the god of death, Osiris, who ruled over the beyond, was the most popular and least disputed of all Egypt's gods. The ancient Jewish religion, on the other hand, completely renounced immortality; the possibility of life continuing after death never receives a mention anywhere. And what makes this all the more remarkable is that of course subsequent experience showed belief in an afterlife to be entirely compatible with a monotheistic religion.

We had hoped that the assumption that Moses was an Egyptian would prove fruitful and enlightening in various directions. However, our first deduction from that assumption, namely that the new religion he gave to the Jews was his own, the religion of Egypt, has foundered on an awareness of the difference between, not to say the conflicting nature of the two religions.

(2)

A curious fact of Egyptian religious history that was only acknowledged and appreciated at a late stage offers us a further prospect here. It remains possible that the religion Moses gave to his Jewish people was indeed his own, was *an* Egyptian religion even if it was not *the* Egyptian religion.

In the glorious eighteenth dynasty, under which Egypt first became a world empire, a young pharaoh mounted the throne around 1375 BC who was initially called Amenhotep (IV) like his father but subsequently changed his name – and not just his name. This king undertook to impose a new religion on his Egyptians, one that ran counter to their thousands of years of tradition and all their familiar habits. It was a rigid monotheism, the first experiment of its kind in the history of the world, so far as we know, and with belief in a single god, as it were inevitably, religious intolerance was born, something that had been unknown to the ancient world before – and for a long time afterwards as well. However, Amenhotep's reign lasted only seventeen years; very soon after his death in 1358 BC the new religion was swept away and the heretical monarch's memory ostracized. The ruins of the new residence that he had built and dedicated to his god, together with the inscriptions on the rock-tombs belonging to it, yield the little that we know about him. Whatever we can learn about this remarkable, indeed unique figure merits the greatest interest.[4]

Everything new has to have its preparations and predeterminants in something earlier. The origins of Egyptian monotheism can almost certainly be traced somewhat further back.[5] In the priests' college of the sun temple at On (Heliopolis), tendencies had been in operation for some time towards developing the idea of a universal god and emphasizing the ethical side of his nature. Ma'at, the goddess of truth, order and righteousness, was a daughter of sun god Re. Under Amenhotep III, the father and predecessor of the reformer, worship of the sun god had already begun to receive a boost, probably in opposition to the power of Amon of Thebes, which had become excessive. An ancient name for the sun god, Aton or Atum, was revived, and in this Aton religion the young king found a movement to hand – one that he did not first need to rouse but was able to join.

Around this time, political conditions in Egypt had begun to have a lasting effect on Egyptian religion. Through the military achievements of the great conqueror Thothmes III, Egypt had become a world power; Nubia to the south and Palestine, Syria and part of Mesopotamia to the north had been added to the kingdom. This imperialism came to be reflected in religion as universalism and monotheism. Now that the pharaoh's pastoral writ ran beyond Egypt to embrace Nubia and Syria as well, godhood must also give up its national confines, and since the pharaoh was the sole, absolute ruler of the world as the Egyptian knew it, so too, presumably, must the Egyptians' new deity become. At the same time it was natural that, as the empire expanded its frontiers, Egypt became more open to foreign influences; not a few royal wives were Asian princesses,[6] and there is even a possibility that direct stimuli in the direction of monotheism had penetrated from Syria.

Amenhotep made no secret of his adherence to the sun cult of On. In the two hymns to Aton that have come down to us in rock-tomb inscriptions (and that he is likely to have composed himself), he extols the sun as creator and preserver of all living things inside and outside Egypt with a fervour not found again until many hundreds of years later in the psalms lauding the Jewish god Yahweh. However, he did not content himself with this astonishing anticipation of the scientific discovery of the effect of solar radiation. There is no doubt that he went a step further, worshipping the sun not as a material object but as a symbol of a divine being whose energy was revealed in its rays.[7]

We shall be doing the king less than justice, however, if we regard him simply as the supporter and patron of an Aton religion that had existed before he came along. What he did went much deeper. He added something new, as a result of which the doctrine of the universal god actually became monotheism: he contributed the exclusivity factor. One of his hymns states this in so many words: 'O thou sole god, beside whom there is no other.'[8] And let us not forget that, when it comes to appreciating the new doctrine, recognizing its positive content alone is not enough; almost as important is its negative side, i.e. recognizing what it rejects. It would also be wrong to assume that the new religion was called into being at a stroke, complete and fully equipped, like Athene from the head of Zeus. On the contrary, there is every indication that, during the reign of Amenhotep, it gained in strength gradually, achieving ever-greater clarity, consistency, brusqueness and intolerance. This development is likely to have taken place under the influence of the vigorous opposition that the priests of Amon mounted against the king's reform. In the sixth year of the reign of Amenhotep, the quarrel had reached a point where the king changed his name, part of which was the now discredited divine name of Amon. He called himself henceforth not Amenhotep but Ikhnaton.[9] However, not only did he eradicate the hated god's name from his own name; he also obliterated it from all inscriptions, including those in which it occurred in the name of his father Amenhotep III. Soon after the change of name, Akhenaton left the Amon-dominated Thebes and built himself a new royal seat downstream, which he named Akhetaton (horizon of Aton). The ruins are today known as Tell el-Amarna.[10]

The king's campaign of persecution hit Amon hardest, but not just Amon. All over the kingdom temples were closed, services banned, temple property confiscated. In fact, the king's zeal went so far as to have the old monuments inspected in order to erase the word 'god' from them whenever it was used in the plural.[11] Not surprisingly, these measures taken by Akhenaton provoked a mood of fanatical vindictiveness among the oppressed priesthood and the dissatisfied people that, after the king's death, found free rein. The religion of Aton had not become popular, in all probability remaining confined to a small group around the king's person. What eventually happened to Akhenaton is shrouded in mystery so far as we are concerned. We hear of one or two short-lived, shadowy successors from his family. His son-in-law Tutankhaton was obliged to move back to Thebes and in his name replace the god Aton by Amon. There followed a period of anarchy, until General Horemheb succeeded in restoring order in 1350. The glorious eighteenth dynasty was no more, and at the same time its conquests in Nubia and Asia had been lost. During this murky interlude the old religions of Egypt had been reinstated. The religion of Aton had been abolished, Akhenaton's residence destroyed and plundered, his memory proscribed as that of a criminal.

It is for a specific reason that at this point we pull out a number of points from the negative characterization of the religion of Aton. First, that everything mythical, magical, and having to do with enchantment is excluded from it.[12] Then the way in which the sun god is portrayed: no longer, as formerly, by a small pyramid and a falcon but (almost soberly, one might say) by a disc from which rays emerge, terminating in human hands. Despite all the artistic exuberance of the Amarna period, a different portrayal of the sun god, a personal image of Aton, has not been found, and we can say with some confidence that none will be found.[13] Lastly, the complete silence about the god of death, Osiris, and his kingdom. Neither hymns nor funerary inscriptions tell anything of what perhaps lay closest to the Egyptian's heart. The contrast with the national religion cannot be illustrated more clearly.[14]

(3)

We should now like to venture the conclusion: if Moses was an Egyptian, and if he passed on his own religion to the Jews, it was Akhenaton's religion, the religion of Aton.

Earlier, we compared the Jewish religion with the Egyptian national religion and noted the contrast between the two. Now we are going to draw a comparison between the Jewish religion and that of Aton, expecting to show that the two were originally identical. We know we are not facing an easy task. It is possible that, because of the vindictiveness of the priests of Amon, we know too little about the religion of Aton. The Mosaic religion is familiar to us only in its final version, as established some 800 years later by the post-exile Jewish priesthood. If despite this unpromising material we find individual indications favouring our assumption, we shall be entitled to rate them highly.

There would be a short cut to proving our hypothesis that the Mosaic religion is none other than that of Aton, and that would be by way of a confession of faith, a proclamation. However, I fear we shall be told that this avenue is not practicable. The Jewish creed is of course: 'Schema Jisroel Adonai Elohenu Adonai Echod'. If it is not merely by chance that the Egyptian Aton (or Atum) is reminiscent of the Hebrew word *Adonai* and the Syrian divine name Adonis but as a result of there having existed, in primeval times, a commonality of language and meaning, the Jewish formula might be translated: 'Hear, O Israel, our god Aton (Adonai) is one god'. Unfortunately, I am quite unqualified to answer this question, nor was I able to find much about it in the literature,[15] but no doubt rather more time needs to be invested in this. Incidentally, we shall have to revisit the problems of the divine name later.

The similarities as well as the differences between the two religions are obvious, without making us much the wiser. Both are forms of a rigid monotheism, and we are inclined from the outset to ascribe the elements of agreement between them to this basic character. In some respects, Jewish monotheism takes an even more robust line than Egyptian, e.g. in banning pictorial images altogether. The key difference (apart from the divine name) lies in the fact that the Jewish religion departs completely from the sun-worship that Egyptian religion continued to follow. In making this comparison with Egypt's national religion, we had gained the impression that, apart from the antithesis in principle, there was an element of deliberate contradiction involved in the way the two religions differed. That impression now seems justified if, in the comparison, we replace the Jewish religion by the religion of Aton, which Akhenaton, as we have seen, developed in a spirit of deliberate hostility to the national religion. We had been justifiably surprised by the fact that the Jewish religion refuses to acknowledge the Beyond and life after death, since such a doctrine would be compatible with the most rigid monotheism. That feeling of surprise fades if from the Jewish religion we go back to the religion of Aton and suppose that the rejection had been adopted from this source, because for Akhenaton it was a necessity in combating the national religion, where Osiris, god of death, played a possibly greater role than any god of the upper world. The fact that the Jewish religion and that of Aton agree on this important point is the first powerful argument in favour of our hypothesis. As we shall hear, it is not the only one.

Moses not only gave the Jews a new religion; he can with equal certainty be said to have introduced the custom of circumcision among them. This fact is of crucial importance as regards our problem and has scarcely ever been acknowledged. The biblical account in fact contradicts it repeatedly, on the one hand tracing circumcision back to ancestral times as a sign of the covenant between god and Abraham, on the other hand narrating in a particularly dark passage that god was angry with Moses for neglecting the hallowed practice, that he wished to kill Moses for it, and that

Moses' wife, a Midianite, saved her threatened husband from god's wrath by swiftly performing the operation. However, these are corruptions that ought not to mislead us; we shall come to understand the reasons for them later. The fact remains that, to the question where the Jews got the custom of circumcision from, there is only one answer: from Egypt. Herodotus, the 'father of history', tells us that the custom of circumcision had long been indigenous to Egypt, and his statements have been confirmed by mummy findings and indeed by paintings on tomb walls. No other eastern Mediterranean people, so far as we know, practised this custom; as regards the Semites, Babylonians and Sumerians, it can safely be assumed that they were uncircumcised. As for the inhabitants of Canaan, we have the word of biblical history itself; it is the prerequisite for the outcome of the adventure of Jacob's daughter with the prince of Shechem.[16]

The possibility that the Jews living in Egypt adopted the practice of circumcision by another avenue than in connection with Moses' inauguration of their religion is one we can reject as wholly without foundation. Bearing in mind, then, that circumcision was practised in Egypt as a universal popular custom and assuming for a moment (as is usually done) that Moses was a Jew who wished to liberate his compatriots from slavery in Egypt and lead them towards developing an independent, self-assured national existence outside the country (as in fact happened), what would have been the point of burdening them at the same time with a custom that, as it were, turned them into Egyptians themselves and would inevitably keep their memories of Egypt fresh for ever, whereas all his efforts must in fact have been focused on the opposite, namely that his people should become estranged from the land of their bondage and overcome their yearning for the 'fleshpots of Egypt'? No, the fact that we took as our starting-point and the assumption that we coupled with it are so irreconcilable as to encourage us to conclude: if Moses gave the Jewish people not only a new religion but also the command to practise circumcision, he was not a Jew himself but an Egyptian, in which case the Mosaic religion was probably an Egyptian religion – specifically (because of its contrast to the national cult) the religion of Aton, with which the later Jewish religion also coincides in a number of remarkable respects.

We remarked that our assumption that Moses was not a Jew but an Egyptian creates a fresh riddle. What in a Jew seemed readily understandable behaviour becomes incomprehensible in the case of an Egyptian. However, if we place Moses in the period of Akhenaton and connect him with that pharaoh, the riddle disappears, revealing a possible motivation that answers all our questions. Let us start from the premise that Moses was a distinguished person of high rank, perhaps truly a member of the royal family, as legend would have it. He was undoubtedly aware of his great talents as well as being an ambitious, energetic man; he may even have nourished the aim of one day leading the nation as ruler of the kingdom. Close to the pharaoh, he was a convinced disciple of the new religion, the basic ideas of which he had made his own. When the king died and reaction set in, he saw all his hopes and prospects destroyed. If he was not prepared to abjure his beloved convictions, Egypt had nothing more to offer him; he had lost his fatherland. In this desperate situation, he found an unusual way out. The dreamer Akhenaton had alienated himself from his people and had allowed his international empire to crumble. It accorded with Moses' energetic nature that he should plan to establish a new empire, to find a new people on whom he intended to confer the religion scorned by Egypt for them to worship. It was, as has been recognized, a heroic attempt to challenge fate, compensating himself in two directions for the losses that the Akhenaton disaster had cost him. He may at the time have been governor of that frontier province (Goshen) in which (back in the days of the Hyksos, possibly?) certain Semitic tribes had settled. He chose those tribes to be his new people – a key decision in the history of the world![17] He reached an understanding with them, placed himself at their head, and took care of their emigration 'with a strong hand'. In complete contrast to the biblical tradition, the suggestion is that this exodus was peaceful and passed off without persecution. Moses' authority made it possible, and a central power that might have prevented it was not present at the time.

According to this construct of ours, the exodus from Egypt would fall into the period 1358–1350, i.e. after the death of Akhenaton and *before* the establishment of state authority by Horemheb.[18] The goal of that emigration can only have been the land of Canaan. That was where, following the collapse of Egyptian dominance, hordes of warlike Aramaeans had burst in, conquering and pillaging – and demonstrating in the process where a capable people could get hold of new land. We know of these warriors from letters found in the archives of the ruined city of Amarna in 1887. There they are referred to as Habiru, and the name somehow passed (no one knows how) to the Jewish invaders (Hebrews) who arrived later and who cannot have been meant in the Amarna letters. The peoples living to the south of Palestine (in Canaan) included the tribes that were the nearest relations of the Jews currently leaving Egypt.

The motivation we have guessed at for the exodus as a whole also covers the start of circumcision. We know how people (nations as well as individuals) react to this age-old and now little-understood custom. Those who do not practise it find it disconcerting and have something of a horror of it, while to those who have adopted circumcision it is an object of pride. They feel it raises them up, almost ennobles them, and they look down with scorn on the rest of mankind, whom they regard as unclean. Even today, Turk reviles Christian as an 'uncircumcised dog'. It is possible that Moses, who as an Egyptian was himself circumcised, shared this attitude. The Jews with whom he was quitting the fatherland were intended to furnish him with a better substitute for the Egyptians he was leaving behind. On no account must they be inferior. He wished to make a 'consecrated people' of them, as the biblical text explicitly says, and as a sign of that consecration he introduced among them, too, the practice that made them at least equals of the Egyptians. Also, it cannot have been other than welcome to him if as a result of that sign they were isolated and prevented from interbreeding with the foreign nations amongst which their migration was to bring them, just as the Egyptians themselves had kept themselves apart from all foreigners.[19]

Subsequently, though, Jewish tradition behaved as if weighed down by the conclusion we drew earlier. If it was conceded that circumcision was an Egyptian custom introduced by Moses, that was almost tantamount to an acknowledgement that the religion Moses handed down to them had also been Egyptian in origin. However, there were good reasons for denying that this was true; it followed that the facts regarding circumcision must also be contradicted.

(4)

At this point I expect the objection that I have presented my construct, which places Moses, the Egyptian, in the time of Akhenaton, which attributes his decision to look after the Jewish people to the political circumstances obtaining in the country at the time, which recognizes the religion that he bestowed or imposed upon his protégés as that of Aton (which had just collapsed in Egypt itself) – that I have put forward this whole framework of conjecture with a far greater degree of certainty than the evidence warrants. I believe the objection is unjustified. Having stressed the element of doubt back in my introduction, placing it before the parenthesis, as it were, I may in that case dispense with repeating it at each point within the parenthesis.

Some of my own critical remarks should serve to continue the discussion. The nucleus of our proposition, the dependence of Jewish monotheism on the monotheistic episode in the history of Egypt, has been suspected and intimated by various authors. I dispense with rehearsing these voices here since none of them is able to explain how that influence may have been exerted. If for us it remains bound up with Moses the man, nevertheless possibilities other than the one we prefer ought also to be looked at. There is no reason to assume that the collapse of the official Aton religion brought the trend towards monotheism in Egypt to a complete halt. The priests' college at On, from which it emerged, survived the catastrophe and was able to draw generations following Akhenaton under the spell of its thinking. Moses' action is thus conceivable even if he did not live at the time of Akhenaton and was not personally influenced by him, even if he was merely a disciple or even a member of the On college. This possibility would shift the time of the exodus, bringing it closer to the usually accepted date (in the thirteenth century [BC]); apart from that, though, it has nothing to recommend it. The insight into Moses' motives would be forfeit, and the way in which the exodus may have been facilitated by the anarchy prevailing in the land would no longer be relevant. Subsequent nineteenth-dynasty kings ruled with a rod of iron. All external and internal conditions favouring the exodus come together only in the period immediately following the heretic king's death.

The Jews possess a rich non-biblical literature containing the myths and legends that took shape down the centuries around the wonderful figure of their first leader and the founder of their religion, both throwing light on and obscuring that figure. Scattered amongst such material there may be bits and pieces of valid tradition that never found room in the Five Books.[20] One such legend charmingly describes how the ambitious nature of the man Moses found early expression in his childhood. When on one occasion the pharaoh took him in his arms and playfully held him up in the air, the three-year-old boy snatched the crown from the pharaoh's head and placed it on his own. Alarmed by this omen, the monarch promptly consulted his sages about it.[21] Elsewhere there is mention of the military victories that Moses secured as an Egyptian commander in Ethiopia and, in the same connection, of his fleeing Egypt because he had reason to fear the envy of a certain party at court or of the pharaoh himself. The biblical account itself attributes to Moses a number of features that one is inclined to believe. It describes him as a hot-tempered man, quick to boil over, telling how in his rage he killed the brutal overseer whom he saw beating a Jewish worker, how in his bitterness at the people's backsliding he smashed the tablets of the law that he had brought down from god's mountain – indeed, how in the end god himself punished him for some act of impatience (we are not told what). The fact that such a quality is hardly praiseworthy might make it historically true. Nor can the possibility be discounted that many of the character traits that the Jews incorporated in their early conception of their god (referring to him as jealous, strict and inexorable) were basically drawn from their recollection of Moses, because in reality it was not an invisible god but the man Moses who had brought them out of Egypt.

Another trait ascribed to him has a particular claim to our interest. Moses, we are told, was 'slow of speech', i.e. had a speech impediment or a speech defect, as a result of which, during the alleged negotiations with the pharaoh, he needed the help of Aaron, who is referred to as his brother. Again, this may be historically true, and it would be a welcome contribution towards bringing the great man's physiognomy to life. But it may have a different, more important significance. The account may commemorate, in a slightly corrupted form, the fact that Moses spoke another language, that he could not communicate with his Semitic neo-Egyptians without an interpreter, at least not in the early days of their relations. Further confirmation, then, of the theory that Moses was an Egyptian.

Here, however, our study appears to have come to a temporary halt. From our assumption that Moses was an Egyptian (whether or not it is proven) we are unable, at the moment, to deduce anything further. No historian can regard the biblical account of Moses and the exodus as anything other than a pious fiction that reworked an ancient tradition to suit its own ends. How the tradition originally ran, we do not know; what the corrupting tendencies were is something we should be delighted to guess at, but ignorance of the events of history keeps us in the dark. The fact that our reconstruction does not accommodate many of the showpieces of the biblical narrative such as the ten plagues, the crossing of the Red Sea,[22] and the law-giving ceremony on Mount Sinai is a conflict that does not disconcert us. However, we cannot remain apathetic at finding ourselves contradicting the findings of the sober historical research of our day.

These recent historians, of whom we should like to acknowledge Eduard Meyer as the representative,[23] agree with the biblical account in one crucial point. They too believe that the Jewish tribes from which the people of Israel eventually emerged did at a certain point in time adopt a new religion. However, this event occurred not in Egypt, nor at the foot of a mountain on the Sinai Peninsula, but at a place called Meribath-Kadesh,[24] an oasis noted for its wealth of springs and wells in the area south of Palestine between the eastern end of the Sinai Peninsula and the western edge of Arabia. There they began to worship a god called Yahweh, probably adopting the practice from an Arab tribe, the Midianites, who lived in the vicinity. The presumption is that other neighbouring tribes were also followers of this god.

Yahweh was of course a volcano god. Now, Egypt has no volcanoes, as everyone knows, and the mountains of the Sinai Peninsula were likewise never volcanic; on the other hand, there are volcanoes, active until quite recently, along the western edge of Arabia. So one of those mountains must have been the Sinai-Horeb that was thought to be where Yahweh lived.[25] Despite all the reworkings that the biblical account has undergone, according to Eduard Meyer the original character study of the god can still be reconstructed: he is a sinister, bloodthirsty demon who walks by night and abhors the light of day.[26]

The intermediary between god and people in this founding of a religion is called Moses. He is the son-in-law of the Midianite priest Jethro, whose herds he was guarding when he received the divine call. He is also visited at Kadesh by Jethro, who gives him instructions.

Eduard Meyer says he never doubted that the story of the sojourn in Egypt and of the disaster suffered by the Egyptians contains a grain of historical truth,[27] but having acknowledged the fact he clearly has no idea how to accommodate and evaluate it. The only thing he is prepared to derive from the Egyptians is the practice of circumcision. He bolsters our earlier line of argument with two important clues; first, the fact that Joshua called upon the people to practise circumcision in order 'to remove from their shoulders the mockery of the Egyptians';[28] secondly, the quotation from Herodotus to the effect that the Phoenicians (presumably the Jews)²⁹ and the Syrians in Palestine themselves admit to having learned circumcision from the Egyptians.³⁰ But he has little time for an Egyptian Moses.

The Moses we know is the ancestor of the priests of Kadesh, i.e. a figure of genealogical legend connected with the cult, not a historical figure. Nor (apart from those who accept tradition lock, stock and barrel as historical truth) have any of those who treat him as a historical person yet managed to give him any kind of content, portray him as a concrete individual, or cite anything he created as constituting his historical achievement.³¹

On the other hand, he constantly stresses Moses' connection with Kadesh and Midian: 'The figure of Moses, which is closely associated with Midian and the places of worship in the desert.'³² 'The fact is, this figure of Moses is inextricably bound up with Kadesh (Massa and Meríba), and making him the son-in-law of the Midianite priest sets the seal on this. The connection with the exodus, on the other hand, and the whole account of his early years are entirely secondary and purely the result of fitting Moses into a coherent, consecutive legendary narrative.'³³ He also points out that subsequently the motifs contained in the story of Moses' childhood were all dropped:

Moses in Midian is no longer an Egyptian and grandson of the pharaoh but a shepherd to whom Yahweh reveals himself. In the plague narratives his earlier connections are no longer referred to, easy though it would have been to make effective use of them, and the order to kill Israelite boys is completely forgotten. In the exodus and the destruction of the Egyptians, Moses plays no part at all, he is not even mentioned. The heroic personality presupposed by the childhood legend is entirely lacking in the adult Moses; he is simply, later on, the man of god, a miracle-worker endowed by Yahweh with supernatural powers [. . .].³⁴

There is no disputing the impression that this Moses of Kadesh and Midian, to whom tradition was even able to attribute the setting-up of a 'brazen serpent' as saviour, is quite other than the exalted Egyptian of our reconstruction, who showed the people a religion in which any kind of magic or spell-casting was strictly taboo. It may be that our Egyptian Moses differs from the Midianite Moses no less than the universal god Aton differs from the demon Yahweh inhabiting the divine mountain. And if we give any measure of credence to the findings of recent historians, we have to admit that the thread we were trying to spin from the assumption that Moses was an Egyptian has now broken once again – this time, it would appear, without hope of re-attachment.

(5)

Surprisingly, here too there is a way out. Attempts to see Moses as a figure going beyond the priest of Kadesh, and to confirm the splendour that tradition extols in him, did not cease even after Eduard Meyer ([Hugo] Gressmann being one example). Then in 1922 [Ernst] Sellin made a discovery that crucially affects our problem.[35] He found in connection with the prophet Hosea (second half of the eighth century [BC]) unmistakable evidence of a tradition to the effect that Moses, the founder of the Jewish religion, met a violent end in an uprising by his stubborn and unruly people. At the same time the religion he had inaugurated was rejected. But this tradition is not confined to Hosea, it crops up again in most of the later prophets – in fact, according to Sellin it became the basis of all subsequent messianic expectations. Towards the end of the Babylonian exile there grew up among the Jewish people the hope that the man who had been so shamefully murdered would return from the dead and lead his repentant people (possibly others, too) into the realm of an endless bliss. The obvious connections with a later founder of a religion do not concern us here.

Again, I am of course in no position to determine whether Sellin interprets the prophetic passages correctly. But if he is right, the tradition he has uncovered merits historical credence for the reason that such stories are not lightly fabricated. There is no tangible motive for such things, but if they really did occur it is hardly surprising that people wished to forget them. We need not accept every detail of the tradition. Sellin believes that Shittim in East Jordan is given as the scene of the crime against Moses. We shall soon see that such a locality is unacceptable so far as our reflections are concerned.

We borrow from Sellin the assumption that the Egyptian Moses was struck dead by the Jews and the religion he had introduced abandoned. This enables us to go on spinning our thread without contradicting credible findings of historical research. However, in other respects we venture to keep our distance from the authors and independently 'blaze [our] own trail'. The exodus from Egypt remains our starting-point. A substantial number of people must have left the country with Moses; an ambitious man, he aimed high, and a small group would not have been worth the effort. Probably the immigrants had dwelt in the land long enough to have grown impressively numerous. But we shall certainly not be mistaken if, like the majority of authors, we assume that only a fraction of the later Jewish nation underwent the Egyptian experience. In other words, the tribe returning from Egypt subsequently, having reached the area between Egypt and Canaan, joined forces with other related tribes that had been settled there for some time. The expression of this unification, from which emerged the people of Israel, was the adoption of a new religion shared by all the tribes, that of Yahweh – an event that according to Eduard Meyer took place at Kadesh under Midianite influence. The nation then felt strong enough to undertake its invasion of the land of Canaan. This version of events is not compatible with the catastrophe of Moses and his religion occurring in East Jordan; it must have happened long before the unification.

There is no doubt that very disparate elements came together to form the Jewish people, but the biggest difference between those tribes must have been whether or not they had lived through the sojourn in Egypt and what followed. Regarding this point, the nation may be said to have proceeded from the unification of two components, and it is in line with that fact that, following a brief period of political unity, it split into two separate parts: the kingdom of Israel and the kingdom of Judah. History loves such restorations in which later fusions are reversed and early divisions reappear. The most impressive example of this kind sprang from the Reformation, of course, when after an interval of more than a thousand years it re-exposed the borderline between the part of the Teutonic world that had once been Roman and the part that had remained independent. As regards the Jewish people, we could not prove so faithful a reproduction of the former state of affairs; our knowledge of the period is too uncertain to allow us to state that the northern kingdom reunited those who had long been settled in the land, the southern kingdom those who had returned from Egypt. However, here too the later break cannot be unconnected with the earlier weld. The former Egyptians were likely to have been fewer in number than the others, but culturally they proved the stronger; they exerted a more powerful influence on the further development of the people, because they brought with them a tradition that the others lacked.

Possibly something else as well, something more tangible than a tradition. One of the greatest riddles of Jewish prehistory is the origin of the Levites. They are traced back to one of the twelve tribes of Israel, the tribe of Levi, but no tradition ever ventured to state where that tribe originally lived or which part of the conquered land of Canaan was allotted to them. They occupy the highest priestly positions, yet they are distinct from the priests. A Levite is not necessarily a priest; it is not the name of a caste. Our premise regarding the person of Moses suggests an explanation. It is not plausible that such a great lord as the Egyptian Moses should go over to what to him was a foreign people unaccompanied. He undoubtedly brought with him his retinue, his immediate followers, his scribes, his servants. They were originally the Levites. The traditional assertion that Moses was a Levite looks like a transparent corruption of the facts: the Levites were Moses' people. This solution is supported by something I mentioned in my earlier essay, namely that only among the Levites do Egyptian names crop up again later.[36] Presumably a good many of these people escaped the disaster that befell Moses himself and the religion he had founded. They multiplied in subsequent generations, having merged with the people amongst whom they lived, but they remained faithful to their lord, preserving his memory and keeping up the tradition of his teachings. At the time of the unification with the Yahweh worshippers they formed an influential and (by comparison) culturally superior minority.

I put it forward as a provisional assumption that two generations, possibly as much as a hundred years, elapsed between the death of Moses and the religious inauguration at Kadesh. I see no way of determining whether the Neo-Egyptians (as I should like to call them here for the purposes of distinction), i.e. the returners, encountered their tribal relatives after the latter's adoption of the religion of Yahweh or in fact before. The second alternative may be thought more likely. So far as the end-result is concerned, it makes no difference. What happened at Kadesh was a compromise in which the part played by the Moses tribes is unmistakable.

Here we can again fall back on the evidence of circumcision, which has repeatedly (as our index fossil, so to speak) performed such invaluable service. This custom became law in the Yahweh religion too, and since it is inseparably associated with Egypt its adoption can only have been a concession to the Moses people, who (or the Levites among them) were loath to renounce this symbol of their sanctification. That much they were determined to salvage from their old religion, and they were prepared in exchange to accept the new deity and what the priests of Midian said on the subject. It is possible that they wrested other concessions too. We have already mentioned that Jewish ritual laid down certain restrictions with regard to using the divine name. Instead of 'Yahweh' people had to say 'Adonai'. It is tempting to bring this rule into our context, but it is a conjecture without further foundation. Banning the use of the divine name is known to be an age-old taboo. Why the ban should have been revived particularly in the Jewish religion is not understood; it is not out of the question that this occurred under the influence of a fresh motive. We need not assume that the ban was observed consistently; for forming theophoric personal names, i.e. for combinations, the name of the god Yahweh remained available (Jochanan, Jehu, Joshua). However, with these names it was a slightly different story. Critical biblical scholarship is known to postulate two sources for the Hexateuch.[37] They are referred to as J and E, because one uses the divine name Yahweh,[38] the other talks about Elohim – Elohim, notice, rather than Adonai, but remember what one of our authors said: 'The different names are a clear indication of originally different gods.'[39]

We allowed the retention of circumcision to stand as proof that on the occasion of the religious inauguration at Kadesh a compromise took place. The substance of that compromise may be gathered from the concurrent accounts of J and E, which in this respect therefore go back to a common source (written record or oral tradition). The dominant tendency was to establish the greatness and power of the new god Yahweh. Since the Moses people set such store by their experience of the exodus from Egypt, Yahweh had to be thanked for this act of liberation, and the event came to be embellished in ways that bore witness to the terrible magnificence of the volcano god – the pillar of smoke, for example, which at night turned into a pillar of fire, the storm that for a time dried up the seabed, with the result that the pursuers were drowned by the returning waters. In the process the exodus and the religious inauguration were brought closer together; the long interval separating them was denied; the giving of the law, too, occurred not at Kadesh but at the foot of god's mountain amid signs of a volcanic eruption. However, this account did a serious injustice to the memory of the man Moses; it had been he, after all, not the volcano god, who had liberated the nation from Egypt. Consequently, Moses was due some compensation, and this was found by shifting him to Kadesh or to Sinai-Horeb and setting him up in place of the priests of Midian. That this solution satisfied a second, irrefutably urgent tendency is something we shall discuss later. In this way a balance had been achieved, as it were: Yahweh, who resided on a mountain in Midian, was shifted towards Egypt, and in return the life and work of Moses were moved to Kadesh and as far as Transjordania. There he became fused with the person of the later religious founder, the son-in-law of the Midianite Jethro, to whom he lent his name of Moses. But of this other Moses we have no personal evidence – with the result that he is completely overshadowed by the other, Egyptian Moses. Unless, of course, we point to the contradictions in the character of Moses found in the biblical account. We are told often enough that he was imperious, irascible, even violent, and yet it is also said of him that he was the gentlest and most patient of men. Clearly, these latter qualities would scarcely have suited the Egyptian Moses, who had such great and mighty plans for his people; perhaps they belonged to the other one, the Midianite. I believe that there are grounds for separating the two persons again and assuming that the Egyptian Moses was never at Kadesh and had never heard the name Yahweh, and that the Midianite Moses had never stood on Egyptian soil and knew nothing of Aton. For the purpose of welding the two persons together, it fell to tradition or myth-making to bring the Egyptian Moses to Midian, and from what we have heard there was more than one explanation for this in circulation.

(6)

We are prepared to hear once again the reproach that we have presented our reconstruction of the prehistory of the people of Israel with too great (unjustifiably great) a degree of certainty. The criticism will not affect us deeply since it finds an echo in our own judgement. We are aware ourselves that our structure has its weak points, but it also has its strong ones. Overall, the impression is overwhelming that this study is worth pursuing in the direction taken. The biblical account before us contains precious, indeed invaluable historical information – which, however, has been corrupted by the influence of powerful distorting tendencies and embellished with the products of poetic invention. In the course of our efforts hitherto we have been able to guess at one of those distorting tendencies. The discovery indicates how we should proceed. We need to uncover other such tendencies. Once we have clues to recognizing the distortions they produce, behind them we shall bring out fresh fragments of the true facts of the case.

Let us first listen to critical biblical scholarship, telling us what it can about how the Hexateuch (the five books of Moses plus the Book of Joshua, which are all that concern us here) came into being.[40] The earliest written source is thought to be J, the Yahwist [or Jahwist], whom a recent authority seeks to identify as the priest Ebyatar, a contemporary of King David.[41] A somewhat later date (it is not known how much later) is given for the so-called 'Elohist', who belonged to the Northern Kingdom.[42] Following the collapse of the Northern Kingdom in 722, a Jewish priest combined bits of J and E and made contributions of his own. His compilation is known as 'JE'. In the seventh century, Deuteronomy, the fifth book, is added, allegedly found in the temple in its entirety, brand-new. The period following the destruction of the temple (586), during the exile and after the return, is believed to have produced the revision called the 'priestly codex'; in the fifth century, the work reached its final form and has remained essentially unchanged ever since.[43]

The history of King David and his time is in all probability the work of a contemporary. It is proper historiography, five hundred years before Herodotus, the 'father of history'. One comes some way towards understanding this achievement if one thinks in terms of our assumption of Egyptian influence.[44] It has even been suggested that the Israelites of that early period, i.e. Moses' scribes, had something to do with inventing the first alphabet.[45] To what extent accounts of earlier periods go back to early records or to oral traditions and how much time, in individual instances, lay between event and record are of course things we do not know. But the text we have before us today also tells us enough about its own fate. Two mutually conflicting treatments have left their mark on it. On the one hand it was seized on by versions that, pursuing secret agendas, falsified it, mutilated it, expanded it, and even turned it into its opposite; on the other hand it was ruled over by a tender piety determined to preserve everything it found therein, regardless of whether such findings tallied or conflicted with one another. As a result, almost every part came to include obvious gaps, awkward repetitions, and tangible contradictions – signs that tell us things we were never meant to know. The corruption of a text is not unlike a murder. The problem lies not in doing the deed but in removing the traces of it. It would be good to give *Entstellung*[46] the double meaning to which it is entitled, although nowadays it makes no use of the alternative. The word should mean not only 'to alter the appearance of' but also 'to move to a different place, to shift elsewhere'. It follows that in many cases of textual corruption we can expect to find that what has been suppressed and what has been denied is still there, hidden somewhere, albeit altered in appearance and wrenched out of context. The trouble is, it will not always be easy to recognize.

The corrupting [corrupting/displacing] tendencies we wish to pin down must have had their effect on traditions back in the days before anything was committed to writing. One of these, possibly the most powerful of all, we have already uncovered. As we said, the setting up of the new god Yahweh at Kadesh made it urgently necessary that something be done to glorify him.[47] To be more precise, he had to be installed, room had to be made for him, the traces of earlier religions needed to be removed. As regards the religion of the resident tribes, this appears to have been achieved with complete success, we never hear of it again. With the return-ers, it was not so simple; the exodus from Egypt, the man Moses and circumcision were things they refused to be robbed of. In other words, they had been in Egypt, but they had left it again, and hence-forth all trace of Egyptian influence was to be denied. The man Moses was dealt with by relocating him to Midian and Kadesh and merging him with the Yahweh priest of the religious inauguration. Circumcision, the most serious sign of Egyptian dependency, had to be retained, but not without an attempt being made, despite all the evidence, to uncouple the custom from Egypt. There is only one way to interpret that mysterious, incomprehensibly stylized passage in Exodus[48] (according to which Yahweh had once grown angry with Moses for having neglected circumcision, whereupon his Midianite wife, by swiftly performing the operation, had saved his life!), and that is as a deliberate contradiction of the perfidious facts of the matter. We shall shortly be hearing of another invention designed to render the awkward exhibit harmless.

It can hardly be described as the appearance of a fresh tendency (rather, it is simply a continuation of the earlier one) when efforts become manifest, straightforwardly denying that Yahweh was a new and for the Jews foreign god. To this end the legends of the forefathers of the people, Abraham, Isaac and Jacob, are roped in. Yahweh affirms that he had already been the god of these forefathers; granted, he is himself obliged to concede that they had not worshipped him under his proper name.[49]

He does not go on to say what other name they used. And here is the occasion for a decisive blow against the Egyptian origin of the custom of circumcision. Yahweh had already demanded it of Abraham, appointing it as a symbol of the covenant between himself and Abraham's descendants. However, this was a particularly clumsy invention. As a sign that is intended to set a person apart from others and place him above them, one chooses something not found in the others rather than something that millions can demonstrate identically. An Israelite transplanted to Egypt would have had to acknowledge all Egyptians as fellow members of the covenant, as brothers in Yahweh. The fact that circumcision was indigenous to Egypt is one of which the Israelites who created the text of the Bible cannot possibly have been unaware. The passage from Joshua mentioned by Eduard Meyer unthinkingly admits as much, yet that fact was at all costs to be denied.

The processes of religious myth-building cannot be expected to pay great attention to logical consistency. Otherwise public feeling might have taken justified exception to the behaviour of a divinity who, having concluded an agreement with the ancestors that laid down obligations on both sides, took no notice of the human contracting partners for hundreds of years before abruptly conceiving the idea of treating the descendants to a fresh revelation. Even more disconcerting is the notion of a god suddenly 'choosing' a people, pronouncing them to be his people and himself their god. It is the only such case, I believe, in the history of human religions. Otherwise god and people belong inseparably together; they are a single entity from the outset. Occasionally one hears of a people adopting a different god but never of a god picking a different people. It may be that we come somewhere near understanding this unique event when we think of the relations that existed between Moses and the Jewish people. Moses had lowered himself to the level of the Jews, making them his people; they were his 'Chosen People'.[50]

Bringing in the forefathers also served another purpose. They had lived in Canaan, and their memory was bound up with specific places in that country. Possibly they were themselves originally Canaanite heroes or local divinities who had then been used by the Israelite immigrants for their own prehistory. Referring to them was a way of asserting one's rootedness in the soil and guarding against the odium that attached to the foreign conqueror. It was a shrewd move, claiming that the god Yahweh was simply giving them back what their forefathers had once possessed.

Later contributions to the biblical text continued the deliberate avoidance of any mention of Kadesh. The site of the founding of the new religion now finally became the divine mountain of Sinai-Horeb. The motive for this is unclear; possibly people did not wish to be reminded of the influence of Midian. However, all subsequent distortions, particularly those of the period of the so-called 'priestly codex', serve a different purpose. It was no longer necessary to alter accounts of past events in the desired direction, for this had been done long before. Now people sought to transport present precepts and institutions back into the past, usually justifying them in terms of Mosaic legislation in order to derive their claim to sanctity and legality from that source. No matter that what people were after here was falsifying the image of the past – the process is not without a certain psychological legitimacy. It reflected the fact that, over the course of a long, long period (some 800 years elapsed between the exodus from Egypt and the finalization of the biblical text under Ezra and Nehemiah), the religion of Yahweh had regressed to a position of agreement, possibly even identity with the original religion of Moses.

And that is the essential outcome, the momentous substance of Jewish religious history.

(7)

Of all the occurrences of the dim and distant past that later writers, priests and historians set out to deal with, one stood out, which the most obvious and highest human motives made it necessary to suppress. This was the assassination of the great leader and liberator Moses, which Sellin deduced by guesswork from hints in the prophets. Sellin's version of events cannot be dismissed as fantasy; it is plausible enough. Moses, being of the school of Akhenaton, used the selfsame methods as the king. He gave orders, he imposed his faith on the people.[51] The teachings of Moses may have been even starker than those of his master; he did not need to establish the link with the sun god, the school of On having no meaning for a foreign people. Like Akhenaton, Moses met the fate that awaits all enlightened despots. Moses' Jewish people were no more capable of tolerating so cerebral a religion, of finding in what it had to offer any satisfaction of their needs, than the eighteenth-dynasty Egyptians had been. The same thing happened in both instances: those who were being treated like children and placed under constraint rebelled and threw off the burden of the religion that had been forced on them. But whereas the docile Egyptians waited until fate had removed the divine figure of the pharaoh, the wild Semites took fate into their own hands and got rid of the tyrant themselves.[52]

Nor can it be alleged that the surviving biblical text leaves us unprepared for such a Mosaic exit. The account of the 'wanderings in the wilderness' (which can stand for the period of Moses' dominance) describes a series of grave rebellions against his authority, which were also (at Yahweh's command) put down by bloody chastisement. It is easy to imagine that one such uprising ended differently from the way the text claims. The people's falling away from the new religion is also related in the text, albeit as an episode. This is the story of the Golden Calf, in which, in a neat turn, the breaking of the tablets of the law (to be understood symbolically: 'he broke the law') is shifted on to Moses himself and motivated by a violent temper tantrum on his part.

There came a time when people regretted the killing of Moses and tried to forget it. Clearly this was the case at the time of the encounter at Kadesh. But if the exodus was moved closer to the religious inauguration at the oasis and Moses was given a role here in place of the other, not only had the demands of the Moses people been met but also the painful fact of his violent elimination had been successfully denied. In reality it is most unlikely that Moses could have played a part in what happened at Kadesh, even had his life not been cut short.

We must try at this point to explain how these events related to one another in time. We have placed the exodus from Egypt in the period after the end of the eighteenth dynasty (1350). It may have taken place at that time or a while later, because the Egyptian chroniclers included the ensuing years of anarchy in the reign of Horemheb, who brought those years to an end and ruled until 1315. The next (but also the only) chronological clue is provided by the stela of Merneptah (1225–15), which boasts of the victory over Isiraal (Israel) and the laying waste of its young crops (?). Any use of this inscription is unfortunately debatable; it has been cited as proof that Israelite tribes were already settled in Canaan at the time.[53] Eduard Meyer rightly infers from the stele that Merneptah cannot have been the pharaoh of the exodus, as had been readily assumed up until then. The exodus must have belonged to an earlier period. The question of the pharaoh of the exodus strikes us as an idle one in any case. There was no pharaoh of the exodus because the exodus took place during an interregnum. But nor does the discovery of the Merneptah stele throw any light on the possible date of the unification and adoption of a new religion at Kadesh. All we can say with certainty is: some time between 1350 and 1215. We suspect that, within that century,[54] the exodus fell very close to the first date, what happened at Kadesh not too far from the second. We should like to claim the greater part of that period for the interval between the two events. The fact is, we need quite a long time until, following the assassination of Moses, passions among the returners had cooled and the influence of the Moses people, the Levites, had become as great as the Kadesh compromise presupposes. Two generations (sixty years, say) would suffice for the purpose – but only just. The deduction from the Merneptah stele comes too early for us, and since we acknowledge that in our structure here one assumption rests only upon another, we concede that this debate exposes a weak side to our construct. Unfortunately, everything about the settlement of the Jewish people in Canaan tends to be similarly hazy and confused. We are left, for instance, with the information that the name on the Israel stele does not refer to the tribes whose destiny we are trying to trace and that came together to form the subsequent people of Israel. Even the name Habiru (=Hebrews) passed down to that people from the Amarna period.

Whenever it took place, this unification of the tribes into a nation as a result of the adoption of a common religion, it might easily have become a thoroughly insignificant occurrence so far as world history is concerned. The new religion could have been swept away on the tide of events, Yahweh might have taken his place in the procession of bygone gods seen by the writer Flaubert, and all twelve tribes of his people might have become 'lost', not just the ten that the English-speaking world has spent so long looking for. The god Yahweh, to whom the Midianite Moses brought a new people at that time, is unlikely to have been an exceptional being in any way. A crude, petty local deity, violent and bloodthirsty, he had promised to give his followers a 'land flowing with milk and honey', and he invited them to exterminate its present inhabitants 'with the edge of the sword'. It may be thought surprising that, despite all the revisions of the biblical accounts, so much was left to allow his original nature to show through. It is not even certain that his religion was a true monotheism, disputing the divinity of the gods of other peoples. Probably it was sufficient that their own god was more powerful than all foreign gods. If then in subsequent years everything turned out differently from the way such beginnings suggested, we shall find the reason for that in one fact and one alone. To a section of the people the Egyptian Moses had given a different, more cerebral notion of divinity, the idea of a single god embracing the whole world, a god who was as all-loving as he was all-powerful, who, loathing all ceremonial and magic, held out for men, as their highest goal, a life lived in righteousness and truth. The fact is, however incomplete our records of the ethical side of the religion of Aton, it cannot be without significance that Akhenaton regularly described himself in his inscriptions as 'living in *ma'at*' (truth, righteousness).[55] In the long run it made no difference that the people, probably only a short while later, rejected Moses' teachings and got rid of the man himself. The Mosaic *tradition* survived, and its influence achieved (albeit only gradually, over the course of centuries) what had been denied to Moses himself. The god Yahweh had received undeserved honour when, after Kadesh, Moses' act of liberation was credited to his account, but he had to pay dearly for that usurpation. The shadow of the god whose place he had taken became stronger than him; at the end of this process of development, the essence of the forgotten Mosaic god had come out from behind his essence and advanced into the light. No one doubts that it was only the idea of this other god that enabled the people of Israel to survive all the blows of fate and has kept it alive into our own day.

The part played by the Levites in the final victory of the Mosaic god over Yahweh can no longer be determined. They had stood up for Moses back when the Kadesh compromise had been reached, when the memory of the master whose followers and fellow countrymen they were was still a living thing. In the centuries that followed they had merged with the people or with the priesthood, and it had been the primary function of the priests to develop and supervise the ritual as well as to guard the holy scriptures and edit them to suit their purposes. But were not all sacrificial practices and all ceremonial basically only magic and sorcery of the kind that Moses' old teachings had unconditionally rejected? There then emerged from among the people an unbroken line of men who were not connected with Moses by descent but were in thrall to the great and powerful tradition that had gradually grown up behind the scenes, and it was these men, the prophets, who tirelessly preached the ancient Mosaic doctrine that god scorned sacrifice and ceremonial, demanding only faith and a life lived in truth and righteousness (*'ma'at'*). The efforts of the prophets had lasting success; the teachings with which they reinstated the old faith became the permanent substance of the Jewish religion. It is honour enough for the Jewish people that it was able to preserve such a tradition and produce men who lent it a voice, even if the stimulus had come from outside, from a great foreigner.

I should not feel confident with this account could I not appeal to the opinions of other, more expert scholars who see the importance of Moses to Jewish religious history in the same light, even if they do not accept his Egyptian origin. Sellin, for example, writes:

So we must now imagine the true religion of Moses, namely belief in the single moral god whom he proclaims, as having been from the outset the possession of a small group within the nation. From the outset we must not reckon to come across it in the official cult, in the religion of the priests, or in the faith of the people. We can only, from the outset, expect that occasionally, here and there, a spark from the spiritual fire that he once lit will re-ignite, that his ideas will not have died out but will very quietly, here and there, have affected belief and morals until such time as, sooner or later, under the stimulus of particular experiences or of persons particularly in thrall to his spirit, they once again burst forth more strongly and gained influence over broader sections of the population. It is from this standpoint that the religious history of ancient Israel should be viewed from the outset. Anyone seeking to reconstruct the Mosaic religion, say, on the basis of the kind of religion that according to the historical documents we find in the life of the people in the first five centuries in Canaan would be committing the gravest methodological error.[56]

Volz is even clearer, writing that 'Moses' towering achievement was at first understood and implemented only very feebly and scantily, until over the centuries he imposed himself more and more, eventually finding like minds in the great prophets, who continued the solitary man's work'.[57]

That would bring me to the end of my study, the sole purpose of which has after all been to insert the figure of an Egyptian Moses into the context of Jewish history. Putting our conclusion in the shortest possible form of words, to the familiar dualisms of that history (*two* peoples coming together to form the nation, *two* kingdoms into which that nation divides, *two* names for god in the source writings of the Bible) we add two new ones: *two* religious inaugurations, the first forced out by the second but later emerging from behind it and coming victoriously to the fore, *two* religious inaugurators, both of whom went by the same name, Moses, and whose personalities we need to separate. And all those dualisms are inevitable consequences of the first, namely that one component of the people had been through what has to be described as a traumatic experience that the other had been spared. Beyond that, there is a very great deal that still needs to be discussed, explained and asserted. In fact, only then could interest in our purely historical study be justified. What accounts for the true nature of a tradition and what gives it its special power, how impossible it is to deny the personal influence of individual great men on world history, how heinous a crime is committed against the wonderful variety of human existence when the only motives people are prepared to recognize are those relating to material needs, from what springs do some ideas, particularly religious ideas, draw the strength to subjugate individuals and nations alike – studying all these things with particular relevance to Jewish history would be a tempting task. Such a continuation of my work would tie in with comments I set down twenty-five years ago in *Totem and Taboo*. However, I no longer feel I have the strength to accomplish it.

Notes

1. [Sigmund Freud,] 'Moses ein Ägypter', in *Imago* XXIII (1937), issue 1 [i.e. the first part of the present essay].

2. We have no idea what numbers were involved in the exodus from Egypt.

3. [On the question of whether or not to capitalize the word 'god', even in a monotheistic context, in an English translation of Freud, may I refer the reader to my note 7 ('Compulsive actions . . .') on page 13.]

4. 'The first individual in human history,' Breasted calls him [J. H. Breasted, *A History of Egypt*, London 1906].

5. What follows is based mainly on the accounts given by J. H. Breasted in his *History of Egypt*, op. cit, [see note 4 above] and *The Dawn of Conscience*, op. cit. [see note 3, section 1] as well as on the relevant sections of *The Cambridge Ancient History*, vol. II.

6. Possibly including Amenhotep's beloved consort Nofretete [Nefertiti].

7. As Breasted puts it: 'But however evident the Heliopolitan origin of the new state religion might be, it was not merely sun-worship; the word Aton was employed in the place of the old word for "god" (*nuter*) and the god is clearly distinguished from the material sun' (J. H. Breasted, *A History of Egypt*, op. cit. [see note 4 above], p. 360). 'It is evident that what the king was deifying was the force by which the Sun made himself felt on earth' (*idem, The Dawn of Conscience*, op. cit. [see section 1, note 3 above], p. 279). A similar assessment of a form of words honouring the god is found in Adolf Erman, *Die Ägyptische Religion* (1905): 'They are [. . .] words intended to express as abstractly as possible that it is not the star itself that is worshipped but the being who reveals himself in it.'

8. J. H. Breasted, *A History of Egypt*, op. cit. [see note 4 above], p. 374.

9. With this name I am following the English spelling (otherwise it would be *Akhenaton*). The king's new name means more or less the same as his old one: 'god is pleased'. Compare our [German] names Gotthold, Gottfried. [Actually, 'Akhenaton' is the most widely accepted English transliteration, so this is the one used in the rest of this essay.]

10. It was there, in 1887, that the correspondence of the Egyptian kings with their friends and vassals in Asia (so important for our knowledge of history) was found.

11. J. H. Breasted, *A History of Egypt*, op. cit. [see note 4 above], p. 363.

12. In *The Life and Times of Akhnaton* (1922) [new and revised edition; first edition, 1910], Arthur Weigall says that Akhenaton [Weigall uses the transliteration 'Akhnaton'] would not hear of a hell against whose horrors people were supposed to seek protection through innumerable magic spells: 'Akhnaton flung all these formulae into the fire. Djins, bogies, spirits, monsters, demigods, demons, and Osiris himself with all his court, were swept into the blaze and reduced to ashes' (pp. 120–1).

13. 'Akhnaton did not permit any graven image to be made of Aton. The

True God, said the king, had no form; and he held to this opinion through-out his life' (A. Weigall, *The Life and Times of Akhnaton*, op. cit. [see note 12 above], p. 103).

14. Adolf Erman, *Die Ägyptische Religion*, op. cit. [see note 7 above], p. 70: 'Nothing more was to be heard of Osiris and his realm.' In Breasted's words: '*Osiris is completely ignored.* He is never mentioned in any record of Ikhnaton or in any of the tombs at Amarna' (*The Dawn of Conscience*, op. cit. [see section 1, note 3 above], p. 291).

15. Only a couple of passages in Arthur Weigall, *The Life and Times of Akhnaton*, op. cit. [see note 12 above]: ['. . . at noon he was Ra; and at sunset he took the name of Atum, a word probably connected with the Syrian Adon (*sic*) . . .' This appears between square brackets because for some reason Freud himself cites only the page reference (p. 12) for this quotation. I am grateful to Frederick W. Bauman of the Manuscript Division of the Library of Congress, Washington DC, for his help over this and other problems concerning Freud's original manuscript of this text.] 'The god Atum, the aspect of Ra as the setting sun, was, as has been said, probably of common origin with Aton, who was largely worshipped in North Syria; and the foreign queen with her retinue may therefore have felt more sympathy with Heliopolis than with Thebes' (p. 19).

16. If we treat biblical tradition so high-handedly and arbitrarily as to use it for confirmation where it suits us and to reject it out of hand where it goes against us, we are well aware that we shall expose ourselves to seri-ous methodological criticism as a result, weakening the evidential value of our remarks. However, it is the only way to deal with material in connec-tion with which one knows for sure that its reliability has been seriously impaired by the influence of corrupting tendencies. One hopes to acquire a degree of justification at some later point by tracking down those secret motives. The fact is, no certainty can be achieved here, and we might add in passing that all other authors have done the same. [The reference in the text is to Genesis 34.]

17. If Moses was a high-ranking civil servant, it is easier for us to under-stand the leadership role that he assumed among the Jews; if he was a priest, the obvious course was for him to figure as founder of a religion. In either case he would have been pursuing his existing occupation. A prince of the royal blood might easily be both governor and priest. In the account given by Flavius Josephus, who accepts the exposition myth but appears to be aware of other traditions than biblical ones, Moses was an Egyptian general who fought a victorious campaign in Ethiopia (*Antiquities of the Jews*).

18. That would be something like a century earlier than is assumed by most historians, who place it in the nineteenth dynasty under Merneptah. Possibly slightly later, because the official record appears to have included the Interregnum in the reign of Horemheb.

19. Herodotus, who visited Egypt around 450 BC, includes in the account of his travels a description of the Egyptian people that bears an astonishing similarity to familiar features of later Jewry: 'They are altogether, in every respect, more pious than other people, from whom they are also distinguished by many of their customs. By circumcision, for instance, which they were the first to introduce, doing so for reasons of cleanliness; also by their abhorrence of pigs, which undoubtedly has to do with the fact that Set wounded Horus in the guise of a black pig, and lastly (and most especially) by their reverence for cows, which they would never eat nor sacrifice, for that would give offence to the cow-horned Isis. That is why no Egyptian man or woman would ever kiss a Greek or use a Greek's knife, roasting-spit, or bowl or eat of the flesh of an otherwise clean ox that had been cut with a Greek knife [. . .] they looked down in haughty narrow-mindedness on other peoples who were unclean and less close to the gods than they' (taken from Adolf Erman, *Die Ägyptische Religion*, op. cit. [see note 7 above], pp. 181 ff.).

We ought not, of course, to overlook parallels in this connection in the life of the Indian people. Who, for that matter, prompted the Jewish writer Heinrich Heine in the nineteenth century AD to complain about his religion as 'the plague we dragged along with us from the Nile Valley, the unhealthy ancient Egyptian faith'?

20. [Otherwise known as the Pentateuch, a collection later adopted as the first five books of the Christian Old Testament.]

21. The same anecdote (in a slightly amended form) occurs in Josephus [see section 1, note 10].

22. [In German, *das Schilfmeer* or 'the Reed Sea'. The 'sea' of Exodus 14 (actually called 'the Red Sea' in English translations of Exodus 15:4 and traditionally referred to by that name) is widely accepted to have been a different topographical feature from what we now know as 'the Red Sea'.]

23. Eduard Meyer, *Die Israeliten und ihre Nachbarstämme* ['The Israelites and their neighbour tribes'], 1906.

24. [Freud calls it 'Meribat-Qadeš'.]

25. There are places in the biblical text where Yahweh is still referred to as having come down from Sinai to Meribath-Kadesh.

26. Eduard Meyer, op. cit. [see note 23 above], pp. 38, 58.

27. Ibid., p. 49.

28. [Cf. Joshua 5:9 (RSV).]

29. [One wonders why Freud made this particular assumption. Meyer's assumption to the same effect is made in a note placed after '. . . die Phoeniker und die Syrer in Palälestina . . .']

30. Eduard Meyer, op. cit. [see note 23 above], p. 449 [Herodotus II: 24].

31. Ibid., p. 451.

32. Ibid., p. 49.

33. Ibid., p. 72.

34. Ibid., p. 47.

35. [Ernst] Sellin, *Mose und seine Bedeutung für die Israelitisch-jüdische Religionsgeschichte* ['Moses and his importance in Israelite-Jewish religious history'], 1922.

36. This assumption accords well with Yahuda's account of the Egyptian influence on early Jewish literature. See [Abraham Shalom] Yahuda, *Die Sprache des Pentateuch in ihren Beziehungen zum Ägyptischen*, 1929 [translated into English by W. Montgomery as *The Language of the Pentateuch*, London 1933].

[Incidentally, Freud is evidently mistaken in believing that this was 'something I mentioned in my earlier essay' – if, that is, he is referring to what is reproduced as the first part of the present text.]

37. [The five books of Moses plus the Book of Joshua.]

38. [Sometimes transliterated as 'Jahveh', and in any case rendered by Freud as *Jahve*.]

39. [Hugo] Gressmann ['Mose und seine Zeit' in W. Bossuet and H. Gunkel, *Forschungen zur Religion und Literatur des Alten und Neuen Testaments* . . ., new series, Issue 1, 1903], p. 54.

40. *Encyclopaedia Britannica*, eleventh edition, 1910. Article: Bible.

41. See [Elias] Auerbach, *Wüste und Gelobtes Land* ['Desert and Promised Land'], 2 vols, Berlin 1932.

42. Jahwist and Elohist were first distinguished by Astruc in 1753.

43. It is an established historical fact that the definitive fixing of the Jewish type was the outcome of the reforming work of Ezra and Nehemiah in the fifth century BC – i.e. after the exile, during the period (favourable to the Jews) of Persian rule. By our calculations, some 900 years had then elapsed since the appearance of Moses. In that reform, serious attention was paid to the regulations aimed at sanctifying the people as a whole, their separation from those living around them was implemented by the ban on intermarriage, and the Pentateuch, the actual 'Book of the Law', received its final form with the completion of the revision known as the 'priestly codex'. However, it seems established that the reform, rather than introducing any fresh tendencies, simply took up and consolidated earlier ideas.

44. See A. S. Yahuda, op. cit. [see note 36 above].

45. If they were under pressure from the ban on images, they even had a motive for abandoning hieroglyphic picture-writing as they prepared their written characters for giving expression to a new language. See also [Elias] Auerbach, op. cit. [see note 41 above], p. 142.

46. [Literally 'displacement', but here translated conventionally as 'corruption' or 'distortion'.]

47. [The reader is respectfully asked to bear in mind that, German being a gendered language, German pronouns associated with the masculine noun *Gott* carry a primarily grammatical connotation; they are less loaded with the 'sexual' baggage that readers of English are used to wrestling with.]

48. [Exodus 4:24–6.]

49. While this makes the restrictions on the use of the new name no easier to understand, it does make them more suspect.

50. Yahweh was undoubtedly a volcano god. For inhabitants of Egypt, there was no reason to worship him. I am certainly not the first to have been struck by the similarity of sound between the name Yahweh and the root of that other divine name Ju-piter (Jove). The name Jochanan, formed in conjunction with the abbreviation of the Hebrew Yahweh (it is like [the German] Gotthold, while the Punic equivalent is Hannibal), became, in the forms Johann, John, Jean, Juan, the most popular forename in European Christendom. By translating it as Giovanni and calling one of the days of the week Giovedi, the Italians bring back to light a similarity that may or may not be highly significant. The possibilities this opens up are far-reaching but at the same time deeply insecure. Apparently, in those dim centuries of which history knows so little, the countries ringing the eastern basin of the Mediterranean were the scene of frequent, violent volcanic eruptions that must have made the most powerful impression on the local inhabitants. [Sir Arthur] Evans supposes that the final destruction of the palace of Minos at Knossos was itself the result of an earthquake. On the island of Crete at that time, as probably throughout the Aegean world, it was the great mother goddess that was worshipped. The perception that she was unable to shield her dwelling against the assaults of a higher power may have contributed towards her having to make way for a male divinity, and here the volcano god had the strongest claim to take her place. Zeus, after all, is still the 'earth-shaker'. There can be little doubt that those early 'dark ages' saw the replacement of mother goddesses by male gods (who may originally have been sons). Particularly impressive is what happened to Pallas Athene, doubtless the local form of the mother goddess, who was demoted by the religious unheaval to the position of daughter, had her own mother wrested from her, and found herself, through her enforced virginity, permanently excluded from motherhood.

51. In those days, of course, any other form of influence was scarcely possible.

52. It is truly remarkable how little, in all the millennia of Egyptian history, is heard of the violent removal or assassination of a monarch. Comparing this situation with Assyrian history, for example, only increases one's amazement. It is possible, of course, that this is because the Egyptians used historiography exclusively for official purposes.

53. Eduard Meyer, op. cit. [see note 23 above], p. 222.

54. [It is not clear why Freud uses the word *Jahrhundert* to refer to a period of 135 years, but see below, p. 264, note 3.]

55. His hymns stress not only the universality and oneness of god but also his loving care for all created beings, inviting joy in nature and enjoyment of its beauty. See also J. H. Breasted, *The Dawn of Conscience*, op. cit. [see section 1, note 3 above].

56. Ernst Sellin op. cit. [see note 35 above], p. 52.

57. Paul Volz, *Mose*, Tübingen, 1907, p. 64.

III

Moses, His People, and Monotheistic Religion
Part One
Foreword I
(before March 1938)

With the boldness of one who has nothing or not much to lose, I propose to set about breaking a well-founded resolution for the second time and follow up the two treatises on Moses in *Imago* (vol. XXIII, nos. 1 and 3) with the endpiece then held back. I closed with a protestation to the effect that I knew my strength would no longer suffice for the purpose; I was referring, of course, to the weakening of the creative faculties that accompanies advanced age,[1] but I also had another obstacle in mind.

We are living in particularly remarkable times. We find to our surprise that progress has forged an alliance with barbarism. Soviet Russia has embarked on an attempt to raise some hundred million oppressed people to superior forms of existence. In a bold move they have been deprived of the 'opiate' of religion and in a wise one given a sensible measure of sexual freedom, but in the process they have been subjected to the cruellest coercion and robbed of any chance of freedom of thought. With similar violence the Italians are being trained up to orderliness and a sense of duty. It comes as something of a relief from an oppressive anxiety to see that in the case of the German people the relapse into almost prehistoric barbarism is able to proceed even without recourse to any forward-looking idea. At any rate, as things have turned out, the conservative democracies have today become the guardians of cultural progress, and curiously the Catholic church (of all institutions!) is mounting a powerful defence against the spread of this threat to civilization. The Catholic church, hitherto the implacable enemy of freedom of thought and of progress towards the discovery of truth!

Here[2] we are living in a Catholic country under the protection of that church, unsure how long such protection will last. However, so long as it is in place we naturally have misgivings about doing something that will inevitably arouse the church's enmity. This is not cowardice but caution; the new enemy, whom we are anxious not to serve in any way, is more dangerous than the old, with whom we have already learned to coexist. The psychoanalytical research that we cultivate is in any case the object of suspicious attention on the part of Catholicism. We are not going to claim that this is so without justification. If our work leads us to a conclusion that reduces religion to a human neurosis and explains its awesome power in the same way as the neurotic compulsion afflicting individual patients of ours, we are sure that we shall bring down upon our heads the greatest displeasure of the powers that rule our lives. Not that we should have anything new to say, anything we had not said quite clearly a quarter of a century ago. However, that has since been forgotten, and it cannot remain without effect if we say the same again today, illustrating it in terms of an example that holds true for all religious inaugurations. It would probably lead to our being banned from practising psychoanalysis. After all, the church is no stranger to such violent methods of repression; it merely feels it as an invasion of its prerogatives that others should deploy them too. The fact is: psychoanalysis, which in the course of my long life has travelled everywhere, still has no home that would be of more value to it than the city in which it was born and grew up.

I do not simply think, I know that I shall permit this other obstacle, namely the external danger, to prevent me from publishing the final part of my study on the subject of Moses. I have tried once again to get rid of the problem by telling myself that my fear is based on an exaggerated view of my own personal importance. Probably the powers that be will be quite indifferent to what I choose to write about Moses and the origin of monotheistic religions.

However, I have no confidence in my judgement here. A more likely outcome, it seems to me, is that malice and sensationalism will make up for what I lack in prestige in the eyes of my fellow men. So I shall not publish this work, but that need not keep me from writing it. Particularly since I had already put it down on paper two years ago now, with the result that I need only revise it and append it to the two earlier essays. May it then be preserved in obscurity until at length the day dawns when it can venture with impunity into the light, or until someone who professes the same conclusions and opinions can be told: there was someone there before, in darker times, who thought as you do.

Notes

1. I do not share the view of my contemporary, Bernard Shaw, that people would only do something worthwhile if they were able to live for three hundred years. Prolonging the span of human existence would achieve nothing; many other radical changes would need to be made to people's living conditions.
2. [Freud was not persuaded to leave Vienna until June 1938.]

Foreword II
(in June 1938)

The quite exceptional difficulties that I was under as I wrote this study bearing on the person of Moses (internal misgivings coupled with external constraints) have led to this third, concluding essay being prefaced by two different forewords that are mutually contradictory – indeed, cancel each other out. The reason is that in the brief period that separates them the writer's external circumstances changed radically. I was then living under the protection of the Catholic church and feared that as a result of my publication I should lose that protection and the followers and students of psychoanalysis in Austria would be barred from working. And then, abruptly, came the German invasion; Catholicism, to borrow a phrase from the Bible, proved a 'broken reed'. Certain that I should now be persecuted not only for the way I think but also on account of my 'race', I joined a large number of friends in leaving the city that since early childhood, for the space of seventy-eight years, had been my home.

I found the most cordial welcome in beautiful, free, big-hearted England. Here I now live, an honoured guest, able to breathe once again now that that pressure has been removed and I may speak and write (I nearly said: think) as I wish or must. I make bold to lay the last section of my essay before the public.

No more external constraints, or at least not of the sort one might shy away from. In the few weeks of my sojourn here I have received countless greetings from friends who were delighted to have me with them and from strangers, even outsiders, who simply wished to voice their gratification at the fact that I have here found freedom and security. And there also, with a frequency surprising to a foreigner, came letters of a different kind, concerned about the state of my soul, seeking to show me the ways of Christ and enlighten me with regard to the future of Israel.

The good people who wrote in this vein cannot have known much about me; but when this work about Moses becomes, through translation, familiar to my new fellow countrymen, I anticipate that I shall also, so far as a number of others are concerned, forfeit not a little of the sympathy they now show me.

With regard to the internal problems, political upheaval and a change of domicile have altered nothing. I still have a feeling of uncertainty in the face of my own work; I miss the sense of oneness and solidarity that ought to exist between the author and his book. It is not that I lack conviction of the rightness of the end-result. I acquired that a quarter of a century ago, in 1912, when I wrote the book *Totem and Taboo*, and since then it has only grown stronger. Since that time I have no longer been in any doubt that the only way to understand religious phenomena is by using the model of the neurotic symptoms of the individual with which we are so familiar to see such phenomena as recurrences of long-forgotten, meaningful events in the prehistory of the human family; I am convinced that in fact they owe their compulsive nature to that source, so that it is by virtue of their content of *historical* truth that they affect human beings. My uncertainty arises only when I ask myself whether I have successfully demonstrated those principles in respect of my chosen example of Jewish monotheism. My critics see this essay based on the man Moses as a dancer balanced on the tip of a single toe. Had I not been able to call upon a particular analytical interpretation of the exposition myth and from there reach across to Sellin's conjecture regarding how Moses met his end, the whole thing would inevitably have remained unwritten. Still, here goes.

I begin by summarizing the findings of my second, purely historical study of Moses. Here they will not be subjected to any further criticism, since they form the premise of the psychological discussions that proceed from them and keep referring back to them.

A

The historical premise

The historical background to the events that have captivated our interest is therefore as follows:

As a result of the conquests of the eighteenth dynasty, Egypt has become an empire. The new imperialism is reflected in the development of the religious ideas not of the nation as a whole but certainly of its dominant, intellectually aware upper class. Under the influence of the priests of the sun god at On (Heliopolis), possibly reinforced by stimuli from Asia, the idea arises of a universal god Aton, to whom restriction to a single country and people no longer attaches. With the young Amenhotep IV, a pharaoh comes to power whose highest interest lies in developing this concept. He elevates the religion of Aton to national status, making this universal god the *One God*; everything told about other gods is deception and lies. With superb implacability he spurns all the seductions of magical thought, rejecting an illusion particularly dear to the Egyptians, namely that of life after death. In an amazing anticipation of later scientific discoveries, he sees the energy of the sun's rays as the source of all life on earth and worships it as symbolizing the power of his god. He takes a pride in his enjoyment of creation and in his life in *ma'at* (truth and righteousness).

This is the first and possibly purest instance of a monotheistic religion in human history; a deeper understanding of the historical and psychological circumstances of its emergence would be of inestimable value. However, care was taken to ensure that not too much information about the religion of Aton should come down to us. Even under Akhenaton's feeble successors, everything that he had created collapsed. The revenge of the priesthoods he had suppressed now raged against his memory, the religion of Aton was abolished, and the seat of the ruler now branded a sinner was sacked and plundered. Around 1350 BC, the eighteenth dynasty died out; following a period of anarchy, order was restored under a commander named Horemheb, who reigned until 1315. Akhenaton's reformation, it seemed, was an episode doomed to oblivion.

That much is history, and it is at this point that our hypothetical sequel begins. Among the people close to Akhenaton was a man who like many others at the time may have borne the name Thothmes.[1] The name itself is not particularly important – only that its second element must have been *mose*. He was a high-ranking, devout adherent of the religion of Aton, but in contrast to the brooding king he was forceful and passionate. For this man, the passing of Akhenaton and the abolition of his religion meant the end of everything he had looked forward to. Only as a renegade or outcast could he go on living in Egypt. He may, as governor of the border province, have come into contact with a Semitic tribe that had migrated thither several generations earlier. Distressed, disappointed and alone, he turned to these foreigners, seeking among them some recompense for what he had lost. He chose them as his people and tried to realize his ideals using them as a medium. Having quit Egypt with them, accompanied by his own retinue, he sanctified them with the sign of circumcision, gave them laws, and introduced them to the teachings of the religion of Aton that the Egyptians had just rejected. It may be that the rules that this man Moses gave his Jews were even harsher than those of his lord and teacher Akhenaton; it may also be that he abandoned the attachment to the sun-god of On to which the latter had clung.

For the exodus from Egypt we have to posit the post-1350 inter-regnum period. The following periods, up until the completed seizure of the land of Caanan, are especially opaque. Out of the obscurity that the biblical account leaves here or rather created here, modern historical research has been able to pluck two facts. The first, discovered by Ernst Sellin, is that the Jews, who, even according to the testimony of the Bible, were stubborn and unruly towards their law-giver and leader, one day rose up against him, struck him dead, and threw off the religion of Aton that he had imposed on them as the Egyptians had done before them. The other, which Eduard Meyer demonstrated, is that these Jews who had returned from Egypt later united with other, closely related tribes in the area between Palestine, the Sinai peninsula and Arabia, and that they there, in a well-watered locality called Kadesh, under the influence of the Arab Midianites, adopted a new religion, worship of the volcano god Yahweh. Shortly afterwards they were ready to burst into and conquer Canaan.

How these two events related to each other and to the exodus from Egypt in time is extremely uncertain. The next historical reference point is provided by a stele of the pharaoh Merneptah (d. 1215), which in an account of military campaigns in Syria and Palestine lists 'Israel' among the defeated. Taking the date of that stele as a *terminus ad quem* leaves something like a hundred years (from after 1350 to before 1215) for the whole sequence of events, beginning with the exodus. However, it is possible that the name Israel did not as yet refer to the tribes whose fate we are tracing and that in reality we have a longer period of time at our disposal. The settlement of what became the Jewish people in Canaan was surely no swift conquest but a process of successive thrusts extending over a prolonged period. Freeing ourselves from the constraint of the Merneptah stele makes it that much easier for us to regard a generation (thirty years) as the time of Moses,[2] subsequently allowing at least two generations (though probably more) to elapse before the unification at Kadesh;[3] the interval between Kadesh and the departure for Canaan need be only a short one; as the previous treatise showed, Jewish tradition had good reason to foreshorten the interval between the exodus and the founding of a new religion at Kadesh; the reverse best serves the interests of our account.

But that is all history, an attempt to fill in the gaps in our historical knowledge, some of it a repetition of the second treatise in *Imago*. Our interest is in the fates of Moses and his teachings, to which the rebellion of the Jews had only apparently put an end. We recognized from the Jahwist's report, which was written around 1000 but was certainly based on earlier records, that with the unification and religious inauguration at Kadesh a compromise emerged, the two parts of which are still clearly distinguishable. One party was concerned only to deny the newness and strangeness of the god Yahweh and enhance his claim to the nation's devotion; the other was unwilling to abandon to him precious memories of the liberation from Egypt and the splendid figure of Moses the leader and did in fact succeed in accommodating both the fact and the man in the new account of prehistory, at least retaining the outward sign of the religion of Moses, namely circumcision, and possibly pushing through certain restrictions in the use of the new divine name. We pointed out that the advocates of these demands were the descendants of Moses' people, the Levites, separated only by a few generations from Moses' own contemporaries and fellow nationals and still bound to his memory by vivid reminiscences. The poetically embellished accounts that we attribute to the Jahwist and his later rival, the Elohist, were the tombs in which the true tidings of those early things, of the nature of the Mosaic religion and the violent removal of the great man, now concealed from the awareness of later generations, were to find eternal rest, so to speak. And if we have guessed the process correctly, there is nothing more mysterious about it than that; but it might very well have meant the final end of the Moses episode in the history of the Jewish people.

What is extraordinary is that this is not in fact the case, that the strongest effects of that experience of the people were to become apparent only subsequently; only bit by bit, over the course of many centuries, did they force their way into reality. In terms of character, Yahweh is unlikely to have differed greatly from the gods of the peoples and tribes living round about; he vied with them, of course, as the peoples themselves fought amongst one another, but in all probability a Yahweh-worshipper of the time would no more have thought of denying the existence of the gods of Canaan, Moab, Amalek, etc. than of denying the existence of the peoples who believed in them.

The monotheistic idea that had flared up with Akhenaton had lapsed back into obscurity, where it was to remain for a long time. Finds on the island of Elephantine, just above the first cataract of the Nile, have yielded the surprising information that there was a centuries-old Jewish military colony there in whose temple, along-side the principal god Jahu, two female deities were worshipped, one bearing the name Anat-Jahu. These Jews were of course cut off from the mother country and had not gone through the same religious development; the government of the Persian Empire (fifth century) informed them of the new religious regulations in force in Jerusalem.[4] Going back to earlier times, we can say that Yahweh certainly bore no resemblance to the god of Moses. Aton had been a pacifist, like his representative on earth (his model, actually), the pharaoh Akhenaton, who stood idly by as the world empire won by his forebears fell apart. For a people on the point of taking violent possession of fresh places to settle, the god Yahweh was undoubtedly more suitable. In fact, all the things that made the god of Moses worth worshipping were quite beyond the compre-hension of the primitive mass.

I have said already (and been happy to refer to others who agree with me here) that the central fact of Jewish religious develop-ment was that, over time, the god Yahweh lost his own character and came increasingly to resemble Moses' old god, Aton. There were still differences, of course, which at first glance one would be inclined to rate as significant, but they are easily explained. In

Egypt, Aton had begun his ascendancy in a happy time of secure possession, and even as the kingdom started to totter his worshippers had been able to turn their backs on the disturbance, continuing to praise and enjoy his creations.

Fate brought the Jewish people a series of difficult ordeals and painful experiences, and their god became a harsh, severe, almost looming figure. He retained the character of the universal god who reigns over all countries and all people, but the fact that his worship had passed from the Egyptians to the Jews found expression in a codicil to the effect that the Jews were his chosen people, whose special obligations would also, in the end, find a special reward. The Jewish people may not have found it easy to reconcile a belief in election by their almighty god with the wretched experiences of their unhappy fate. But they refused to be put off, they intensified their own feeling of guilt in order to stifle their doubts about god, and it may be that they pointed in the end to 'god's mysterious wisdom', as the pious among them still do today. If it occurred to them to wonder why he sent more and more men of violence by whom they were conquered and abused – the Assyrians, the Babylonians, the Persians – they nevertheless acknowledged his might in the fact that all these wicked enemies were themselves defeated in turn and their kingdoms disappeared.

In three important respects the later Jewish god eventually came to correspond to the old Mosaic god. The first, decisive respect is that he really did come to be acknowledged as the only god, alongside whom any other was inconceivable. Akhenaton's monotheism was taken seriously by a whole people – indeed, so closely did they embrace that idea that it became the chief content of their inner life, leaving them with no interest in anything else. On this point the people and the priesthood that had risen to prominence in their midst were agreed, but whereas the priests' entire activity consisted in developing the ceremonial for his worship, they found themselves in conflict with intense currents within the people that sought to revive two other aspects of Moses' teaching about his god. The voices of the prophets tirelessly proclaimed that god despised ceremonial and sacrifice, demanding only that people believe in him and live their lives in truth and righteousness. And in extolling the simplicity and sanctity of the desert life they were undoubtedly acting under the influence of the Mosaic ideal.

It is time we raised the question of whether it is in fact necessary to invoke the influence of Moses on the final shaping of the Jewish conception of god or whether it is not sufficient to assume a spontaneous development in the direction of a higher spirituality during a cultural life extending over centuries. Regarding this potential explanation, which would bring our whole guessing game to an end, two things need to be said. Firstly, it explains nothing. Identical circumstances did not lead the undoubtedly very gifted Greek people to monotheism but to a loosening up of polytheistic religion and the beginnings of philosophical thought. In Egypt, as we understand it, monotheism had grown up as a side-effect of imperialism; god was a reflection of the pharaoh, who held absolute sway over one enormous international empire. In the case of the Jews, political conditions were highly unfavourable as regarded the idea of the exclusive national god developing into that of the universal ruler of the world, and what gave this tiny, powerless nation the temerity to pass itself off as the great lord's favourite child? The question of the emergence of monotheism among the Jews would thus remain unanswered, or one would settle for the usual answer, namely that it was simply the expression of that people's special religious genius. Genius is notoriously inscrutable and irresponsible, and for that reason it ought not to be invoked as an explanation until all other solutions have failed.[5]

There is also the obtrusive fact that Jewish reporting and historiography themselves show us the way in that they assert most decisively (this time without internal contradiction) that the idea of a single god had been given to the people by Moses. If there is one objection to the credibility of this assurance, it is that the priestly version of the text before us obviously traces far too much back to Moses. Such institutions as ritual prescriptions, which unmistakably belong to a later age, are presented as Mosaic injunctions, clearly with the intention of adducing authority for them. For us that undoubtedly gives grounds for suspicion, but it is not sufficient for rejection, the reason being that the underlying motive for such exaggeration is plain to see. The priestly account seeks to establish a continuum between its own present and Mosaic antiquity; it sets out to deny the very thing that we have described as the most striking fact of Jewish religious history, namely that between Moses' giving of the law and subsequent Jewish religion there is a yawning gulf, which was initially plugged with Yahweh worship and only later gradually filled in. The priestly account employs every means to dispute that process, although its historical correctness is beyond all doubt; the special treatment that the biblical text underwent left intact more than sufficient evidence to prove it. The priestly version was here attempting something similar to the corrupting tendency that turned the new god Yahweh into the ancestral deity. Allowing for this motive behind the priestly codex, it becomes hard for us to withhold belief from the claim that it really was Moses himself who gave his Jews the idea of monotheism. It should be that much easier for us to agree because we can say where Moses got the idea from, which was something the Jewish priests were undoubtedly no longer aware of.

Someone might at this point ask: what good does it do us, deriving Jewish monotheism from Egyptian? It merely shifts the problem on slightly; regarding the origin of monotheism we are none the wiser. The answer is that this is not a question of profit, it is a question of research. And it may be that we shall learn something from discovering what actually occurred.

B

Latency period and tradition

In other words, we profess the belief that the idea of a single god, the rejection of ceremonial as magically effective, and the emphasis on the ethical demand in god's name were in fact Mosaic teachings that at first went unheeded but then took effect following a lengthy intermediate period and eventually won permanent acceptance. How is this kind of delayed effect to be explained, and where do similar phenomena occur? What strikes one immediately is that they occur quite often in a wide variety of areas and probably come about in a multiplicity of more or less easily understandable ways. Let us, for example, take what happens to a new scientific notion such as Darwin's theory of evolution. Initially it meets with bitter rejection, it is vehemently disputed for several decades, but in no more than a generation it is acknowledged as a major step forward towards the truth. Darwin himself is honoured with a tomb or cenotaph in Westminster. Such a case leaves us little to puzzle out. The new truth arouses instances of affective resistance, these allow themselves to be championed by arguments capable of disputing the evidence in favour of the unwelcome theory, the battle of opinions goes on for some time; there are supporters and opponents from the outset, both the number and the influence of the former increasing steadily until in the end they gain the upper hand; never at any point during the struggle does anyone forget what is at issue. It scarcely surprises us to find that the whole sequence of events has taken quite a long time, doubtless because we fail to appreciate adequately that we are dealing with a process of mass psychology.

It is not hard to find a fully corresponding analogy for this process in the inner life of the individual. This would be when a person learns something as new that, on the basis of certain proofs, he is asked to acknowledge as true but that conflicts with certain of his desires and offends a number of his cherished convictions. He will then show some reluctance, look around for reasons to doubt the new theory, and struggle with himself for a while before eventually admitting: yes, that's the way it is, though I do not find it easy to accept, in fact I feel awful about having to believe it. All we learn from this is that it takes time for the mental work of the 'I' to overcome objections that are upheld by powerful affective charges.[6] The resemblance between this case and the one we are trying to understand is not very great.

The next example we turn to seems to have even less in common with our problem. It happens, say, that a person leaves the scene where he has experienced a frightening accident (e.g. a rail crash), apparently unharmed. Over the next few weeks, however, he develops a series of severe psychological and motor symptoms that can only be put down to his shock, to the shake-up, or to whatever else took effect at the time. The person now has a 'traumatic neurosis'. That is a wholly incomprehensible, i.e. quite new fact. The time that elapsed between the accident and the first appearance of the symptoms is the 'incubation period' – transparently, an allusion to the pathology of infectious diseases. We shall inevitably be struck, subsequently, by the fact that, despite the two cases being fundamentally different, in one respect there is nevertheless some correspondence between the problem of traumatic neurosis and that of Jewish monotheism. Namely in the characteristic that might be called *latency*. The fact is, according to our soundly based assumption there was, in Jewish religious history, a long period following the break with the religion of Moses in which nothing is heard of the monotheistic idea, the repudiation of ceremonial, and the heavy stress on the ethical. This prepares us for the possibility that the solution to our problem should be sought in a particular psychological situation.

We have already described on a number of occasions what happened at Kadesh when the two sections of what was to become the Jewish nation came together to adopt a new religion. On the part of those who had been in Egypt, memories of the exodus and of the figure of Moses were still so strong and fresh as to demand inclusion in an account of antiquity. These were perhaps the grandsons of people who had actually known Moses, and some of them still felt they were Egyptians and bore Egyptian names. However, they had good motives for suppressing the memory of the fate that their leader and law-giver had encountered. The behaviour of the others was dictated by their intention to magnify the new god and dispute his foreignness. Both parties had the same interest in denying that a previous religion had existed amongst them and what had been its content. As a result, there came about that initial compromise that was no doubt soon enshrined in writing; the people from Egypt had brought writing and the taste for recording history with them, though a long time was to pass before historiography acknowledged an inexorable commitment to the truth. Initially, it had no qualms about shaping its accounts in accordance with its needs and tendencies at the time, as if the concept of falsification had not yet occurred to it. In the circumstances, a conflict was able to emerge between the written record and oral transmission of the same material, namely the *tradition*. What had been omitted or amended in 'scripture' might very well be preserved intact in this 'tradition'. Tradition complemented and at the same time contradicted historiography. It was less subject to distorting tendencies; much of it may even have been wholly exempt therefrom and could therefore be more truthful than the account that was fixed in writing. However, its reliability suffered from its being less constant and less specific than the written record, liable to undergo a wide variety of changes and disfigurements as a result of being passed on from one generation to another by oral communication. Such a tradition might meet with various fates. Our first expectation would be that it would be overcome by the written record, failing to assert itself alongside the latter, becoming more and more obscure, and eventually passing into oblivion. Other fates are possible, however; one is that the tradition itself ends in a fixed written form, and we shall have occasion to deal with others, too, at a subsequent point.

As regards the phenomenon of latency in Jewish religious history with which we are concerned, we now, potentially, have the explanation that the facts and content deliberately denied by official historiography, so to speak, never in fact got lost. Knowledge of them lived on in traditions that were preserved among the people. Sellin assures us that even concerning Moses' end there was a tradition current that flatly contradicted the official account and came much closer to the truth. The same, presumably, applied with respect to other matters that had apparently met their death with Moses – i.e. to much of the content of the Mosaic religion that the vast majority of Moses' contemporaries had found unacceptable.

But the curious fact we come across here is that those traditions, rather than weakening with time, became stronger and stronger as the centuries went on, forcing their way into later versions of the official record of events and eventually proving powerful enough to influence decisively the way the nation thought and acted. However, what conditions made that outcome possible for the moment elude our knowledge.

It is so curious, this fact, that we feel justified in taking a further look at it. It holds the key to our problem. The Jewish people had abandoned the religion of Aton brought to them by Moses and turned to the worship of another god who differed little from the *baalim* of neighbouring peoples. All efforts by later tendencies failed to obscure this shameful sequence of events. However, the religion of Moses had not vanished without trace; a kind of memory of it had survived, a possibly dulled and distorted tradition. And it was this tradition of a great past that, continuing to exert influence from the background, as it were, gradually gained more and more power over people's minds and eventually succeeded in transforming the god Yahweh into the Mosaic god and bringing the religion of Moses, which had come in many centuries ago and then been abandoned, back to life. That a forgotten tradition should have so powerful an effect on the inner life of an entire people is not an idea we are familiar with. We find ourselves here in an area of mass psychology in which we do not feel at home. We are on the lookout for analogies, for facts that are at least similar in kind, albeit in other areas. We believe they can be found.

In the period in which, among the Jews, the religion of Moses was preparing a comeback, the Greek nation was in possession of a rich store of tribal legends and hero myths. The ninth or eighth centuries, it is believed, saw the emergence of the two Homeric epics that drew their material from this body of legends. Given our present-day understanding of psychology, it would have been possible to ask long before Schliemann and Evans: where did the Greeks get it from, all the legend material that Homer and the great Attic dramatists worked up in their masterpieces? The answer would have had to be: probably this nation, in its early history, experienced a period of outward brilliance and cultural splendour that was overwhelmed in some historical catastrophe, and of that period these legends preserved a dim tradition. Recent archaeological research has confirmed this conjecture, which at the time was undoubtedly denounced as excessively bold. It uncovered the evidence of the magnificent Minoan–Mycenaean civilization that probably came to an end on the Greek mainland before 1250 BC. Later Greek historians scarcely mention it. There is the odd comment – that there was once a time when Cretans ruled the waves, that there was a king called Minos who had a palace with a labyrinth – but that is all; otherwise, nothing remains of it but the traditions taken up by poets and playwrights.

National epics have come to light in connection with other peoples too – the Germans, the Indians, the Finns. It is up to literary historians to investigate whether their emergence allows us to posit the same conditions as in the case of the Greeks. I believe such an investigation will yield a positive result. The condition or requirement as we understand it is: a piece of prehistory that must appear immediately afterwards as rich in content, important and splendid, possibly always heroic, but that lies so far back in the past, belongs to so remote a time, that for subsequent generations only a dim and incomplete tradition bears witness to it. People have expressed surprise that the epic as artistic genre disappeared in later times. Perhaps the explanation is that the requirement for it no longer came about. The old material had been worked up, and for all other eventualities the writing of history had taken the place of tradition. The greatest heroic deeds of modern times have proved incapable of inspiring an epic, but even Alexander the Great had a right to complain that he would never find a Homer.

Long-gone eras hold a great, often mysterious attraction for the human imagination. Whenever men are dissatisfied with their present (and that is pretty often), they turn to the past in the hope that this time they will succeed in bringing about the never quite extinct dream of a golden age.[7] Probably they are still under the spell of their childhood, which a not unpartisan memory reflects back at them as a time of undisturbed bliss. If all that remains of the past are the incomplete, hazy recollections we call tradition, this constitutes a special incentive for the artist, for he is then at liberty to fill in the gaps in memory as his imagination desires and to shape the image of the time he is seeking to reproduce in accordance with his own intentions. One might almost say: the more indistinct tradition has become, the more use it is to the poet. So as far as the significance of tradition for poetry is concerned we need not be surprised, and the analogy of the conditionality of the epic will make us more inclined to accept the disconcerting assumption that in the case of the Jews it was the Moses tradition that transformed the worship of Yahweh, bringing it more into line with the old Mosaic religion. In other respects, though, the two cases are still too different. In one the outcome is a poem, in the other a religion, and with regard to the latter we have assumed that under the impetus of tradition it was reproduced with a fidelity to which the case of the epic can of course not provide the counterpart. This leaves enough of our problem unresolved to justify the need for more appropriate analogies.

C

The analogy

The only satisfactory analogy for the curious process that we have discovered in Jewish religious history lies in an area apparently far removed; however, it is extremely complete – indeed, almost identical. Here too we find the phenomenon of latency, the appearance of incomprehensible manifestations demanding explanation, and the requirement for an early experience subsequently forgotten. We also find the characteristic of compulsion imposing itself by overwhelming the logical thinking of the psyche – a trait that in connection with the origin of the epic, for example, did not enter into consideration.

This analogy is found in psychopathology in connection with the origin of human neuroses – that is to say, in a field that belongs to the psychology of the individual, whereas religious phenomena of course come under mass psychology. As we shall see, the analogy is not as surprising as would appear at first glance. In fact, it is more in the nature of a postulate.

The impressions, experienced early on and subsequently forgotten, to which we attribute such great importance for the aetiology of neuroses we refer to as *traumas*. It is an open question whether the aetiology of neuroses in general should be regarded as traumatic. The obvious objection is that not in every case can a manifest trauma be deduced from the early history of the neurotic individual. Often one must be content to say that nothing else is present but an exceptional, abnormal reaction to experiences and demands that affect all individuals and are processed and dealt with by them in different, what we should call normal ways. Where no other explanation is available than hereditary, constitutional predispositions, one is understandably tempted to say that the neurosis is not acquired but developed.

However, two points stand out in this connection. The first [see I below] is that the origin of the neurosis invariably goes back to very early childhood impressions.[8] Secondly [II], it is true that some cases are described as 'traumatic' because the effects unmistakably go back to one or more powerful impressions from that early period that escaped normal processing, so that one might say that, had those impressions not occurred, the neurosis itself would not have come about. It would be sufficient for our purposes, in fact, if the analogy we are after had to be confined to such traumatic cases. But the gap between the two groups appears not unbridgeable. It is entirely possible to combine both aetiological conditions in a single view; it depends only on what is defined as traumatic. If the experience may be assumed to have acquired its traumatic character purely as a result of a quantitative factor, in other words if the blame in all cases may be assumed to lie with an excess of demand, if the experience gives rise to unusual, pathological reactions, it is a simple matter to conclude that in one constitution something acts as a trauma that in another constitution has no such effect. This leads to the idea of a sliding scale, what we call a *complemental series*, in which two factors come together to fulfil the aetiology, with a little less of one being balanced out by a bit more of the other; as a general rule the two work together, and only at the two extremities of the scale can there be any question of a simple motivation. Considered in this light, the distinction between traumatic and non-traumatic aetiology can be left on one side as unimportant so far as the analogy we are looking for is concerned.

It may be useful at this point, despite the risk of repetition, to bring together the facts contained in what we regard as an eloquent analogy. They are these: it has emerged for our study that what we call the phenomena (symptoms) of a neurosis are the consequences of certain experiences and impressions that, precisely for that reason, we recognize as aetiological traumas. We now face two tasks: firstly, to seek out the common characteristics of those experiences, and secondly to seek out the common characteristics of neurotic symptoms. There is no need, in this connection, to avoid certain schematizations.

I a) All these traumas belong to early childhood, approximately up to the age of five. Impressions from the time when a child is first learning to speak stand out as particularly interesting; the second to fourth years appear to be the most important, though at what point after birth this period of predisposition begins cannot be established with any certainty.

b) The relevant experiences have as a rule been completely forgotten; they are not accessible to memory, falling into the period of infantile amnesia, which is usually perforated by isolated scraps of recollection – what we call covering memories.[9]

c) They relate to impression of a sexual and aggressive nature and also, undoubtedly, to early instances of damage to the 'I' (narcissistic disorders). Note in this connection that such young children do not distinguish sharply between sexual and purely aggressive actions, as they do later (sadistic misunderstanding of the sexual act). The predominance of the sexual impulse is of course very conspicuous and calls for theoretical appreciation.

These three points (early occurrence within the first five years, the fact of having been forgotten, sexual-aggressive content) belong closely together. Traumas are either personal physical experiences or sensory perceptions, usually of things seen and things heard, i.e. experiences or impressions. The interconnectedness of the three points is established by a theory, a product of the work of analysis that can alone convey knowledge of the forgotten experiences or, to put it more starkly but less correctly, recall them to memory. Theoretically, in contrast to popular opinion a person's sex life (or what corresponds thereto subsequently) flowers early, that early flowering coming to an end around the age of five and being followed by the so-called latency period (up until puberty), in which no further development of sexuality occurs – indeed, what has been achieved is undone. This theory is confirmed by anatomical study of the growth of the internal genitalia; it leads one to suppose that man is descended from a type of animal that reached sexual maturity in five years, and it prompts the suspicion that the postponement and two-stage beginning of our sex life is very closely bound up with the history of how the human race emerged. Man appears to be the only creature with this kind of latency and delayed sexuality. Studies of primates, which so far as I know have not been done, would be indispensable as regards testing the theory. Psychologically, it cannot be a matter of indifference that the years of infantile amnesia coincide with this early period of sexuality. Possibly it is this state of affairs that constitutes the true precondition for the possibility of neurosis, which is after all in a sense a human prerogative and, looked at in this light, seems to be a 'survival' of primitive times in the same way as certain parts of our physical anatomy.[10]

II As regards the shared properties or peculiarities of neurotic phenomena, two points need to be stressed:

a) The effects of trauma are of two kinds: positive and negative. The former are efforts to bring the trauma back to the fore, to recall the forgotten experience or, even better, to make it real, reliving a repetition of it, even if it was no more than an early affective relationship, resurrecting it in a similar relationship with a different person. Such efforts are summarized as *fixation* on the trauma and as *repetition compulsion*. They may be absorbed into the so-called normal 'I' and as permanent tendencies of the same bestow upon it immutable character traits, despite the fact or rather precisely because of the fact that their true justification, their historical origin, has been forgotten. For instance, a man whose childhood has been spent in immoderate (and since forgotten) attachment to his mother may spend his entire life looking for a woman on whom he can make himself dependent, having her feed and sustain him. A girl who in early childhood was the object of a sexual seduction may arrange her later sex life in such a way as repeatedly to provoke similar assaults. It is easy to guess that, with the aid of such insights, we go beyond the problem of neurosis to reach an understanding of character-formation in general.

The negative reactions pursue the opposite goal, namely that nothing shall be remembered of the forgotten traumas and nothing repeated. We may summarize them as *defensive reactions*. Their principal expression are what we call *avoidances*, which may grow into *inhibitions* and *phobias*. Such negative reactions also make enormous contributions towards shaping character; basically, they are just as much fixations on the trauma as their counterparts, only these are fixations in the opposite direction. Strictly speaking, the symptoms of neurosis are compromise formations in which both currents proceeding from traumas meet in such a way that now one direction, now the other finds overwhelming expression in them. As a result of these opposing reactions, conflicts arise that are normally incapable of reaching a settlement.

b) All these phenomena (symptoms, restrictions of the 'I', and stable character changes) possess a *compulsive character* – that is to say, in connection with great psychical intensity they demonstrate a high degree of independence from the organization of the other mental processes, which are adapted to the demands of the real outside world, obeying the laws of logical thought. They are not or not sufficiently influenced by external reality, having no concern for it or for representing it psychically, with the result that they easily enter into active conflict with both. They are a state within a state, so to speak, an unapproachable party, not available for collaboration, that is nevertheless capable of getting the better of the other, 'normal' party and pressing it into its service. If this happens, an internal psychical reality has gained the upper hand over the reality of the external world and the way is open for psychosis. Even if the situation does not reach that point, the practical importance of such circumstances can scarcely be overestimated. The inhibitedness and practical incapacity of persons in thrall to neurosis constitute a very significant factor in human society and can be seen as a direct expression of such persons' fixation on an early fragment of their past.

And now, what is it about latency that is inevitably of particular interest to us in terms of an analogy? The childhood trauma can be immediately followed by a neurotic outbreak, a childhood neurosis, full of defensive endeavours, with symptoms taking shape. It may last for some time, possibly provoking disorders, but it may also run a hidden course and be overlooked. In it, as a rule, defence predominates; certainly changes to the 'I', rather like the formation of scar tissue, are left behind. Only rarely will the childhood neurosis experience a smooth transition into the adult neurosis. Much more often it will be replaced by a period of apparently undisturbed development, which is assisted or rendered possible by the intervention of the physiological latency period. Only later does the transformation occur whereby the final neurosis becomes manifest as a delayed effect of the trauma. This happens either with the onset of puberty or some time afterwards – in the former case, because the drives strengthened by physical maturation can now resume the struggle in which they had initially succumbed to defence mechanisms; in the latter, because the reactions and modifications to the 'I' engendered in connection with such defence now turn out to be a nuisance as regards performing the new life tasks, with the result that severe conflicts now arise between the demands of the real outside world and the 'I', anxious to preserve the organization so laboriously acquired in the defensive struggle. The phenomenon of latency as characterizing neurosis between the first reactions to the trauma and the later onset of illness must be acknowledged as typical. The illness may also be seen as an

attempt at healing, a striving to reconcile with the rest of the 'I'
the parts that had split away under the influence of the trauma
and to combine them into an entity that will have power against
the outside world. However, such an attempt rarely succeeds without the work of analysis coming to its aid, and even then not always:
quite often it ends in a total ravaging and shattering of the 'I' or
in its being overwhelmed by the part that had split away early on,
dominated by the trauma.[11]

To gain the reader's conviction it would be necessary to give
detailed accounts of large numbers of neurotic life stories.
However, given the sprawling and problematic nature of the object,
that would completely alter the character of this essay. It would
turn into a treatise about the theory of neurosis and even then
probably only touch the minority of people who have chosen the
study and practice of psychoanalysis as their life's work. Since I
am here addressing a wider audience I have no alternative but to
ask readers to grant a certain provisional credibility to the explanations given in abbreviated form above, granting for my own part
that they need only accept the conclusions to which I will lead
them if the teachings on which those conclusions are based turn
out to be true.

I can try, nevertheless, to recount an individual case that illustrates with particular clarity a good many of the properties of neurosis to which I have referred. A single instance cannot of course be
expected to reveal everything, and readers must not be disappointed if in terms of content it departs a long way from that for
which we are seeking an analogy.

The small boy who, as so often in petty-bourgeois families,
shared his parents' bedroom in his early years had repeated, indeed
regular opportunities to observe, at an age where he was just learning to talk, what happened between his parents sexually, seeing
much and hearing even more. In his subsequent neurosis, which
breaks out immediately after his first spontaneous emission, the
earliest and most irksome symptom is disturbed sleep. He becomes
abnormally sensitive to noises in the night and cannot, once awake,
go back to sleep. Such insomnia was a true compromise symptom,

on the one hand an expression of his defence against those noctur-
nal perceptions, on the other hand an attempt to recreate the state
of wakefulness in which he could eavesdrop on those impressions.

Prematurely roused to aggressive virility by such observation,
the child began to excite his little penis manually and perform various sexual assaults upon his mother, identifying with the father in
whose place he was putting himself as he did so. Things went so
far that, eventually, he heard his mother forbid him to touch his
penis; he further heard her threaten to tell his father and, as punishment, deprive him of the sinful member. This threat of castration
had an extraordinarily powerful traumatic effect on the boy. He
abandoned his sexual activity and altered his character. Instead of
identifying with the father he feared him, adopted a passive attitude towards him, and by occasional naughtiness provoked him to
acts of corporal punishment that for the boy possessed a sexual
significance, enabling him, through them, to identify with the
mistreated mother. The mother herself he clung to with increasing anxiety, as if he could not manage without her love for a
moment, seeing her love as a shield against the threat of castration emanating from the father. In this modified version of the
Oedipus complex he spent the latency period, which remained free
of obvious disturbances. He became a model child and enjoyed
great success at school.

Thus far we have followed the immediate effect of the trauma
and confirmed the fact of latency.

The advent of puberty brought the manifest neurosis and revealed
the second main symptom: sexual impotence. He had forfeited the
sensitivity of his member, tried not to touch it, dared not approach
a woman with sexual intent. His sexual activity remained confined
to psychical masturbation with sado-masochistic fantasies in which
it is not hard to recognize echoes of his early observations of parental
coitus. The thrust of heightened virility that puberty brings with it
was expended in furious hatred of the father and obstreperous behaviour towards him. This extreme, self-destructively inconsiderate relationship with his father was also to blame for the young man's lack
of success in life and for his clashes with the outside world. He was

unable to achieve anything in his profession because his father had forced him into that profession. He also made no friends and was never in favour with his superiors.

When, burdened with these symptoms and inabilities, he finally found a wife following his father's death, character traits came to prominence almost as the core of his being that made dealings with him a difficult task for anyone close to him. He developed a totally selfish, despotic and brutal personality that clearly needed to oppress and offend others. He was a faithful copy of his father as the latter's image had formed itself in his memory – a revival, in other words, of the father-identification to which he had once, as a small boy, resorted from sexual motives. In this hard case we recognize the *recurrence* of what had been repressed, which in addition to the immediate effects of the trauma and the phenomenon of latency we have described as being among the key features of a neurosis.

D

Application

Early trauma – defence – latency – onset of neurotic disorder – partial recurrence of what had been repressed: such was the formula we established for the development of a neurosis. The reader is now invited to take the step towards assuming that something similar occurred in the life of the human race as in that of the individual. In other words, that here too events took place of a sexually aggressive nature that left lasting traces but were usually repelled and forgotten and that later, following an extended latency, took effect and gave rise to phenomena similar in structure and tendency to symptoms.

We believe that we can detect the presence of these processes, and we wish to demonstrate that their symptom-like consequences are religious phenomena. Because since the emergence of the idea of evolution there can be no further doubt that the human race has a prehistory, and because this is unknown, i.e. forgotten, such a conclusion almost has the weight of a postulate. If we find that the effective and forgotten traumas relate in the one case as in the other to life in the human family, we shall welcome this as a highly desirable, quite unexpected bonus not required by our discussions hitherto.

I set out these claims a quarter of a century ago in my book *Totem and Taboo* (1912) and need only repeat them here. The construct proceeds from something Charles Darwin said and brings in a suggestion put forward by Atkinson. It says that, in primitive times, primitive humans lived in small hordes, each dominated by a powerful male. The time cannot be indicated, the connection with what we know as the geological eras has yet to be established, probably the creatures concerned had not advanced very far in the development of language. An important element in the construct is the assumption that the fates to be described affected all primitive humans – that is to say, all our forebears.

History is narrated in magnificent poetry as if things took place on a single occasion that in reality extended over millennia and during that prolonged period were repeated countless times. The powerful male was lord and father of the entire horde, enjoying unlimited power, which he wielded in violent ways. All female creatures were his property, the women and daughters from his own horde and possibly also those stolen from other hordes. The fate of sons was a hard one; if they roused the father's envy, they were killed or castrated or driven out. They had to rely on living together in small communities and obtaining women by abduction, with one or another individual then managing to work his way up to a similar position to that of the father in the primitive horde. For natural reasons a special position arose for youngest sons. Protected by his mother's love, the youngest son was able to profit from his father's ageing and replace him after his demise. Both the expulsion of elder sons and the preferential treatment accorded to younger sons are believed to find echoes in legends and folk tales.

The next decisive step towards changing this first type of 'social' organization is thought to have been when the expelled brothers who were living in a community got together, overpowered the father, and according to the custom of the time ate him raw. No one need take offence at such cannibalism, for it extends a long way into later periods. What is important, though, is that we ascribe to these early humans the same emotional attitudes as we are able, through the medium of analytical research, to ascertain among today's primitives, namely our children. In other words, that they not only hated and feared the father but also worshipped him as an exemplar, and that in reality each of them wished to take his place. The act of cannibalism then becomes comprehensible as an attempt, by swallowing a piece of him, to secure identification with him.

Presumably, the murder of the father was followed by a considerable period of time during which the brothers fought one another for the father's inheritance, which each wished to gain for himself alone. An understanding of the risks and unsuccessfulness of these struggles, recollection of the jointly executed act of liberation, and the reciprocal emotional ties that had formed during the period of expulsion led eventually to an agreement amongst them, a kind of social contract. There came into being the first form of social organization with *renunciation* [in the sense of 'forgoing'] *of drives*, recognition of mutual *obligations*, appointment of certain *institutions* held to be absolute (sacred) – the beginnings, in other words, of morality and law. Each individual renounced the ideal of acquiring the paternal position for himself, renounced possession of his mother and sisters. Hence the *incest taboo* and the requirement for *exogamy*. A large part of the absolute power released by eliminating the father passed to women, ushering in the period of *matriarchy*. The memory of the father lived on in this period of the 'league of brothers'. A powerful, perhaps at first always also a feared animal was found as father-substitute. Such a choice may seem strange to us, but the gulf that humans later created between themselves and animals did not exist for primitives, nor does it exist for our children, whose animal phobias we can understand as fear of the father. In relations with the totem animal the original ambivalence of the emotional relationship to the father is preserved in full. On the one hand, the totem was seen as physical ancestor and protective deity of the clan, to be worshipped and spared; on the other hand, a feast day was appointed on which it was arranged that the totem should meet the same fate as the first father. It was killed and eaten jointly by all comrades (the totemic meal described by Robertson Smith). This great feast day was in reality a triumphant celebration of the allied sons' victory over the father.

Where does that leave religion? In my opinion, we have every right to see in totemism, with its worship of a father-substitute, the ambivalence engendered by the totemic meal, the appointment of commemorations and of bans, violation of which is punishable by death – we are entitled, as I say, to see in totemism the first manifestation of religion in human history and to confirm its association, from the outset, with social structures and moral obligations. Here we can give only the briefest survey of subsequent developments in religion. They undoubtedly march in parallel with cultural advances made by the human race and with changes in the structure of human communities.

The next advance away from totemism is the humanization of the worshipped being. In place of animals, human gods appear, their provenance from the totem undisguised. Either the god still takes animal form or is at least depicted with an animal's face, or the totem becomes the god's favourite, inseparable companion, or legend has the god kill the very animal that was in fact only a preliminary stage in that god's development. At a point in this development that is not easy to determine great mother-goddesses appear, probably earlier than the male gods but subsequently surviving for some time alongside them. Meanwhile, a major social change has occurred. Matriarchy has been replaced by a restored patriarchal order. Of course, the new fathers never achieved the omnipotence of the first father. There were many of them, living together in larger units than the hordes had constituted. Needing to get on well with one another, they remained constrained by social rules. Probably the mother-goddesses emerged at the time when matriarchy was in decline to compensate neglected mothers. Male gods first appear as sons alongside great mothers, only later assuming

clear characteristics of father-figures. These male gods of polytheism mirror the circumstances of a patriarchal age. They are many
in number, mutually restricting one another, occasionally subordi-
nating themselves to a higher supreme deity. However, the next
step leads to the topic that concerns us here, the recurrence of the
sole, single, boundlessly dominant father-god.

Granted, this historical overview is sketchy and at many points
insecure. But anyone seeking to dismiss our version of prehistory
as pure fantasy would be gravely underestimating the richness and
evidential value of the material that has gone into it. Large parts
of the past, here gathered into a whole, are historically proven:
totemism, male leagues. Others have survived in superb replicas.
For instance, more than one author has been struck by how faithfully the rite of Christian communion, in which believers ingest
the flesh and blood of their Lord in symbolic form, echoes the
meaning and content of the ancient totemic meal. Many remnants
of forgotten prehistory have been preserved in legends and folk
tales, and analytical study of the inner life of children has supplied
an unexpectedly rich store of material to plug the gaps in our
knowledge of primitive times. As contributions towards understanding the enormous significance of the paternal relationship I
need only cite animal phobias, the apparently extraordinary fear
of being eaten by one's father, and the tremendous intensity of
castration anxiety. Nothing about our construct is pure invention;
there is nothing that cannot stand on solid foundations.

If our account of prehistory is accepted as broadly credible, the
teachings and rites of religion offer two recognizable elements: on
the one hand fixations on ancient family history and survivals of
the same, on the other hand restorations of things past, recurrence
of things forgotten after lengthy intervals. It is the latter, hitherto
overlooked and therefore not understood, that I want to prove
here from at least one impressive example.

It is worth stressing particularly that every element returning
from oblivion imposes itself with especial force, exerts an incomparably powerful influence on human masses, and asserts an irresistible claim to truth, against which logical objection is powerless.

In the style of the *credo quia absurdum*. This remarkable characteristic can be understood only on the model of the delusions of
psychotics. We grasped long ago that the delusional idea contains
a piece of forgotten truth that on its recurrence has had to put up
with distortions and misunderstandings, and that the compulsive
conviction engendered for the delusion stems from this nucleus of
truth and spreads to the errors in which it is shrouded. This kind
of content of what must be termed *historical* truth is something
we must also concede to the doctrines of religions, which though
they possess the character of psychotic symptoms are mass
phenomena and as such are spared the curse of isolation.

No other piece of religious history has become so transparent
to us as the establishment of monotheism in Judaism and its continuation in Christianity – with the exception of the likewise seam-
lessly comprehensible development from animal totem to human
god with his regular companion. (Even with the four Christian
evangelists, each has his favourite animal.) If for the moment we
allow the world dominance of the pharaohs to have occasioned the
emergence of the idea of monotheism, we see that, detached from
its native soil and transferred to a foreign people, the idea took
hold of that people after a long period of latency, was guarded by
that people as their most precious possession, and subsequently,
in return, kept that people alive by giving them the pride of having
been chosen. It is the religion of the first father, bound up with
the hope of reward, of honour, ultimately of world domination.
The latter wish-fantasy, which the Jewish people gave up long ago,
lives on today among the enemies of that people in the belief in
the conspiracy of the 'wise men of Zion'. We propose to set out
in a later section how the special peculiarities of this monotheistic religion borrowed from the Egyptians inevitably affected the
Jewish people and placed a lasting stamp on its character as a result
of the rejection of magic and mysticism, the encouragement of
advances in intellectuality/spirituality[12] and the invitation to subli-
mations, how the Jewish people, blessed by possession of the truth,
overwhelmed by their awareness of having been chosen, came to
place a high value on things intellectual and to strees the ethical,

and how the wretched fate and the real disappointments of that people contrived to reinforce all these tendencies. For now, though, let us pursue developments in a different direction.

The reinstatement of the first parent in his historic rights was a great step forward, but it could not be the end. The other pieces of the prehistoric tragedy also pressed for recognition. What this process set in motion is not easy to guess. Apparently, a growing sense of guilt seized the Jewish people, and possibly the entire civilized world of the time, as a precursor of the recurrence of the repressed content. Until a member of that Jewish people found in the justification of a politico-religious agitator the occasion for a new religion (Christianity) to break away from Judaism. Paul, a Roman Jew from Tarsus, seized on that sense of guilt and correctly traced it back to its prehistoric source. He called it 'original sin', a crime against god that could be atoned for only by death. It was through this original sin that death had entered the world. In reality, the crime worthy of death had been the murder of the subsequently deified first parent. However, the murder was not remembered; instead, its atonement was fantasized, and that enabled this fantasy to be greeted as message of redemption (gospel). A son of god had allowed himself to be killed as an innocent man, thus taking upon himself the guilt of all. It had to be a son, because it was the father who had been murdered. Probably traditions from eastern and Greek mysteries had influenced the development of the redemption fantasy. The core of it appears to have been Paul's own contribution. He was in the truest sense a religiously minded person; the dark traces of the past lurked in his mind, ready to break through into more conscious regions.

That the redeemer had sacrificed himself without guilt was a clearly tendentious distortion creating problems for any logical understanding, because how could a man innocent of the original murder take the murderers' guilt upon himself by allowing himself to be killed? In historical reality, no such contradiction existed. The 'redeemer' could not be anyone but the chief culprit, the leader of the league of brothers that had overpowered the father. Whether there was such a chief rebel and leader is a question that must in my opinion remain unresolved. It is entirely possible, but some account must also be taken of the fact that every individual in the league of brothers undoubtedly wished to do the deed on his own, thus giving himself a special position and creating a substitute for the father-identification that had to be given up and was becoming submerged in the community. If there was no such leader, Christ is the heir to a wish-fantasy that remained unfulfilled; if there was, he is the successor to and reincarnation of that person. But regardless of whether what we have here is fantasy or recurrence of a forgotten reality, this is certainly where the origin of the idea of the hero is to be found, the hero who indeed constantly rebels against the father and who in some form or another kills him.[13] So is the true explanation for the otherwise almost undemonstrable 'tragic guilt' of the hero in drama. There is little doubt that the hero and the chorus in Greek drama represent this same rebellious hero and the league of brothers, and it is not without significance that in the Middle Ages theatre begins anew by portraying the story of the Passion.

We have already said that the Christian ceremony of holy communion, in which the believer swallows the flesh and blood of the saviour, repeats the content of the ancient totemic meal – only in its loving sense, of course, expressive of worship, not in its aggressive sense. However, the ambivalence that dominates the father-relationship became clearly apparent in the end-result of the religious reform. Supposedly meant to appease the father-god, it ended up dethroning and getting rid of him. Judaism had been a father-religion; Christianity became a son-religion. The ancient figure of god the father faded in importance behind Christ; Christ the son took his place – completely, just as in those primitive times every son had yearned to do. Paul, the continuer of Judaism, also became its destroyer. He undoubtedly owed his success primarily to the fact that, with the idea of redemption, he exorcized men's sense of guilt, but also to the circumstance that he relinquished the chosenness of his people and its visible sign, circumcision, with the result that the new religion was able to become universal, encompassing the whole human race. This step on Paul's part may have been partly prompted by personal revenge directed against the resistance that his reform encountered in Jewish quarters; nevertheless, it restored one of the characteristics of the old religion of Aton, removing a constriction that it had acquired during the process of transfer to a fresh vehicle, the Jewish people.

In many respects the new religion meant a cultural regression in comparison with the older Jewish religion, as indeed is regularly the case when new groups of people of a lower level force their way in or are admitted. The Christian religion did not maintain the high degree of spiritualization that Judaism had attained. It ceased to be strictly monotheistic, it borrowed many symbolic rites from adjacent nations, it reinstated the great mother-goddess, and it found room for large numbers of polytheism's divinity figures in transparent disguises, albeit in subordinate positions. Above all, it did not, as the religion of Aton and the Mosaic religion that followed had done, seal itself off against the inroads of superstitious, magical and mystical elements, which were seriously to impede the spiritual development of the next two thousand years.

The triumph of Christianity was a second victory of the priests of Amon over Akhenaton's god after an interval of one and a half millennia and in an expanded theatre. Even so, in terms of the history of religion, i.e. in relation to the recurrence of repressed material, Christianity was a step forward and the Jewish religion, from then on, a kind of fossil.

It would be worth taking the trouble to understand how it happened that the idea of monotheism was able to make so deep an impression on the Jewish people in particular and cause them to cling to it so tenaciously. I believe these questions can be answered. Fate had brought the Jewish people closer to the great feat and outrage of prehistory, the killing of the father, by having it repeat the same on the person of Moses, who was an outstanding father-figure. It was a case of 'doing something' instead of remembering, such as occurs frequently during analytical work on neurotics. However, to the stimulus towards remembering given them by Moses' teaching they reacted by denying their action; they stalled at recognition of the great father, preventing themselves

from accessing the point at which Paul was later to start the continuation of primitive history. It is scarcely a matter of indifference
or indeed accidental that the violent killing of another great man
also became the point of departure for Paul's religious innovation.
This was a man whom a small band of disciples in Judaea regarded
as the son of god and the heralded messiah, to whom a fragment
of the childhood history ascribed to Moses was later also transferred but about whom we actually know little more for certain
than we do about Moses himself – for example, we do not know
whether he really was the great teacher portrayed in the gospels
or whether it was not rather the fact and circumstances of his death
that determined the importance his person acquired. Paul, who
became his apostle, never met him personally.

The killing of Moses by his Jewish people, which Sellin identified from traces it had left in the tradition and which interestingly
the young Goethe also took up without any proof whatsoever,[14]
thus becomes an essential element in our construct, an important
connecting link between the forgotten events of prehistory and the
late reappearance in the form of monotheistic religions.[15] It is an
attractive conjecture that remorse over the killing of Moses was
the impulse behind the wish-fantasy of the messiah, who was to
return and bring his people salvation and, as promised, world domination. If Moses was that first messiah, Christ became his substitute and successor, and it was with a certain historical justification
that Paul could proclaim to the nations: Behold, the messiah really
did come, for he was murdered before your very eyes. Then, too,
there is a grain of historical truth in the resurrection of Christ,
because he was the returning first parent of the primitive horde,
transfigured and as son having taken the father's place.

The poor Jewish people, which with its customary stubbornness
went on denying the murder of the father, has paid a high price
for it over the centuries. The reproach has repeatedly been levelled
at it: you killed our god. And that reproach is quite right, if properly translated. It then runs, related to the history of religions: you
refuse to *admit* that you murdered god (the prototype of god, the
first parent, and his subsequent reincarnations). There should be

a supplement: all right, we did the same, but we *admitted* it and have since received atonement. Not all the reproaches with which anti-Semitism persecutes the descendants of the Jewish people can invoke a similar justification. A phenomenon of the intensity and permanence of people's hatred of the Jews must have more than one reason, of course. A whole series of reasons can be guessed at, some clearly derived from reality and needing no interpretation, others lying deeper, flowing from secret springs that one would readily acknowledge as the specific motives. Of the former, the reproach of foreignness is probably the least tenable, because in many places currently dominated by anti-Semitism the Jews are among the oldest sections of the population or even predate the present inhabitants. This is true of the city of Cologne, for example, to which Jews came with the Romans before it was occupied by Teutons. Other grounds for hatred of Jews are stronger, such as the fact that they usually live as minorities among other nations, because the sense of community among human groups, to be complete, needs hostility towards an alien minority, and the numerical weakness of such outsiders invites their repression. Quite unforgivable, however, are two other peculiarities of Jews. Firstly, they differ in many respects from their 'host peoples'. Not radically, since they are not, as their enemies allege, Asians of foreign race but are usually made up of remnants of Mediterranean peoples and heirs of Mediterranean culture. But they are different none the less, often indefinably different from Nordic peoples in particular, and it is a curious fact that mass intolerance often finds stronger expression against small differences than against fundamental ones. Even more powerful in its effect is the second point, namely that they defy all oppression, the cruellest persecutions have failed to exterminate them – indeed, they demonstrate instead an ability to prove themselves in commercial life and, where they are admitted, make valuable contributions to all branches of cultural attainment.

The deeper motives for hatred of Jews are rooted in the remote past, they operate out of the unconscious of nations, and I am prepared to believe that initially they will not appear credible. I venture to suggest that envy of the nation that called itself the first-born, favourite child of god the father still reigns among other nations; it has yet to be overcome – just as if they had given credence to the claim. Also, among the customs by which the Jews kept themselves apart, that of circumcision made an unpleasant, uncomfortable impression that can presumably be explained by its providing a reminder of the dreaded castration threat, thus touching on a bit of the prehistoric past that people wished to forget. And finally, the most recent motive in this series: it should not be forgotten that all the nations currently distinguished by their hatred of Jews became Christian only in recent historical times, often having been forced into it by violent coercion. They were all, one might say, 'imperfectly baptized'; beneath a thin veneer of Christianity they remained what their ancestors had been, subscribing to a barbaric polytheism. They had still not overcome their resentment at the new religion that had been foisted on them, but they had shifted that resentment on to the source from which Christianity came to them. The fact that the gospels tell a story that takes place among Jews and in fact concerns only Jews made such a shift easier for them. Their hatred of Jews is basically hatred of Christians, and no one need be surprised that in Germany's National Socialist revolution this close relationship between the two monotheistic religions finds such clear expression in the hostile treatment of both.

E

Difficulties

It may be that the above has successfully set out the analogy between neurotic processes and religious events, thus indicating the unsuspected origin of the latter. Out of this transposition from individual to mass psychology there arise two difficulties differing in kind and merit, and these we must now address. The first is that we are here dealing with only one case from the richly varied phenomenology of religions, throwing no light on the rest. The author must regretfully concede that he is unable to provide more than this single sample, that his expertise is insufficient to render the investigation complete. He can, from his limited knowledge, add that for example the case of the inauguration of the Mohammedan religion strikes him as an abbreviated repetition of that of the Jewish religion, in imitation of which it arose. In fact, it seems the prophet originally intended to embrace Judaism fully for himself and his people. Among the Arabs, the recovery of the one great first father engendered an extraordinary heightening of self-confidence that led to great secular successes but that also went no further. Allah showed himself much more grateful to his chosen people than Yahweh had been towards his. However, the internal development of the new religion soon came to a halt, possibly because it lacked the extra depth that, in the case of the Jews, had been occasioned by the killing of the religious inaugurator. The apparently rationalistic religions of the east are at heart ancestor worship – in other words, they stop at an early stage in their reconstruction of the past. If it is true that among present-day primitives recognition of a supreme being is found to be the sole content of their religion, this can only be interpreted as a stunting of religious development and placed alongside the countless cases of rudimentary neuroses encountered in that other field. Why in neither case did things go further is beyond our understanding. We must contemplate putting this down to the individual gifts of those peoples, the direction of their activity, and their general social circumstances. Incidentally, a good rule of analytical work is to be satisfied with explaining what is present and not trying to explain what failed to come about.

The second difficulty associated with this transposition to mass psychology is far more significant since it throws up a fresh problem of principle. The question arises, in what form is effective tradition present in the life of peoples, a question that does not arise in connection with the individual because here it is answered by the existence of memory-traces of things past in the unconscious. Let us go back to our historical example. We based the compromise at Kadesh on the continued existence of a powerful tradition among those who had returned from Egypt. This case holds no problem. According to our assumption, such a tradition rested on conscious memories of oral communications that those living at the time had received from their forebears (only two or three generations back), who had taken part in and been eye-witnesses of the events concerned. But can we believe the same with regard to later centuries, namely that the tradition was always based on knowledge passed on in the normal fashion, handed down from father to son? Who the persons were who preserved such knowledge and propagated it orally can no longer be explained in the same way as in the previous case. According to Sellin, the tradition of the assassination of Moses had always been present in priestly circles until it finally found written expression, which was the only thing that enabled Sellin to find out about it. However, it can have been known only to a few; it was not common knowledge. And is that sufficient to account for its influence? Can one attribute to knowledge held by a few the power to gain such a lasting hold over the masses, once they become aware of it? Rather, it seems as if something must also have been present in the unsuspecting mass that was somehow related to the knowledge of the few and that responded to it when it found expression.

It becomes even more difficult to pass judgement when we turn to the analogous case from prehistory. That there had been a first father with the familiar qualities and the fate that had befallen him had undoubtedly been forgotten over the centuries; nor can any relevant oral tradition be assumed, as in the case of Moses. So in what sense is there any question of a tradition at all? What form can it have taken?

To simplify matters for those readers who are reluctant or lack the preparation to plunge into a complicated set of psychological facts, I shall give prior notice of the outcome of the investigation that now follows. In my opinion, the identity between individual and mass is in this respect almost complete; in masses, too, the impression of the past lies preserved in unconscious memory-traces.

In the case of the individual, we believe we see clearly. In the individual, the memory-trace of early experiences lies preserved – only it takes a particular psychological form. The individual may be said always to have known it in the same way as one knows that which has been repressed. We have formed certain ideas (ideas easily corroborated by analysis) as to how something can be forgotten and how, after a while, it can reappear. What has been forgotten has not been obliterated but only 'repressed', memory-traces of it are present in perfect freshness but they have been isolated by 'counter-charges'.[16] They are unable to communicate with other intellectual processes, they are unconscious, not accessible to consciousness. Another possibility is that certain parts of what has been repressed have withdrawn themselves from the process; they remain accessible to memory, they occasionally emerge into consciousness, but even then they are isolated, like foreign bodies unconnected with the other. It may be so, but it need not be so; repression may also be complete, and this is what we shall be assuming in what follows.

This repressed material retains its impulse, its aspiration to break through into consciousness. It achieves its goal under three conditions: 1) if the strength of the counter-charge is lowered by pathological processes affecting the other part, the so-called 'I', or by a different distribution of charge energies within that 'I' such as regularly occurs in sleep; 2) if the drive elements attached to repressed material receive special reinforcement, the best example of which is the processes accompanying puberty; 3) if in the course of living experience impressions are received or experiences occur that are so similar to what has been suppressed that they are able to reawaken it. The living then draws strength from the latent energy of the repressed, and the repressed comes out from behind the living, with its help, to take effect. In none of these three cases does the previously repressed rise smoothly to consciousness, unchanged; it must always suffer distortions that bear witness to the influence of the residual resistance arising out of the counter-charge or the modifying influence of living experience or both.

A distinction that has served us as a marker and signpost is whether a mental process is conscious or unconscious. The repressed is unconscious. It would be a pleasing simplification indeed if that sentence could also be inverted – that is to say, if the difference in the properties conscious (c.) and unconscious (unc.) coincided with the distinction: belonging-to-the-'I' and repressed. The fact that such isolated and unconscious things exist in our inner life would be new and important enough. In reality, the situation is more complicated. It is true that everything repressed is unconscious, but it is no longer true that everything belonging to the 'I' is conscious. We are beginning to notice that consciousness is a fleeting quality that only temporarily attaches to a psychical process. Consequently, for our purposes we have to replace 'conscious' by 'capable of becoming conscious', calling this quality 'preconscious' (pre-c.). We then say more correctly: the 'I' is essentially pre-conscious (virtually conscious), but parts of the 'I' are unconscious.

This latter observation teaches us that the qualities to which we have confined ourselves hitherto are inadequate as regards finding our way in the darkness of the inner life. We need to introduce a different distinction – no longer qualitative but [in the medical sense] *topical* and (which makes it particularly valuable) at the same time *genetic*. We now separate in our inner life (which we understand as an [in the political sense] apparatus made up of a number of authorities, districts and provinces) a region that we call the *'I'* as such from another that we term the *'It'*. The 'It' is the older part; the 'I' has developed from it like an outer layer or rind as a result of the influence of the outside world. In the 'It' our original drives engage; everything that happens in the 'It' takes place unconsciously. The 'I' coincides, as we said before, with the area of the preconscious; it contains parts that normally remain unconscious. Psychical processes in the 'It' are governed by quite different laws of development and reciprocal influence from those that prevail in the 'I'. In actual fact, it is the discovery of those differences that led us to our new perception and that justify it.

The *repressed* should be attributed to the 'It' and is also subject to the mechanisms of the same, differing from the 'It' only in terms of origin. The differentiation occurs in the early years, while the 'I' is developing out of the 'It'. Then part of the content of the 'It' is taken up by the 'I' and raised to preconscious status; another part, unaffected by this transfer, remains in the 'It' as the unconscious proper. However, in the further course of formation of the 'I' certain psychical impressions and processes in the 'I' are excluded as a result of a defence process; the character of preconsciousness is taken away from them, so that they are once again degraded to the status of components of the 'It'. This, then, is the 'repressed' in the 'It'. As regards communication between the two mental provinces, we assume therefore that on the one hand the unconscious process in the 'It' is raised to the level of preconsciousness and incorporated in the 'I', and that on the other hand preconscious material in the 'I' is able to make the reverse journey and be returned to the 'It'. It is outside our present area of interest that later on a separate area becomes marked off in the 'I' – that of the 'Above-I'.

All this may appear very far from simple, but once one has become familiar with the unusual three-dimensional conception of the mental apparatus, picturing it can no longer present any particular difficulties. I would simply add that the psychical topics developed here has nothing to do with the anatomy of the brain; in fact, it only touches on it at one point. The unsatisfactory aspect of this idea, which I feel as keenly as anyone, stems from our total ignorance of the *dynamic* nature of mental processes. We tell ourselves that what distinguishes a conscious idea from a preconscious one and the latter from an unconscious one cannot be anything else but a modification, possibly also a different distribution of psychical energy. We talk about charges and hypercharges but beyond that we lack any kind of knowledge and even any kind of starting-point for a usable working hypothesis. Regarding the phenomenon of consciousness, we can further state that it originally depends on perception. All sensations arising from the perception of pain, tactile, aural and visual stimuli are most immediately conscious. Thought-processes and whatever may be their analogue in the 'It' are in themselves unconscious and acquire access to consciousness by association with residual memories of perceptions of sight and hearing along the language-function route. In animals, who lack language, such relationships must be simpler.

The impressions of the early traumas from which we emerged are either not translated into the preconscious or are quickly, as a result of repression, returned to the 'It' state. Residual memories of them are then unconscious and operate from within the 'It'. We believe we can follow their further fate well, provided that they relate to things experienced personally. However, a fresh complication appears when we become aware of the probability that the psychical life of the individual is affected not only by personal experience but also by material contributed at birth, items of phylogenetic origin, an *archaic inheritance*. This then prompts the questions: what does this consist in, what does it contain, where is the evidence for it?

The most immediate and surest answer is: it consists in certain predispositions common to all living creatures – in other words, in the ability and inclination to go down specific developmental roads and react in a special way to certain types of arousal, impressions and stimuli. Since experience shows that there are differences in this respect among individual humans, the archaic inheritance includes those differences; they represent what is acknowledged as the *constitutional* element in the individual. Now, since in their early years at least all people experience more or less the same things, they also react to those things in similar ways, and a doubt might arise as to whether those reactions, together with their individual differences, ought not to be ascribed to the archaic inheritance. That doubt should be dismissed: our knowledge of the archaic inheritance is not enriched by the fact of such similarity.

Meanwhile, analytical research has contributed a number of findings that give us something to think about. The first of these is the universality of language symbolism. The symbolic representation of one object by another (the same thing happens with a child's 'business') is something all our children are familiar with. It almost goes without saying. We are unable to prove how they learned it, and in many instances we have to concede that it cannot possibly have been learned. This is a case of natural knowledge that the adult has subsequently forgotten. Adults may use the same symbols in their dreams, but they do not understand the symbols unless the analyst interprets them, and even then they are reluctant to give credence to the translation. When adults use one of the very many expressions in which this symbolism has become enshrined, they have to admit that the true meaning of the expression eludes them completely. Such symbolism also has no regard for differences of language; studies would no doubt show that it is ubiquitous, the same for all peoples. Here, then, we have an apparently certain case of archaic inheritance from the period of the development of language, yet a different explanation could still be attempted. It could be said that these are thought-relationships between ideas that came into being during the historical development of language and that now need to be repeated each time an individual goes through the process of language development. It would then be a case of transmission of a thinking predisposition like any other drive predisposition and again not a new contribution to our problem.

However, the work of analysis has brought something else to light, the scope of which extends beyond what has been said hitherto. When we study reactions to early traumas we are quite often surprised to find that, rather than keeping strictly to actual personal experience, they depart from it in a way that accords much more closely with the pattern of a phylogenetic occurrence and is altogether explicable only in terms of the influence of the latter. The behaviour of the neurotic child towards its parents in the Oedipus complex and the castration complex contains a wealth of such reactions, which individually seem unjustified and only become comprehensible phylogenetically, through being related to the experience of earlier generations. It would be a thoroughly worthwhile undertaking to collect the material to which I am able to refer in this context and place it before the public. Its evidential value seems to me to be great enough to venture a step further and say straight out that a person's archaic inheritance comprises not only predispositions but actual content, memory-traces of the experience of earlier generations. That would significantly increase both the range and the importance of the archaic inheritance.

On closer reflection, we must face the fact that for a long time we have acted as though the inheritance of memory-traces of ancestral experience, independently of direct participation and the influence of education by example, were beyond question. In speaking of the continuance of an ancient tradition in a people, of the formation of a national character, what we usually had in mind was this kind of inherited tradition rather than one passed on by communication. Or at least we made no distinction between the two, failing to be clear in our own minds how bold we were being in not doing so. Our situation is made more difficult, of course, by the current attitude of biological science, which refuses to have anything to do with transmission of acquired characteristics to descendants. However, we confess in all modesty that we are unable, even so, to dispense with this factor in biological development. The same thing is not involved in both instances, of course: in the one case, acquired characteristics that are hard to grasp, in the other, memory-traces of external impressions – something tangible, so to speak. But it will probably be the case that we cannot, when it comes down to it, imagine one without the other. If we accept the continued existence of such memory-traces in the archaic inheritance, we bridge the gulf between individual and mass psychology, enabling us to treat peoples like individual neurotics. Granted, we currently have no firmer evidence of memory-traces in the archaic inheritance than the residual phenomena left over from analytical work, requiring derivation from phylogenesis, yet that evidence seems to us firm enough to postulate such a state of affairs. If it is not so, neither in analysis nor in mass psychology shall we get a step further along the road we have taken. It is an unavoidable audacity.

We are also doing something else here. We are reducing the gulf that earlier periods of human superiority opened up much too widely between humans and animals. If the so-called instincts [*Instinkte*] of animals, which allow them from the outset to conduct themselves in the new living situation as if it were an old one with which they had long been familiar – if this instinctual life of animals admits of any explanation at all, it can only be that they bring the experiences of their kind into their own new existence, that they have retained within themselves memories of things their fore-bears lived through. Basically, what we are saying is that it is no different with human animals. Corresponding to the animal's instincts is the human animal's archaic inheritance, however much the latter differs in scope and content.

Having said which, I have no hesitation in pronouncing that humans have always known (in that special way) that they once had a first father and that they struck him dead.

Two further questions need answering here: firstly, under what conditions does such a memory enter the archaic inheritance; secondly, in what circumstances is it able to become active, i.e. to emerge from its unconscious state in the 'It' and penetrate consciousness, albeit in an altered, distorted form? The answer to the first question is easily framed: if the event was important enough or occurred frequently enough or both. In the case of patricide, both conditions are met. With regard to the second ques-tion, a multitude of influences must be considered, not all of which are necessarily known, and even a spontaneous sequence of events is conceivable, analogously to what happens in connection with many neuroses. However, what is undoubtedly of crucial impor-tance is the arousal of the forgotten memory-trace by a lived, actual repetition of the occurrence. Such a repetition was the assassina-tion of Moses; later, the alleged judicial murder of Christ, bring-ing these events to the fore as regards causation. It is as if the genesis of monotheism could not have occurred without these inci-dents. One is reminded of the poet's words: '*Was unsterblich im Gesang soll leben, muß im Leben untergehen*' ['Whatsoever would live on in undying song, in life must meet its end'].[17]

Finally, an observation that contributes a psychological argument. A tradition based only on communication would not be able to gener-ate the compulsive nature that attaches to religious phenomena. It would be listened to, weighed up, and possibly rejected like any other piece of external information, never attaining the privilege of release from the compulsion of logical thought. It must first have suffered the fate of repression, it must first have experienced the state of dwelling in the unconscious before being able, on its return, to develop the sorts of powerful effect, bringing masses under its spell, that we have witnessed with astonishment (and hitherto without comprehension) in connection with religious tradition. And that consideration weighs heavily in persuading us that things really did happen the way we have sought to describe them – or at least similarly.

Notes

1. It was the name, for example, of the sculptor whose workshop was discovered at *Tell el-Amarna*.

2. This would correspond to the forty-year sojourn in the wilderness of the biblical text.

3. So something like 1350/40–1320/10 for Moses, 1260 or more probably later for Kadesh, and before 1215 for the Merneptah stele.

4. Elias Auerbach op. cit. [see p. 214, note 41], vol. 2, 1936.

5. The same consideration applies in respect of the remarkable case of William Shakespeare of Stratford.

6. [I make no apology for 'affective' (it is the technical term that all psychologists use to describe things pertaining to the emotions), but 'charges' (for *Bezetzungen*) does ask for some explanation, which the reader will find elsewhere in the present volume, in *Mass Psychology and Analysis of the 'I'* p. 51, note 6.]

7. This was the situation on which Macaulay based his *Lays of Ancient Rome*. In them, he casts himself in the role of a bard who, saddened by the arid party struggles of the present, holds up to his listeners the self-sacrificial courage, unity and patriotism of their forebears.

8. In other words, it is nonsense to claim to be practising psychoanalysis if one excludes precisely these early times from investigation and consideration, as happens in certain quarters.

9. [*Deckerinnerungen* are of course usually rendered in English as 'screen memories'. However, 'screen' has several meanings; I want to make it clear that Freud had only one in mind: his *Deckerinnerungen* hide something from view.]

10. [In Freud's text, *Überbleibsel* is followed by the English word 'survival' in parentheses.]

11. [The printed text has *Traum* ('dream'), which is a misprint for *Trauma*.]

12. [The German word is *Geistigkeit*, and I use this somewhat cumbrous device to draw the reader's attention to two things: a) as 'intellectuality', the term bears none of the unfortunately negative connotations (dryness, verging on aridity) that have become attached to what Freud regarded as a thoroughly positive quality; b) as 'spirituality', the term bears only the 'non-material' connotation of its first *Concise Oxford Dictionary* definition. I only use the device once, afterwards rendering the term with the more usual 'spirituality'. May I respectfully ask the reader to 'clean' the term of any specifically religious connotations?]

13. Ernest Jones points out that the god Mithras, who kills the bull, may represent this leader, boasting of his deed. We know how long Mithras worship fought for ultimate victory with the young Christian religion.

14. [Johann Wolfgang von Goethe] *Israel in der Wüste* ['Israel in the wilderness'], vol. 7 of the Weimar edition, p. 170.

15. On this subject, see also the famous expositions of Frazer in *The Golden Bough*, vol. III, *The Dying God*, 1911.

16. [*Gegenbesetzungen*. See *Mass psychology* . . ., p. 51, note 6.]

17. Schiller, *Die Götter Griechenlands* ['The Gods of Greece'].

Part Two
Summary and Restatement

The part of the present study that now follows cannot be launched upon the public without extensive explanations and apologies. The fact is, it is no more than a faithful, often literal restatement of the first part, shortened in many critical investigations and added to by extra material relating to the problem of how the special character of the Jewish people emerged. I realize that this type of presentation is as inappropriate as it is inartistic; it has my own wholehearted disapproval.

Why did I not avoid it? The answer to that is not hard for me to find, but neither is it easy to confess. I was not in a position to remove the traces of the admittedly unusual manner in which this study came about.

The fact is, it was written twice. First, several years ago in Vienna, where I did not believe I could possibly publish it. I decided to leave it be, but it tormented me like an unlaid ghost, and I hit on the solution of making two parts of it self-contained and publishing them in our journal *Imago*: the psychoanalytical prelude to the whole thing ('Moses an Egyptian') and the historical construct based thereon ('If Moses was an Egyptian . . .'). The rest (namely the material that was actually offensive and risky: the application to the origin of monotheism and the perception of religion as a whole) I kept back – for ever, as I thought. Then in March 1938 came the unexpected German invasion, forcing me to leave my homeland but also freeing me from the worry that my publication might provoke a ban on psychoanalysis in a place where it was still tolerated. Very soon after reaching England, I found the temptation irresistible to make the pearls of wisdom I had withheld available to the world, and I began to rework the third part of the study to follow on from the two that had already appeared. This of course involved a certain amount of rearrangement of material. However, I was unable to accommodate all the material in this second revision; on the other hand, I could not make up my mind to dispense entirely with the earlier version, which led me to the expedient of joining a whole section of the first account on to the second, unchanged, even though this involved the disadvantage of extensive repetition.

I was able to find some consolation in the thought that the things I am dealing with are in fact so new and so important (regardless of how far my account of them is correct) that it cannot be bad if the public is obliged, in this connection, to read the same material twice. Some things should be said more than once – in fact, they cannot be said often enough. However, the reader must be left free to choose whether to linger over the subject or to return to it. There should be no trickery whereby in one and the same book the reader is served up the same stuff twice. The thing remains clumsy, and one ought to take the blame for it. Unfortunately, a writer's creativity does not always obey his will; the work turns out as it may, often presenting itself as independent of (indeed, almost alien to) the person who wrote it.

a) The People of Israel

If it is clearly realized that a method such as ours – taking from traditional material what strikes us as useful, rejecting what does not suit us, and assembling the individual elements in accordance with their psychological plausibility – if it is clearly realized that such a technique offers no guarantee of finding the truth, one is right to ask: why undertake such a study in the first place? The answer has to do with the outcome. If the stringency of the requirements of a historico-psychological investigation is much reduced, it may become possible to explain problems that have always seemed worth attention and in the wake of lived events force themselves on the observer anew. We know that, of all the peoples who lived around the Mediterranean basin in ancient times, the Jewish people is almost the only one that still exists today in name and probably also in substance. With unprecedented powers of resistance it has defied misfortunes and persecutions, developed particular character traits, and in the process acquired the hearty dislike of all other peoples. Where this Jewish capacity for survival comes from and how the Jewish character relates to the fortunes of the Jews – these are matters we should like to know more about.

Let us begin with a character trait of Jews that dominates their relations with others. There is no doubt that they have a particularly high opinion of themselves, considering themselves to be more distinguished, more advanced, and generally superior to others, from whom they are also set apart by many of their customs.[1] They are also imbued with a special confidence in life such as is granted by secret possession of some precious asset, a kind of optimism; the pious would call it trust in god.

We are aware of the reason for this behaviour and know what their secret treasure is. They really do believe they are god's chosen people, they feel they are particularly close to god, and this makes them proud and confident. We have it on good authority that even back in Hellenistic times they behaved as they do today – in other words, the Jewish character was already fully formed at that time, and the Greeks amongst whom and alongside whom the Jews lived reacted to that character in just the same way as today's 'host nations'. Their reaction (it might have been felt) suggested they too believed in the preferential status that the people of Israel claimed for themselves. The declared favourite of the feared father need not be surprised at the envy of its siblings, and where such envy can lead is very finely illustrated by the Jewish legend of Joseph and his brothers. The course of world history seemed to justify Jewish presumption, because when god subsequently decided to send the human race a messiah and redeemer he once again chose him from among the Jews. The other nations would then have had occasion to say to themselves: Truly, they were right, they are god's chosen people. However, what happened instead was that the redemption of those nations by Jesus Christ only served to increase their hatred of the Jews, while the Jews themselves derived no advantage from this second 'choosing' since they did not acknowledge the redeemer.

On the basis of our earlier discussions, we are now in a position to say that it was the man Moses who stamped the Jewish people with this trait that was to be of such significance for all time to come. He raised their self-esteem by assuring them that they were god's chosen people, he imposed observance of the sabbath on them, and he made them promise to keep themselves apart from others. Not, of course, that other nations lacked self-esteem at the time. Just as today, every nation of the ancient world regarded itself as better than every other. But through Moses the self-esteem of the Jews became anchored in religion; it became part of their religious belief. Through their particularly intimate relationship with their god, they acquired a share in his greatness. And since we know that behind the god who chose the Jews and liberated them from Egypt stands the person of Moses, who had done exactly that, ostensibly at god's command, we make bold to say: It was the man Moses and he alone who created the Jews. It is to him that this people owes its toughness – but also much of the hostility that it has encountered and encounters still.

b) The great man

How is it possible for one person to have so exceptional an effect as to transform inert individuals and families into a nation, moulding that nation's definitive character and sealing its fate for thousands of years? Is not such an assumption a step backwards into the kind of thinking that allowed creation myths and hero-worship to arise, into a time when writers of history were concerned only with recounting the deeds and destinies of individual persons, rulers or conquerors? The modern tendency is much more in the direction of tracing the events of human history back to more hidden, general, impersonal forces, the compelling influence of economic relations, changes in eating habits, advances in the use of materials and tools, migrations brought about by population increase and climate change. In this, the only role played by individuals is that of spokesmen or representatives of mass yearnings that had of necessity to find expression and found it in such persons more by chance than anything else.

These are thoroughly justified viewpoints, but they prompt us to issue a reminder about a significant discrepancy between the way in which our cognitive apparatus is focused and how the world that our thinking seeks to encompass is set out. All our need for causality requires (and it is imperious) is that each occurrence should have *one* demonstrable cause. However, in the real world beyond ourselves this is hardly ever the case. Instead, each thing that happens appears over-determined, emerging as the effect of a number of convergent causes. Alarmed at the apparently limitless complexity of events, our scholars settle for one connection in preference to another; they posit opposites that do not exist, that result only from the severance of more comprehensive interrelations.[2] So when studying a specific case provides proof of the towering influence of a single individual, our conscience need not reproach us with having, in making such an assumption, slapped down the theory of the importance of those other universal, nonpersonal elements. Basically, there is room for both. However, in the case of the origin of monotheism we can point to no other external factor than to the one we have already mentioned, namely that this development is bound up with the establishment of closer relations between different nations and the building up of a major empire.

So we protect the place of the 'great man' in the chain or rather the network of causality. But it may not be entirely pointless to ask under what conditions we award this title. To our surprise, we find this is not entirely an easy question to answer. An initial formulation – if a person possesses in particularly high degree the qualities that we esteem – is clearly inappropriate in every respect. Beauty, for example, and physical strength, however enviable, confer no claim to 'greatness'. So the qualities in question must be of the mind; these must be psychical and intellectual assets. In the latter case a doubt assails us: are we really, if a person is exceptionally skilful in a particular field, going to call him a great man for that reason alone? Certainly not a chess master or a virtuoso on a musical instrument, but also not (or not readily) an outstanding artist or scholar. We are happy to say in such a case that the person is a great writer or painter or mathematician or physicist, a pioneer in the field of this or that activity, but we hold back from dubbing him a great man. If we have no hesitation in declaring Goethe, for instance, or Leonardo da Vinci, or Beethoven, to have been great men, something else must be prompting us, something other than admiration for their marvellous creations. Were it not for just such examples, probably the idea would suggest itself that the title 'a great man' was mainly reserved for men of action (conquerors, generals, rulers), acknowledging the greatness of their

271

achievements and the power of their influence. But this too is unsatisfactory, and it is wholly contradicted by our verdict on so many worthless individuals whose influence upon contemporaries and posterity is beyond dispute. Not even success can be selected as an indicator of greatness if one thinks of the vast numbers of great men who, rather than enjoying success, met a miserable end.

So one is inclined, provisionally, to decide that it is not worth trying to find a clearly defined meaning for the term 'great man', conceding that it is simply a loosely employed and somewhat arbitrarily conferred acknowledgement of the outsize development of certain human qualities in rough approximation to the original meaning of the word 'greatness'. Also, we should do well to remember that we are less interested in the nature of the great man than in the question of how he influences his fellows. But we shall keep this investigation as brief as possible because it threatens to take us well away from our goal.

Let us accept, then, that the great man influences his fellows in two ways: through his personality and through the idea he champions. That idea may highlight an old wish-figment of the masses or hold up to them a fresh target, or it may bring the common man under its spell in some other way. Sometimes (and this is certainly the more natural case) the personality is alone influential, with the idea playing a very minor role. Why the great man should achieve importance in the first place has always been clear to us. We know that the mass of humanity has a powerful need for an authority that it can admire, before which it bows down, and by which it is governed, possibly even abused. The psychology of the individual has taught us where this need on the part of the mass comes from. It is the yearning for the father that inhabits everyone from childhood on, for the same father whom the hero of legend boasts of having overcome. And at this point we may begin to realize that all the traits with which we furnish the great man are paternal traits, and that it is in such correspondence that the essence of the great man (which we have sought in vain) consists. Firmness of thought, strength of will, and vigour of deed belong to the father-image, but so above all do the self-sufficiency and independence of the great man, his divine insouciance, which may extend to ruthlessness. He must be admired, he can be trusted, but he will also, ineluctably, be feared. We should have let the words be our guide: who else but the father was, in the child's eyes, the 'great man' going to have been!

Without a doubt it was a mighty father exemplar who in the person of Moses stooped to the level of the poor Jewish slaves in order to assure them that they were his beloved children. And no less overwhelming in its effect on them must have been the idea of a single, everlasting, almighty god in whose eyes they were not too lowly for him to conclude a covenant with them and who promised to look after them if they continued loyally to worship him. No doubt it became difficult for them to distinguish the image of the man Moses from that of his god, and in this their suspicions were correct, for Moses may have imbued the character of his god with traits of his own such as a violent temper and a certain inexorability. And if they then happened to strike this their great man dead, they were simply repeating an atrocity that in primeval times had been directed as a sanction against the divine king and that went back, as we know, to an even older example.[3]

If, on the one hand, the figure of the great man has thus grown for us into the divine, on the other hand it is time to recall that the father, too, was once a child. As we have been saying, the great religious idea that the man Moses championed was not his own; he had borrowed it from his king, Akhenaton. And Akhenaton, whose greatness as a religious inaugurator is unambiguously proven, may have been responding to stimuli that had come down to him through his mother or by some other route (from the Near or Far East).

We cannot trace the chain back further, but if these first links have been identified correctly, the monotheistic idea returned like a boomerang to its country of origin. This makes it seem a fruitless exercise to seek to identify an individual as entitled to the credit for a new idea. Clearly, many people were involved in its development and made contributions towards it. On the other hand, it would obviously be unjust to break off the chain of causation at

Moses, neglecting the part played by his heirs and continuators, the Jewish prophets. The seed of monotheism had failed to sprout in Egypt. The same might have happened in Israel, once the nation had thrown off this difficult and demanding religion. But out of the Jewish people there repeatedly rose up men who refreshed the fading tradition, breathed new life into the exhortations and expectations of Moses, and sought tirelessly to restore what had been lost. Through the steadfast endeavours of centuries and eventually as a result of two major reforms (one before, the other after the Babylonian exile), the people's god Yahweh was transformed into the god whose worship Moses had imposed upon the Jews. And it is evidence of a special psychical aptitude in the mass that had become the Jewish nation that it was able to bring forth so many people who were prepared to shoulder the hardships of the Moses religion for the reward of election and possibly other similarly exalted prizes.

c) *Progress in spirituality*

To achieve lasting psychical effects on a people it is clearly not enough to assure them that they have been chosen by the deity. Their election must also be proved to them in some way, if they are to believe it and draw consequences from that belief. In the Moses religion, the exodus from Egypt served as that proof; god (or Moses, speaking in god's name) referred endlessly to that mark of favour. Pesah [the feast of the Passover] was instituted to seal the memory of that event, or rather an old-established feast was invested with the substance of that commemoration. But it was only a memory. The fact was, the exodus belonged to a dim and distant past. In the present, signs of god's favour were very sparse; the sorts of thing that happened to god's people rather indicated his disfavour. Primitive peoples tended to topple their gods or even flog them if the gods failed in their duty of guaranteeing the people victory, prosperity and contentment. Kings have always been treated no differently from gods; this is evidence of an ancient identity, of having sprung from a common root. So modern peoples, too, tend to drive out their kings if the brilliance of the latter's rule is tarnished by defeats and the concomitant losses of land and money. But why the people of Israel clung ever more obsequiously to their god, the worse they were treated by him, is a problem that, for the time being, we must simply accept.

It may prompt us to examine whether the Moses religion did in fact bring the people nothing but the heightened self-esteem resulting from their awareness of having been chosen. And the next factor is truly not hard to find. That religion also gave the Jews a very much grander idea of god or, as one might say more plainly, the idea of a grander god. Anyone believing in that god had, as it were, a share in his greatness, might feel personally exalted. To a non-believer, this is not entirely self-evident, though it may become easier to grasp if we think of the kind of elation that grips a Briton in a foreign land rendered unsafe by rebellion, a feeling that wholly eludes the citizen of a small country at the heart of continental Europe. The Briton, you see, knows that his government will send a gunboat if so much as a hair of his head is touched, and he also knows that the rebels are well aware of that fact, whereas the small country does not even have any gunboats. In other words, pride in the greatness of the British Empire is partly rooted in an awareness of the greater security and protection that the individual Briton enjoys. It may be that with the idea of the very grand god the situation is not dissimilar, and since a person is hardly going to claim to help god run the world, pride in god's grandeur melds with pride at having been chosen.

Among the precepts of the Moses religion there is one that is of greater significance than at first appears. It is the ban on making an image of god – the compulsion, in other words, to worship a god one cannot see. We suspect that, on this point, Moses outdid the severity of the religion of Aton; he may simply have wished to be more consistent (it meant his god had neither name nor countenance), or this may have been a fresh precaution against magical abuses. But if the ban was accepted, it had to be far-reaching in its effects. The fact was, it implied a downgrading of sensory perception in favour of what must be termed an abstract idea, a triumph of spirituality over sensuality – strictly speaking, a piece of drive-renunciation with its inevitable psychological consequences.

To find something credible when at first glance it appears implausible, we need to recall other processes of the same nature in the development of human culture. The earliest of these, possibly the most important, is almost lost in the mists of time. Its very striking effects compel us to say that it occurred. In our children, in adult neurotics, and in primitive peoples we come across the mental phenomenon we call belief in the 'omnipotence of thought'. In our judgement, this is to overrate the influence that our mental (in this case, intellectual) acts can have on changing the external world. Basically, of course, all sorcery (the forerunner of our technique) rests on this premise. All the magic of words also belongs in this context, as does belief in the power associated with knowing and pronouncing a name. It is our assumption that the 'omnipotence of thought' was the expression of humanity's pride in the development of language, which resulted in such an extraordinary furtherance of intellectual activities. The new realm of spirituality beckoned, in which ideas, memories and logical processes were what counted, in contrast to the inferior psychical activity that consisted of direct perceptions by the sensory organs. It was undoubtedly one of the most important stages in the emergence of the human race.

Another, far more comprehensible process confronts us from a later age. Under the influence of external factors that we need not go into here (and that are also, in part, insufficiently known), the matriarchal social order happened to be replaced by the patriarchal, which naturally involved the overthrow of traditional legal relationships. An echo of this revolution survives, it is believed, in Aeschylus's *Oresteia*. However, this switch from mother to father also points to a victory of spirituality over sensuality – a cultural advance, in other words, since maternity is proven by the evidence of the senses, while paternity is an assumption constructed on a conclusion and a premise. The preference elevating thought above sensory perception proves a momentous step.

Some time between the two cases just mentioned, another one occurred that appears to be most closely related to the case we have been examining in connection with the history of religion. Human beings felt compelled to acknowledge 'spiritual' powers as such – i.e. powers that cannot be grasped by the senses, in particular by sight, yet nevertheless manifest undoubted, even super-powerful effects. If we can rely on the testimony of language, it was air in motion that provided the model for spirituality, because the spirit borrowed the name of a breath of wind (*animus, spiritus*; Hebrew: *ruach*). With that the discovery of the soul[4] was also given as the spiritual principle in the individual. Observation found air in motion in the breath of the human being, which ceases with death; even today, in German, a dying person 'breathes out his/her soul'. But now humanity had been given access to the spiritual realm; humans were prepared to attribute the soul they had discovered in themselves to everything else in nature. The whole world became 'be-souled', and science, which came along so much later, had its hands full 'de-souling' part of the world again; it has still not finished the job even today.

As a result of the Mosaic ban, god was raised to a higher level of spirituality and the way opened for further changes to the idea of god, about which we shall have more to say later. First, though, let us look at another effect of it. All such advances in spirituality are successful in increasing individual self-esteem, making people proud, with the result that they feel superior to those others who have remained in thrall to sensuality. We know that Moses communicated to the Jews the elation of being a chosen people; the dematerialization of god added a new and precious element to the nation's secret treasure-store. The Jews steered a steady course for things spiritual; the nation's political misfortune taught them to rate the only possession left to them, namely their literature, at its true value. Immediately following the destruction of the temple in Jerusalem by Titus, Rabbi Jochanan ben Zakkai sought permission to open the first Torah academy in Jabneh. Henceforth it was holy scripture and the spiritual effort surrounding it that held the scattered nation together.

That much is generally known and accepted. All I wished to add is that this typical development of the Jewish character was ushered in by Moses' ban on worshipping god in visible form.

The pre-eminence accorded to spiritual endeavours through some 2,000 years in the life of the Jewish people was of course not without effect; it helped curb the brutality and tendency to violence that so often appear where the development of physical strength is the popular ideal. The harmonious cultivation of spiritual and physical activities that the Greeks achieved was denied to the Jewish people. Torn between them, they at least opted for the things of higher worth.

d) Renunciation of drives

It is not self-evident, nor is it immediately comprehensible why an advance in spirituality, a downgrading of sensuality, should increase a person's as well as a nation's self-esteem. That seems to presuppose a specific scale of values and another person or agency administering it. For an explanation, let us turn to an analogous case from the psychology of the individual, a case we have come to understand.

If the 'It' generates in a human being a drive-demand of an erotic or aggressive nature, the simplest and most natural thing is for the 'I', which has the mental and muscular apparatus at its disposal, to satisfy it by some action. This satisfaction of the drive is experienced by the 'I' as pleasure, as non-satisfaction would undoubtedly have become a source of displeasure. Now, it may happen that the 'I' refrains from satisfying the drive in the light of external obstacles, namely if it sees that the action concerned would involve serious risk to the 'I'. This kind of foregoing of satisfaction, this renunciation of a drive as a result of external restraint (as we say: in obedience to the reality principle), is never pleasurable. Renouncing the drive would result in a constant tension of displeasure if it failed to reduce the strength of the drive itself by shifting energies. But drive renunciation may also be enforced for other (as we rightly say) *internal* reasons. In the course of the development of the individual, some of the inhibiting forces in the external world become internalized; an authority is formed within the 'I' that sets itself up against the rest as a critical, nay-saying observer. We call this new authority the 'Above-I'. Henceforth the 'I', before effecting the drive-satisfactions demanded by the 'It', has to take account not only of the perils of the outside world but also of the opposition of the 'Above-I', and it will have all the more reasons for neglecting to satisfy drives. However, whereas renouncing a drive for external reasons simply creates displeasure, doing so for internal reasons, out of obedience to the 'Above-I', has a different 'economic' effect.[5] As well as the inevitable displeasure consequence, it brings the 'I' a pleasure gain – a substitute satisfaction, so to speak. The 'I' feels elated, it takes pride in renouncing the drive as in an estimable achievement. We believe that we understand the mechanics of this pleasure gain. The 'Above-I' is the successor to and representative of the parents (and upbringers) who supervised the individual's actions in his or her first period of life; it continues their functions almost without alteration. It keeps the 'I' in permanent dependence, exerting constant pressure on it. Just as in childhood, the 'I' is worried about placing the sovereign being's love on the line; the 'I' experiences the sovereign being's praise as liberation and gratification, the sovereign being's reproaches as qualms of conscience. If the 'I' has offered the 'Above-I' the sacrifice of renouncing a drive, it expects to be rewarded for this by being more loved by the 'Above-I'. Awareness of meriting that love is experienced by the 'I' as pride. Back when authority had yet to be internalized as the 'Above-I', it was possible for the relationship between imminent loss of love and drive-demand to be the same. It gave a feeling of security and satisfaction when, out of love for its parents, a child successfully renounced a drive. The peculiarly narcissistic nature of pride was unable to accept this good feeling until the authority concerned had itself become part of the 'I'.

What does this explanation of satisfaction through drive renunciation give us as regards understanding the processes we are trying to examine, namely the heightening of self-esteem in connection with advances in spirituality? Very little, it would seem. The circumstances are quite different. There is no drive renunciation involved, and there is no second person or authority to please whom the sacrifice is made. The latter statement very soon gives us pause for thought. The great man can in fact be said to be the authority, to please whom the deed is done, and since the great man himself owes his effect to his similarity with the father, it can come as no surprise that in mass psychology the role of 'Above-I' devolves upon him. In other words, this would also apply to the man Moses in relation to the Jewish people. On the other point, however, a proper analogy refuses to emerge. Progress in spirituality consists in a person, contrary to direct sensory perception, opting for the so-called 'higher' intellectual processes – memories, reflections, deductions. It consists, for instance, in the decision that fatherhood is more important than motherhood, even though it is not, like the latter, demonstrable by the evidence of the senses. The child shall therefore bear the father's name and inherit his estate. Or: our god is the greatest and most powerful, despite the fact that he is as invisible as the storm and the mind.[6] Repudiating a sexual or aggressive drive-demand would seem to be something quite different from this. Nor, in connection with many advances in spirituality (the victory of patriarchy, for example), can any authority be pointed to that supplies the criterion for what is to be deemed superior. In this case, it cannot be the father, for it is only as a result of the advance that he is promoted to the status of authority. So one is faced with the phenomenon that, in the development of the human race, sensuality is gradually overcome by spirituality, and that as a result of each such advance human beings feel proud and uplifted. One cannot, however, say why this should be so. Subsequently, it further transpires that spirituality is itself overcome by the wholly mysterious emotional phenomenon of belief. What we have here is the famous *credo quia absurdum*, and even a person who has managed this regards it as a supreme achievement. Possibly what all these psychological situations have in common is something else. Possibly people simply describe as superior the thing that is more difficult, and the pride they feel is merely narcissism boosted by awareness of a difficulty overcome.

Clearly such discussions can bear little fruit, and it might be thought that they have nothing whatsoever to do with our investigation into what stamped the character of the Jewish people. That would be an undiluted advantage so far as we are concerned, but a certain affiliation to our problem is in fact revealed by something that will occupy us even further at a later stage. The religion that began with the ban on making an image of god increasingly developed over the centuries into a religion of drive renunciation. Not that it was to demand sexual abstinence, contenting itself with a marked restriction of sexual freedom. But god is wholly removed from sexuality and elevated into an ideal of ethical perfection. Ethics, however, means restriction of drives. The prophets are tireless in reminding their hearers that god asks nothing of his people but upright and virtuous conduct – in other words, abstention from all drive-satisfactions that our present morality continues to condemn as depraved. And even the requirement to believe in him seems to take second place to the seriousness of such ethical demands. Drive renunciation thus appears to play a prominent role in religion, even though it did not figure obviously in it from the outset.

Here, however, there is room for an objection intended to obviate a misunderstanding. Drive renunciation, together with the ethics founded thereon, may not seem to be part of the essential content of religion, but genetically speaking it is very closely bound up with it. Totemism, the first form of religion that we recognize, brings with it as essential components of the system a number of commandments and prohibitions that of course signify neither more nor less than renunciations of drives: worship of the totem, which includes a ban on harming or killing it, exogamy, involving renunciation of the passionately desired mothers and sisters in the horde, and the granting of equal rights to all members of the league of brothers, i.e. restricting the tendency towards violent rivalry amongst them. In such rules we need to see the earliest beginnings of a moral and social order. It has not escaped our notice that two different motivations are at work here. The first two bans are in the interests of the father who has been done away with; they perpetuate his wishes, as it were. The third commandment, that of the equality of all members of the league of brothers, disregards the wishes of the father, finding its justification in an appeal to the need to preserve indefinitely the new order that came into being following the father's removal. Otherwise a relapse into the previous state would have become unavoidable. This is the distinction between the social commandments and the rest, which may be said to stem directly from religious connections.

In the abbreviated development of the human individual the essential element of this process is reproduced. Here, too, it is the authority of the parents (essentially, that of the absolute father wielding the power to punish) that calls on the child to renounce drives and sets out for the child what is permitted and what is forbidden. That which in the child elicits a 'well done' or a 'naughty' is subsequently, when society and the 'Above-I' have taken the place of the parents, termed 'good' or 'evil', virtuous or depraved. However, it is still the same thing: renunciation of drives under pressure from the authority that has replaced yet perpetuates the father.

Such insights receive further reinforcement when we set out to examine the curious concept of sacredness. What in fact do we see as 'sacred' – over and above other things that we value and recognize to be important and significant? On the one hand, the sacred is unmistakably bound up with the religious. This is stressed insistently: everything religious is sacred, it is the very core of sacredness. On the other hand, our verdict is shaken by numerous attempts to claim the character of sacredness for so many other things (persons, institutions, routines) that have little to do with religion. Such efforts serve obvious tendencies. Let us start with the prohibitory character that attaches so firmly to the sacred. The sacred is clearly something that may not be touched. A sacred prohibition has a very strong affective stress but in fact no rational justification. Because why, for instance, should it be so especially serious a crime to commit incest with one's daughter or sister; why should this be so much worse than any other kind of sexual inter-course? When one asks about the reason for this, one will undoubt-edly be told that all our feelings revolt against it. But all that means is that the ban is deemed to be self-evident; no one knows how to justify it.

The emptiness of such an explanation can be demonstrated quite easily. What allegedly offends against our most sacred feel-ings was normal usage (a sacred custom, one might almost say) in the ruling families of ancient Egypt and other early peoples. It was taken for granted that the pharaoh should find his first and highest-ranking wife in his sister, and the late successors to the pharaohs, the Greek Ptolemies, unhesitatingly followed their example. We are inclined, on the whole, to conclude instead that incest (in this case between brother and sister) was a privilege denied to ordinary mortals but reserved for the gods' royal repre-sentatives – as indeed the worlds of Greek and Teutonic legend likewise took no offence at such incestuous relations. Conceivably, the scrupulous observance of equality of birth in our high nobil-ity is a relic of this ancient privilege, and it is possible to say that, as a result of generations of inbreeding in the highest strata of society, Europe is today ruled by members of a single family and one other.

The reference to incest among gods, kings and heroes also helps to deal with another attempt to explain fear of incest biologically, tracing it back to a dim sense of the harmfulness of inbreeding. However, it is not even certain that there is any risk of harm as a result of inbreeding, let alone that primitive peoples were aware of this and reacted against it. And uncertainty about determining permitted and forbidden degrees of relationship similarly fails to support the assumption of any 'natural feeling' as lying at the origin of fear of incest.

Our reconstruction of prehistory urges a further explanation on us. The exogamy commandment, of which fear of incest is the negative expression, accorded with the father's intention and perpetu-ated that intention after his removal. Hence the strength of its affective emphasis and the impossibility of a rational justification

– its sacredness, in other words. We confidently expect examination of all other cases of sacred prohibition to lead to the same result as in the case of the fear of incest, i.e. that the sacred is in origin simply the continued intention of the first father. This would also throw some light on the hitherto incomprehensible ambivalence of the words that express the concept of sacredness. It is the same ambivalence as dominates the relationship with the father generally. The Latin word *sacer* means not only 'sacred', 'consecrated', but also something we can only translate as 'loathsome', 'abhorrent' (*'auri sacra fames'*).[7] But the will of the father was not only something that might not be touched, something that must be held in high esteem; it was also something one trembled at, since it demanded a painful renouncing of drives. When we hear that Moses sanctified his people (made them 'sacred') by introducing the custom of circumcision, we now understand the deep significance of that claim. Circumcision is the symbolic substitute for the castration with which the first father, out of the fullness of his absolute power, had once threatened his sons, and whoever accepted that symbol was saying that he was prepared to bow to the father's will, even if the father imposed the most painful sacrifice upon him.

To return to ethics, we can say this in conclusion. Some ethical precepts are justified on rational grounds by the need to define the rights of the community in relation to the individual, the rights of the individual in relation to society, and those of individuals in relation to one another. However, the things that appear to us as wonderful, mysterious, mystically self-evident about ethics are qualities ethics owes to its connection with religion, to its origin in the will of the father.

e) The truth content of religion

How enviously do we, the poor in faith, look upon those researchers who are convinced of the existence of a supreme being! For that great spirit the world holds no problems, for it has itself created all the world's institutions. How comprehensive, exhaustive and definitive are the doctrines of believers, compared to the laboured, meagre, fragmentary attempts at explanation that are the most we can manage! The divine spirit, itself the ideal of ethical perfection, instilled in human beings knowledge of that ideal and at the same time the urge to align their nature with it. They sense immediately what is higher and nobler, what lower and meaner. Their sensory lives are attuned to their distance from the ideal at any particular time. It gives them great satisfaction when, as it were at the perihelion, they come closer to it; they pay the price of extreme listelessness when, at the aphelion, they have moved away. Everything is so simply, so unshakeably laid down. We can only feel regret if certain life experiences, certain observations of the world, make it impossible for us to accept the premise for such a supreme being. As if the world were not baffling enough, we face the fresh task of understanding how those others might acquire belief in the divine being and where such faith draws its immense power, capable of besting 'reason and science'.

Let us go back to the more modest problem that has occupied us hitherto. We were trying to account for the peculiar character of the Jewish people, which is probably also what has enabled it to survive to this day. We found that the man Moses moulded that character by giving the Jews a religion that so raised their self-esteem that they felt superior to all other peoples. They subsequently preserved themselves by keeping their distance from those others. Interbreeding did little harm here because what held them together was an ideal factor, namely joint possession of certain intellectual and emotional assets. The Moses religion had this effect for three reasons: 1) it allowed the people to share in the splendour of a new idea of god; 2) it maintained that that people had been chosen by this great god and destined to receive proofs of his special favour; and 3) it required the people to make an advance in spirituality that, besides being significant enough in itself, paved the way for a respect for intellectual work and for further renunciation of drives.

This is our finding, and though loath to take any of it back we cannot conceal from ourselves that it is somehow unsatisfactory. The cause fails, as it were, to match the outcome; the fact we wish to explain appears to be of a different order of magnitude from everything we explain it by. Could it be that all our investigations up to now have not uncovered the entire motivation but only a superficial skin, as it were, beneath which another, highly significant element awaits discovery? Given the extraordinary complexity of all causation in life and history, we had to be prepared for something of the kind.

Access to that deeper motivation would arise at a specific point in the foregoing discussions. The religion of Moses did not exert its effects directly but in a remarkably oblique fashion. This is not to say, it did not take effect immediately but needed a long time, hundreds of years, to develop its full effect, for that much goes without saying when what is at issue is the moulding of a national character. No, the qualification relates to a fact that we have taken from Jewish religious history or, if you will, brought into it. We said that, after a certain time, the Jewish people rejected the Moses religion – whether completely, or whether a small number of its precepts were retained, we cannot tell. In assuming that, during the long period of the conquest of Canaan and of struggle with the peoples who lived there, the Yahweh religion did not differ essentially from worship of the other *baalim*, we are on firm historical ground, despite all the efforts of subsequent tendencies to obscure this shameful state of affairs. However, the Moses religion had not vanished without trace; a kind of memory of it had been preserved, hazy and distorted, possibly backed up, so far as individual members of the priestly caste were concerned, by ancient records. And it was that tradition of a splendid past that continued as it were to ferment in the background, gradually gaining more and more power over people's minds and eventually succeeding in transforming the god Yahweh into the god of Moses and bringing the religion of Moses, installed many centuries previously and then abandoned, back to life.

In an earlier section of this study we discussed what assumption seems irrefutable if we are to find such an achievement on the part of tradition comprehensible.

f) Recurrence of the repressed

There are a great many similar processes among those that analytical study of the inner life has taught us. Some are termed pathological; others are included in the wide spectrum of normality. However, that hardly matters since the boundaries between the two sorts are not sharply drawn, the mechanisms are to a great extent the same, and it is far more important whether the relevant changes take place within the 'I' itself or whether they stand over against the 'I' as alien, in which case they are called symptoms. From this wealth of material I shall begin by picking out cases relating to character development. The girl has placed herself in diametrical opposition to her mother, cultivating all the qualities that she misses in her mother and avoiding everything reminiscent of her mother. We may add that, like every female child, in early childhood she identified with her mother and is now vigorously rejecting her. However, when this girl marries and becomes a wife and mother herself, we should not be surprised to find that she begins increasingly to resemble the mother of whom she has made an enemy until eventually the mother-identification that she had once overcome is unmistakably re-established. The same thing happens with boys, and even the great Goethe, who at the height of his genius undoubtedly looked down on his stiff, pedantic father, developed traits in old age that belonged to his father's character. The outcome can be even more striking where the contrast between the two persons is sharper. A young man whose fate it became to grow up alongside a worthless father initially developed (in defiance of his father) into a capable, dependable, honourable person. On his attaining the prime of life, his character underwent an abrupt reversal and he behaved henceforth as if he had taken that same father as his model. In order not to lose the link with our subject, we need to bear in mind that at the beginning of every such development there stands an infantile identification with the father. This is then repudiated, even overcompensated for, and by the end has re-established itself.

It had long been common knowledge that the experiences of the first five years have a determining influence on life that nothing subsequent can resist. Regarding the way in which these early impressions assert themselves against all influences of more mature years, much valuable information might be communicated that does not belong in this context. Probably less known, however, is that the strongest influencing of a compulsive nature stems from impressions affecting the child at a time when we must deem its psychical equipment incapable, as yet, of fully taking things in. The fact itself cannot be in any doubt, and so disconcerting is it that we can perhaps make it easier to understand by drawing a comparison with a photographic exposure that, after a certain delay (long or short), can be developed and turned into a picture. People delight in pointing out that an imaginative writer, with the boldness permitted to the poet, beat us to this uncomfortable discovery. E. T. A. Hoffmann used to trace the wealth of figures available to him for his tales to the jumble of images and impressions received during a week-long post-coach journey that he had made as a baby at his mother's breast. What children have experienced and not understood at the age of two they usually never remember, except in dreams. Only as a result of psychoanalytical treatment may it become known to them, but at some later stage it will irrupt into their lives in the form of compulsions, directing their actions, imposing sympathies and antipathies upon them, and quite often dictating their choice of lover, which so often defies rational justification. There is no mistaking the two points at which these facts touch on our problem: firstly, in the remoteness of the time that is here seen as the truly decisive moment;[8] [for example,] in the special condition of recall that in connection with such childhood experiences we term 'unconscious'. In this we expect to find an analogy with the condition that we should like to ascribe to tradition in the inner life of the [Jewish] people. It was not easy, I admit, bringing the concept of the unconscious into mass psychology.

[Secondly,] regular contributions to the phenomena we are looking for are provided by the mechanisms that lead to the formation of neuroses.[9] Here, too, the decisive events occur in early
childhood, but in this case the accent lies not on the time but on
the process that counters the occurrence, on the reaction to it.
This can be set out schematically, as follows:

In consequence of the experience a drive-demand arises that
asks to be satisfied. The 'I' refuses such satisfaction, either because
it is paralysed by the size of the demand or because it sees it as a
threat. The first of these reasons is the more original one; both
come down to avoiding a dangerous situation. The 'I' averts the
threat through the process of repression. The drive impulse is
somehow inhibited, the occasion with its associated perceptions
and imaginings forgotten. However, that does not conclude the
process; either the drive has retained or reassembled its strength
or that strength is reawakened by a fresh occasion. It then renews
its demand, and since the avenue of normal satisfaction remains
closed to it by what we might call the repression scar, it carves out
a new avenue for itself at some weak point towards a 'substitute
satisfaction', which now appears as a symptom without the consent
but also without the comprehension of the 'I'. All phenomena of
symptom-formation can rightly be described as instances of 'recurrence of the repressed'. However, their distinguishing characteristic is the extensive distortion that the recurring material has
undergone in comparison with the original. Some may think that
with the last group of facts we have strayed too far from any similarity with tradition. However, this should not be a matter for regret
if it brings us close to the problem of drive-renunciation.

g) *Historical truth*

We have pursued all these psychological digressions in order to
make it more plausible to us that the Moses religion should have
exerted its influence on the Jewish people simply as tradition.
Probably, all we have achieved is a degree of probability. But let

us assume we had managed full proof; the impression would still remain that we had satisfied the qualitative factor of the requirement only, not the quantitative as well. Everything about the emergence of a religion (the Jewish religion certainly included) is touched by a magnificence that our previous explanations have not covered. Another element must have been involved for which there are few analogies and no equivalent – something unique, something of the same order of magnitude as what became of it, as the religion itself.

Let us try approaching the object from the opposite side. We understand that primitive man needs a god as creator of the world, head of the tribe, and personal provider. Such a god has his place behind the dead fathers of whom tradition still has something to tell. The person of a later time, our own time, behaves in the same way. He too remains infantile and in need of protection, even as an adult, believing he cannot do without the support of his god. That much is beyond dispute, but it is less easy to understand why there should be only one god, why this particular advance from henotheism to monotheism should acquire such overwhelming importance. Granted, as we have said, the believer shares in the greatness of his god, and the greater the god the more reliable the protection he can offer. But the power of a god does not necessarily depend on his being unique. Many peoples saw it only as glorifying their supreme deity if he ruled over other, subordinate gods, and not as diminishing his greatness if others existed besides him. Also, of course, it meant a sacrifice of intimacy if that god became universal and concerned himself with all lands and all nations. One shared one's god with foreigners, so to speak, and it became necessary to compensate by making the reservation that his preference lay with oneself. It may also be asserted that the idea of there being only one god itself implies an advance in spirituality, but the point cannot possibly be rated so highly.

The pious, in fact, know an adequate way of plugging this obvious gap in motivation. They say that the reason why the idea of a single god had so overwhelming an effect on people was because it was part of the eternal *truth* that, after long obscurity, finally emerged into the light and in consequence inevitably swept all men along with it. We have to admit that some such element is at last commensurate with the greatness of the object as well as of the outcome.

We too should like to adopt this solution. However, we come up against a misgiving. The pious argument rests on an optimistic, idealistic premise. It has not been possible to establish otherwise that the human intellect has a particularly fine 'nose' for the truth and that the human mind has a particular inclination towards recognizing the truth. On the contrary, we have tended to find that our intellect very easily and without any warning goes astray, and that nothing more readily attracts our belief than that which, without regard to the truth, meets our wish delusions. So we must add a certain reservation to our assent. We too believe that the solution invoked by the pious contains the truth – but not the *substantive* truth; it contains the *historical* truth. And we claim the right to correct a certain distortion that that truth underwent on the occasion of its recurrence. In other words, we believe not that a single great god exists today but that there was a single person in primeval times who must have appeared huge at the time and who then came back into people's memories elevated to divine status.

We had assumed that the Moses religion had been rejected initially, had fallen into semi-oblivion, and had then broken through as tradition. We now assume that that sequence of events was at that point recurring for the second time. When Moses brought the people the ideal of the one god, it was not something new but constituted a revival of an experience from the earliest days of the human family, an experience that had long since disappeared from conscious human memory. Yet it had been so important, had generated or paved the way for such far-reaching changes in the life of humanity, that one cannot help thinking it had left some kind of permanent trace, comparable to a tradition, in the human mind.

We have learned from the psychoanalysis of individuals that their earliest impressions, gathered at a time when the child had scarcely learned to speak as yet, at some time or other display effects of a compulsive nature without themselves having been consciously remembered. We consider ourselves entitled to assume the same with regard to the earliest experiences of humanity as a whole.

Among those effects (we allege) was the appearance of the idea of a single great god, which has to be acknowledged as a distorted, yes, but thoroughly legitimate memory. Such an idea is in the nature of a compulsion; it needs to be believed. To the extent to which it is distorted, it can be described as a *delusion*; in so far as it occasions a recurrence of things past, it has to be called *truth*. Even psychiatric delusions contain a grain of truth, and the patient's conviction spreads from that truth to the delusional cladding.

What follows until the end is a slightly altered repetition of what was said in Part One.

In 1912, I tried in *Totem and Taboo* to reconstruct the ancient situation from which such effects proceeded. In this I made use of certain theoretical ideas of Charles Darwin, Atkinson, but particularly W. Robertson Smith, combining them with discoveries and indications from psychoanalysis. From Darwin I borrowed the hypothesis that human beings originally lived in small hordes, each under the tyranny of an older male, who appropriated all the females and who either chastised or got rid of the young males, including his own sons. From Atkinson I took a continuation of this account, according to which the patriarchal system ended in a rebellion of the sons, who united against their father, overpowered him, and together ate him. Pursuing Robertson Smith's totem theory, I supposed that subsequently the patriarchal horde gave way to the totemistic fraternal clan. In order to be able to live together in peace, the victorious brothers renounced the women on whose account they had struck the father dead, imposing exogamy upon themselves. The might of the father having been broken, families were set up under the matriarchal system. The sons' ambivalent emotional attitude towards their father retained its force through all future development. In the father's place, a specific animal was installed as totem; this was regarded as progenitor and tutelary spirit, it must not be harmed or killed, but once a year the entire male community gathered for a feast at which the normally worshipped totemic animal was torn to pieces and eaten by everyone present. No one was allowed to exclude himself from this meal; it was the solemn repetition of the act of patricide with which social order, the moral law and religion had first come into being. The correspondence between Robertson Smith's totemic feast and the Christian Last Supper had occurred to many authors before it occurred to me.

I still stand by this reconstruction. I have had to listen to repeated bitter reproaches that in later editions of the book I did not modify my views, despite the fact that more recent ethnologists have unanimously rejected Robertson Smith's ideas and certain of them have put forward other, quite different theories. My response must be that I am well aware of these alleged advances. However, I am convinced neither of the correctness of such innovations nor of the errors of Robertson Smith. Contradiction is not the same thing as refutation, nor is innovation necessarily progress. Above all, though, I am not an ethnologist; I am a psychoanalyst. It was my right to extract from the ethnological literature what I could use for my analytical work. The works of the brilliant Robertson Smith gave me valuable points of contact with the psychological material of analysis, offering links through which to exploit it. I never concurred with his opponents.

h) Historical development

I cannot reiterate the contents of *Totem and Taboo* in detail here, but I must try to fill in the lengthy period between that assumed primitive era and the victory of monotheism in historical times. Once the combination of fraternal clan, matriarchy, exogamy and totemism had become established, a development began that must be described as the gradual 'recurrence of the repressed'. We use the term 'repressed' here in the figurative sense. We are talking about something past and forgotten, something that has been outgrown in the life of a people, something that we venture to equate with the repressed in the inner life of the individual. In what psychological form this past material was present during the period of its obscurity is something we cannot say at the moment. We do not find it easy to transfer the concepts of individual psychology to mass psychology, and I do not believe anything is to be gained by introducing the concept of a 'collective' unconscious. The contents of the unconscious are in any case collective, being the joint property of humanity. So for the time being we resort to employing analogies. The processes we are studying here on the scale of national life are very similar to those familiar to us from psychopathology – very similar but not exactly the same. In the end we fall back on the assumption that the psychical deposit from that primitive era had become part of the human inheritance, needing only to be aroused in each new generation, not acquired afresh. The example we have in mind here is that of the undoubtedly 'innate' symbolism that stems from the period when language is being developed, that all children are familiar with despite having received no instruction, and that is the same in the case of every nation, language differences notwithstanding. What we may still lack in certainty, we gain from other findings of psychoanalytical research. We learn that, in a number of significant relations, our children react not in accordance with their own experience but instinctively, like animals, in a way that is explicable only by phylogenetic inheritance.

Recurrence of the repressed takes place slowly and anything but spontaneously; it occurs under the influence of all the changes in living conditions with which the cultural history of humanity abounds. Here I can neither provide an overview of those dependencies nor furnish more than a patchy record of the stages of that recurrence. The father once again becomes the head of the family, not nearly so absolute as was the father of the primal horde. The totem animal gives way to the god in what are still very clear transitions. At first, the man-shaped god still has the animal's head; subsequently, he turns himself for preference into that specific animal; then the animal becomes sacred to him and his favourite companion or, having killed the animal, he adopts its epithet himself. Between the totem animal and the god, the hero arises, often as a prelude to deification. The idea of a supreme godhead seems to appear at an early stage – only dimly at first, without any involvement in the daily concerns of humanity. As tribes and peoples combine to form larger units, the gods too organize themselves into families and hierarchies. One of them is often raised to the position of sovereign over gods and humans. Hesitantly, the further step is then taken of acknowledging only one god, and finally the decision is made to attribute all power to a single god and to tolerate no other gods apart from him. Only then was the glory of the father of the primal horde restored; only then could the affects relating to him arise again.

The initial effect of this encounter with something that had been so long missed and yearned for was overwhelming; it was exactly as the tradition of the Mount Sinai law-giving describes. Admiration, reverence and gratitude for having found favour in his sight – the Moses religion knows nothing but such positive feelings towards the father-god. Belief in his total supremacy and subjection to his will can have been no less absolute in the case of the helpless, intimidated son of the father of the horde. In fact, they become fully comprehensible only when transferred to the primitive, infantile milieu. Childish feelings are on an entirely different scale from adult feelings in terms of their intensity and inexhaustibility; only religious ecstasy is capable of bringing these things back. Rapturous submission to god, then, is the closest reaction to the recurrence of the great father.

The direction of this father-religion was thus set for all time, but that did not conclude its development. An essential ingredient of the father-relationship is ambivalence; it was inevitable that, as time went by, another feeling should seek to find expression, namely the hostility that had once driven the sons to kill the father they so admired and feared. In the context of the Moses religion there was no room for direct expression of murderous father-hatred; only a powerful reaction to that hatred was able to come out, the feeling of being at fault because of that hostility, the guilty conscience at having sinned against god and doing so still, unceasingly. This feeling of being at fault, which the prophets unremittingly kept alive and which soon formed an integral component of the religious system, had a different, superficial motivation that cleverly masked its true origin. Things were going badly for the nation, the hopes invested in god's favour refused to come true, it was not easy to cling to the supremely popular illusion of being god's chosen people. If that bliss was not to be relinquished, the feeling of guilt at one's own sinfulness offered a welcome let-out for god. The Jews felt they deserved no better than to be punished by him because they did not keep his commandments, and in their need to assuage that feeling of guilt, which was inexhaustible and flowed from springs that lay so much deeper, those command-ments must be made ever harsher, ever more meticulous, and at the same time ever more petty. In a fresh fit of moral asceticism, the Jewish people imposed more and more drive-renunciations upon themselves and in the process, at least in theory and precept, reached ethical heights that had remained inaccessible to the other people of the ancient world. This upward development is some-thing that many Jews regard as the second major characteristic and the second great achievement of their religion. It should be clear from what we have been discussing how it is connected with the first, the idea of the one god. However, that ethic cannot deny its origin in feelings of guilt at a suppressed hostility to god. It has the incomplete, inconclusive character of compulsive neurotic reaction-formations; it also, one imagines, serves the hidden purposes of punishment.

Subsequent developments go beyond Judaism. The rest of what recurred of the tragedy of the first father was no longer remotely compatible with the Moses religion. Not for a long time had that era's awareness of guilt been confined to the Jewish people; as a vague sense of unease, a premonition of doom for which no one could give a reason, it had seized all the peoples of the Mediter-ranean. Present-day historians speak of an ageing of the civilization of antiquity; I suspect they have only grasped incidental causes of and contributors to that mood of mass disgruntlement. The reso-lution of this depressed situation came from Judaism. Irrespective of the many approximations and preparations all around, it was after all a Jewish man, Saul of Tarsus (who as a Roman citizen called himself Paul), in whose mind the realization first broke through: the reason why we are so unhappy is that we killed god the father. And it is entirely understandable that the only way in which he could grasp this piece of truth was in the delusional guise of the good news or 'gospel': we are saved from all sin, one of us having laid down his life in atonement for us. This way of putting it made no mention of the killing of god, of course, but a crime that had to be atoned for by a sacrificial death could only have been a murder. And the link between the delusion and historical truth was provided by the assurance that the victim had been god's son. With the power that filled it from the source of historical truth, this new belief overthrew all obstacles; the bliss of having been chosen was now replaced by the liberation of being redeemed. However, on its return to human remembrance, the fact of the killing of the father had to overcome greater resistance than had the other fact that had constituted the substance of monotheism; it also had to undergo greater distortion. The unnameable crime was replaced by the assumption of what is actually a somewhat vague original sin.

Original sin and redemption by sacrificial death became the cornerstones of the new religion established by Paul. Whether the fraternal horde that had risen up against the first father really had contained a ringleader and instigator of the murder or whether this figure was a later figment of the imaginations of poets seeking to glorify their own persons, which then became incorporated in the tradition – these must remain open questions. After Christian dogma had burst the bounds of Judaism, it absorbed components from many other sources, dropping certain features of pure monotheism and seeking in many particulars to ingratiate itself with the rituals of the other Mediterranean peoples. It was as if Egypt was once again taking vengeance on the heirs of Akhenaton. A feature worth noting is how the new religion tackled the problem of the old ambivalence in the father-relationship. While its primary content was reconciliation with god the father and atonement for the crime committed against him, the other side of the emotional relationship came out in the way in which the son, who had undertaken to make such atonement, himself became a god alongside and in fact in place of the father. Having proceeded from a father-religion, Christianity became a son-religion. The disaster of having had to do away with the father was not one it could escape.

Only a section of the Jewish people accepted the new dogma. Those who rejected it are still called Jews today. As a result of that divorce they became even more sharply separated from others than before. From the new religious community, which in addition to Jews absorbed Egyptians, Greeks, Syrians, Romans, and eventually even Teutons, they had to listen to the reproach that they had killed god. In full, the accusation would have run: You refuse to acknowledge that you killed god, whereas we admit it and have been purged of that guilt. It is easy, then, to see how much truth lies behind the accusation. Why the Jews found it impossible to take the step forward implicit (despite all the distortion) in admitting to having murdered god – that would be material for a separate investigation. In a way, they thereby shouldered a tragic guilt; they have been made to pay dearly for it.

Our study has perhaps thrown a certain amount of light on the question of how the Jewish people acquired the qualities that characterize it. Less light has fallen on the problem of how the Jews have managed to retain their characteristic identity into the present day. However, exhaustive answers to such an enigma cannot, by rights, be either asked for or expected. A contribution (to be assessed in accordance with the reservations mentioned at the outset) is all I am able to offer.

(1938)

Notes

1. The insult, so common in the ancient world, that Jews were 'unclean' (see [the third-century BC Greek priest historian] Manetho) is probably in the nature of a projection: 'They keep such a distance from us, as if we were unclean.'

2. However, I object to the misconception that holds that what I am trying to say is that the world is so complicated that any statement made will inevitably hit upon part of the truth. Not so: our thinking has retained the freedom to discover dependencies and connections that have no correspondence in reality, and clearly it values that gift very highly, making plentiful use of it both inside and outside science.

3. Cf. Frazer, *loc. cit.* [see p. 265, note 15].

4. [The context will make clear why I have chosen to render *Seele* as 'soul' in this passage.]

5. [See *Mass psychology* . . ., p. 51, note 3.]

6. [With some relief, I return to translating *Seele* by 'mind'.]

7. [The Latin quotation reads 'O cursed lust of gold' in the Jackson translation of the *Aeneid*. The German words translated here as 'loathsome' and 'abhorrent' are *verrucht* and *verabscheuenswert*.]

8. Again, let a writer speak. To explain his attachment, he invents: '*Du warst in abgelebten Zeiten meine Schwester oder meine Frau*' ['In times long gone you were my sister or my wife'] (Goethe, vol. IV of the Weimar edition, p. 97).

9. [And I must admit to having 'cheated' here. My 'secondly' has no equivalent in the original German text; I have inserted it in an attempt to avoid confusing the reader.]

A Comment on anti-Semitism

[This article first appeared in issue 7 (25 November 1938) of *Die Zukunft: Ein neues Deutschland, ein neues Europa*, a German journal published in Paris. The title was followed by the words: *The article below is the first publication from the pen of Sigmund Freud since his exile from Vienna.*]

Studying the statements in press and literature occasioned by the latest Jewish persecutions, I came across an article that struck me as so extraordinary that I selected excerpts from it to use myself. In it the writer said something like this:

Let me begin by saying that I am a non-Jew, so it is not any egoistical involvement that prompts what I have to say. However, I have taken a lively interest in the anti-Semitic eruptions of our day, paying particular attention to the protests against them. Those protests came from two sides: ecclesiastical and secular – the first in the name of religion, the second appealing to the dictates of humanity. The former were few in number and slow in coming, but they did come at last; even his Holiness the Pope said something. Frankly, in the pronouncements of both sides there was something I missed, something at the beginning and something else at the end. I now wish to try adding it myself!

I believe all such protests could be prefaced by a specific introduction, and it would run like this: 'All right, I don't like Jews either. To me, there's something foreign about them, something antipathetic. They have many unpleasant characteristics and major defects. I also think the influence they have on ourselves and our affairs is predominantly harmful. Clearly, compared to our own, theirs is an inferior race; everything they do suggests this.' And then, *without contradiction*, what those protests really contain could follow. *However*, we profess a religion of love. We are supposed to love even our enemies as ourselves. We know that the Son of God laid down his earthly life to release *all* people from the burden of sin. He is our pattern, and that is why it is an offence against what He stood for and against the precepts of the Christian religion when we consent to seeing the Jews despised, mistreated, robbed and driven into destitution. We should protest against these things, regardless of how much or how little the Jews merit such treatment. The same is said by the secularists, who believe in the gospel of humanity.

I have to say that all these pronouncements leave me dissatisfied. As well as the religion of love and humanity there is also a religion of truth, and it is this that comes off badly in such protests. The truth is that for long centuries we have treated the Jewish people unjustly, and that we are still doing so in unjustly condemning them today. Anyone amongst us who does not begin to confess our guilt has failed in his duty in this matter. The Jews are no worse than we are; they have somewhat different characteristics and different faults, but on the whole we have no right to look down on them. In fact, in some respects they are better than us. They need less alcohol than we do to find life bearable, the offences of brutality, murder, robbery and sexual violence are great rarities with them, they have always had great respect for intellectual attainment and interests, their family life is warmer, they look after their poor better, charity is for them a sacred duty. Nor may we in any sense call them inferior. Since we permitted them to share in our cultural endeavours, they have made valuable contributions in all fields of science, the arts and technology; they have amply repaid our tolerance. So is it not about time we stopped tossing them favours when they have a right to justice?

So decisive a stance on the part of a non-Jew naturally made a deep impression on me. But now I must make a rather curious confession. I am a very old man, my memory is no longer what it was. I cannot recall where I read the article I have quoted and whose name appeared below it. Possibly a reader of this journal can help me here?

It has just been suggested to me that I am probably thinking of the book by Count Heinrich Coudenhove Calergi (some such title as *Das Wesen der Antisemitismus* ['The essence of anti-Semitism']), which contains precisely what the author I am looking for missed in the recent protests, and more besides. I know the book, it came out in 1901 and was reissued by his son in 1929 with a laudable Introduction. But that cannot be it, I have in mind a shorter statement, something recent. Or am I completely wrong, is there no such thing, and has the work of the two Coudenhoves *really* remained quite without influence on our contemporaries?

(1938)